W9-AUJ-089

Praise for *God's Angry Man*

"Private Joe Haan was a Minnesota boy who endured the unendurable and emerged a great man. A poet and musician, a Purple Heart hero of WWII, and a self-educated man who rose from the bleakness of the Depression. This is a book of hard-earned wisdom."

—Garrison Keillor

"*God's Angry Man* achieves exactly what we strive towards here at The National WWII Museum: to tell the story of the war through the eyes of those citizen soldiers who were there. Through his Uncle Joe's eloquent letters, poems and other writings, B. Wayne Quist has given the reader a unique perspective on the war that changed the world."

—Gordon H. "Nick" Mueller, PhD
President and CEO, The National World War II Museum
New Orleans, Louisiana

"Private Joe Haan's violent combat experience in Patton's Third Army in WWII is noted most vividly through his writings penned while sharing a foxhole with a dead German soldier in Alsace-Lorraine, France. Awarded the Bronze Star for valor behind enemy lines during the Battle of the Bulge and wounded in hand-to-hand combat in 1945, Joe was decorated with the Purple Heart. This is an inspirational true story of one man's victory in his struggle for survival. A remarkable journey . . . a must read."

—Lieutenant General Thomas G. McInerney, USAF (Ret)
Former Assistant Vice Chief of Staff, United States Air Force

"Here's the story of one of Tom Brokaw's Greatest Generation. Like his compatriots, Joe Haan's life was characterized not only by what he achieved, but by what he survived. What makes this book unique is that here is a voice from the underside of that era, one of the forgotten and discarded children who refused to go quietly, but fought defiantly against the odds for his place in the sun."

—Reverend J. Leland Mebust
Sr. Pastor (Retired), Ascension Lutheran, Towson, MD, PhD
Princeton Theological Seminary

"*God's Angry Man: The Incredible Journey of Private Joe Haan* speaks to the life of every orphan who rose to challenge the world and conquer its every obstacle; through his poetry and perseverance, Joe Haan expressed a deep understanding of life."

—Odeh A. Muhawesh
Adjunct Professor, University of St. Thomas, MN

"Joe's ethos is an anomaly given his time and locality, a rare breed for his age. Yet through this work Joe's inspiration is clear and in context. At the Orphanage Museum, it is held that there are 10,635 stories of the Minnesota State Public School for Dependent and Neglected Children, one for each child passing through its doors . . . Joe's path is distinctive and clearly illustrated through his stark verse."

—Daniel J. Parrish Moeckly
Curator and Historian, Owatonna Orphanage Museum, MN

"Some books tell stories, some describe events. *God's Angry Man* is one of those rare books that combines a fascinating tale with the unfolding of momentous historical events of the 20th century."

—Norm Cull
Retired Ironworker, Spokane, WA

God's Angry Man

God's Angry Man

The Incredible Journey of Private Joe Haan

B. Wayne Quist

Brown Books Publishing Group
Dallas, Texas

God's Angry Man:
The Incredible Journey of Private Joe Haan

This book was published, manufactured and distributed in the United States of America by Brown Books Publishing Group.

Brown Books Publishing Group
16200 N. Dallas Parkway, Suite 170
Dallas, Texas 75248
Tel: 972-248-9500
www.brownbooks.com

A New Era in Publishing™

Hardcover ISBN-13: 978-1-934812-68-6
Hardcover ISBN-10: 1-934812-68-4
Paperback ISBN-13: 978-1-934812-69-3
Paperback ISBN-10: 1-934812-69-2

LCCN: 2010923214

Author contact information:

waynequist@joehaan.com

www.joehaan.com

This book is dedicated

to the memory of

Joe Haan,

his wife and sons,

brothers and sisters,

nieces and nephews,

to his many friends, comrades, and admirers—

and to all children around the world

who suffer indignity and injustice

from cruel and loveless institutions and people.

B. Wayne Quist
August 2010

***"Suffering makes men think,
thinking makes men wise."***

—Joe Haan

Table of Contents

Prologue to Joe's Story xiii

Survival Lesson xv

Introducing Joe Haan xvi

I. Spawned of the Tree of Life 1
- To Whom It May Concern
- Letter to Tim Carlson
- Letter to Wendy from "God's Angry Man"

II. "Fish (Fly-Replete in Depth of June . . .)" 11
- Heaven
- The First Idealist—"A Jellyfish Swam in a Tropical Sea"
- Evolution—"When You Were a Tadpole and I Was a Fish"

III. The Last Iconoclast 21
- Shadow of the Past—the Ghost

IV. Growing Up Poor in St. Paul, 1918–1925 31
- The Haan Family
- Oblivion
- The Roaring Twenties
- An Alcoholic Father
- The Mermaid
- Death of a Sainted Mother
- The Vagabond Road: "Small Frail Hands on a Coffin Gray"

V. The Orphanage, 1926–1928 49
- Equality Dead

VI. A Cruel German Farmer, 1928–1936 59
- Notes on the Farm
- Paradise Disorganized

VII. Riding the Rails, 1936–1939 93
- Pickett's Charge—July 3, 1863
- The Bivouac of the Dead
- Fido's Fate

VIII. Northwoods CCC Camp, 1940–1941. 113
On the Nature of Things
War

IX. Army Life, 1942–1945 127
Private Joe Haan—A Soldier's Memoir
Gott Mit Uns
Memories of Death
Sharing a Foxhole with Friedrich Hofman
Bronze Star Medal & Purple Heart
Soldier's Lament
Those That I Fight
The Open Mouth of Hell

X. After the War, 1946–1992 201
High Steel
Ode to Corporal William Cunningham, 2nd Wisconsin Infantry
Remembering Joe at Vicksburg
Dominican Republic Notes
San Pedro, Dominican Republic

XI. Joe's Poems and Songs 241
1. Salute to the Stars
2. The Question
3. Oblivion
4. Thinker
5. Fido's Fate
6. Death of a Galaxy
7. The Particle
8. Futility I
9. Free Thought
10. Futility II
11. A Star's Terminus
12. The 4th Dimension
13. Birth of a Sun
14. Volcano
15. Pestilence
16. Dinosaur Feast
17. Equality Dead
18. The Carnivore
19. The Nucleus
20. Deception
21. Over Population
22. Quantum Jump to Within
23. The Spoiler Man
24. The Slaves

25. Leopard's Feast
26. Paradise Disorganized
27. Prejudice
28. Escape Smilodon
29. The Mermaid
30. Evolution, or Geological Time
31. Heresy's Crime
32. Death of the Gods
33. Conflict of the Gods
34. Stars' Atomic Divinity
35. The Axis Tilts
36. Cockroach: Blattaria Supremus
37. Allosaurus
38. The Coconut Cartel
39. The Round Game
40. Why Soldier Why
41. Love Lost
42. Infidelity
43. The Latin Lament
44. Suzanna

XII. Joe's Epilogue 293
Mr. Flood's Party

XIII. "The Greatest Generation"—An Afterword 299
Blasphemy
Reminiscence from Alaska

XIV. Joe's Story in Pictures 313

Acknowledgments 371

Appendix 373
1. Haan Family Genealogy
2. Joe's Little Blue Books
3. XOTÄNEF Caveman Language

Bibliography 387

Index 391

About the Author

"Sometimes man is so completely confounded by the enigma of life that he attempts to escape into a cocoon of myth and falsity, never to emerge into the light of knowledge."

—Joe Haan,
Notebook I "The Last Iconoclast"

Prologue to Joe's Story

*Joe Haan—Evolutionist—Metaphysicist—Stargazer—
Steel Worker—Taxidermist—Geologist—Artist—
Paleontologist—Workingman's Poet—Thinker & Teacher*

This book was composed and stitched together from the writings of Joe Haan, old letters from the '30s and '40s, historical documents, war records, Joe's Army files, and from recollections of Joe's friends and relatives. Together, these materials paint a portrait that by all accounts is an accurate portrayal of "god's angry man." The language of the narrative tries to capture Joe's spirit; the poetry and letters are pure, unadulterated *Joe Haan*, straight from his soul and direct from Joe to his pencil, paper, and this book.

Joe loved to recite his poetry, as well as other materials he memorized over the years, and this is why his poems are enhanced when read aloud. Everyone who knew Joe remembers his lively recitations and commentary, especially when he was motivated with a little beer or wine.

To all who contributed to this volume, a special thanks—to Tim Carlson, Paul Quist, Julia Quist, David Mahmood, Wendy Haan, Peter Haan, and especially to Joe's sons, James and Jack Haan—and of course, to Joe himself. To James Haan, we owe a special debt of gratitude for making this book possible by saving Joe's poems, art collections, notes, and war materials, and for carrying on the spirit of Joe in his daily life. And to David, a special thanks in bringing the book to the public.

Joe would often start his discussions—they were really extended lectures or monologues—by talking about the "big picture" of life and the lessons of survival he learned along the road of hard knocks he had traveled from 1918 to 1945. Joe's "Survival Lesson" is a good introduction to Joe, for he firmly believed that to live—to survive as a species—mankind must adapt and evolve as new challenges are faced in the "cosmic shooting gallery of life."

—B. Wayne Quist
Minnetonka, Minnesota, August 2010

Survival Lesson

—Joe Haan to Paul Quist

Our earth has made four and a half billion trips around its sun—
Forever long, has it evolved—
Oozing life, some three billion years ago,
Surviving extinctions, cooling, warming—
Asteroids, volcanic eruptions, ever-changing climates.

Time, and time again, adversity altered earth's life forms,
From single-celled organisms,
To viruses, algae, and to grasses,
Fishes, amphibians, great dinosaurs,
Mammals, apes, and other primates.

"Spawned of the Tree of Life,"
Heroic homosapien man first stepped forth,
A mere 130,000 years ago, spreading out from Africa—
Into Asia and Europe some 80,000 years later—
Taking another 40,000 years to learn to farm;

Moving into the Americas just 12,000 years past—
Surviving earthquakes, floods, hurricanes,
Ice ages, drought, starvation, lethal viruses,
And ever-warring tribes of fellow men.

The lessons of life on Earth are these—
To live, mankind must adapt,
The species must evolve, to thus survive,
For written in the code of mankind's DNA,
Immutable imprints of survival therein do reside.

Introducing Joe Haan

Joe was born February 26, 1918,
Nearly completing his 74th trip around the sun
When he died in Houston January 7, 1992.
Orphaned, indentured, little school or fun,
Molded by a mother's sad and early end,
Events of life unfolded without mend—
"Small Frail Hands on a Coffin Gray,"
Etched in his heart a will to never pray,
Grim memories of war, the savage fray,
"Resting on the Corpse of Friedrich Hofman,"
New dead who speak, yet now no longer can.

Joe was a rarity, an exploding star,
An erupting nova—natural, without par,
"A bright, magnificent constellation,"
Said Walt Whitman of another, without proportion.
Joe's inventive mind, his powerful, inductive mind,
His manmade selfless soul, eternally kind,
With physical, intellectual power,
He used natural gifts that would not sour.
As scientist, artist, workingman's poet,
Committed to truth as he would know it.

A true contrarian throughout his life—
Working ever hard, amidst all strife,
Warring with hypocrisy and cruelty,
Journeying daily with heartless incredulity—
Cantankerous, fiercely loyal to prejudice and principle,
Always for the common man, ever evincible,

Declaring science and religion cannot coexist,
Empirical observation enforced with a fist,
For when it came to his own ideas,
More fearless, was he, than bravest Phintias,
Unyielding, independent, courageously ignoring
All pieties and orthodoxies, never ever boring.

Sternly intolerant of ignorance, falsity, oppression,
Stupidity—the uninformed—Joe Haan's obsession,
The rigors of cerebral inquisition,
Through self-made education, his position,
Without demeaning, never compromising standards,
Forever yanking at the biggest, hardest lanyards:

The vanity of religion—can there be a god?
Unadulterated skepticism—do we exist?
If I do, then why?—who are we, and who am I?
What is truth?—why do humans kill?
Are we but animals, and nothing more?
What then, is death, but the end?
What lies beyond that great beyond?

Joe liked people who would think,
Stood up for themselves, would not sink,
Fought for ideas they had worked out,
And the ideals they came about.
He had a fundamental decency,
A plebian modesty, self-confident, creative,
With fierce honesty, loyal to people in his life—
Comrades, buddies, sons and wife,
A righteously good friend and companion,
Leader of higher primates from life's canyon:

To those who liked him not,
They knew not him;
To those who feared his wrath,
They found a higher ground;
(As did a Houston iron man)
And to those he loved—
He was a glowing beam of sun.

Joe drifted into his long goodnight in January 1992,
On his last trip around the sun, fighting for his cause,
Chasing Gobi Desert dinosaurs because
His impermeable beliefs remained, unchanged,
Challenging traditional values, and custom—
Unhinged, overturning, ever fierce-some,
His language, now preserved and never gone,
In this brief memory of Joe Haan,
—The last iconoclast—god's angry man.

—B. Wayne Quist
Minnetonka, Minnesota, August 2010

I

Spawned of the Tree of Life

"Sometimes man is so completely confounded by the enigma of life that he attempts to escape into a cocoon of myth and falsity, never to emerge into the light of knowledge."

— Joe Haan

Joe's life was an extended crucible—a constant fight for the survival of the fittest. He was the ultimate survivor, like a primeval animal in the wild, stalking his next meal. Few were better at it than he was, for out of necessity Joe developed keen insights, intuition, and instincts. He informed himself in many fields of knowledge—from astronomy, archeology, poetry, and philosophy to farming, fishing, trapping, steelwork, and taxidermy. Like Leonardo, Joe was a "disciple of experience," and he was a survivor.

I was spawned of the Tree of Life,
And ate the fruit with little strife,
I knew not then who I were—
(With so simple of mind, I did not care)
I roamed the forest, roamed the plain,
Knew not whence, or where I came.
As time passed by, I stood upright,
Learned to hunt, to kill, and to fight;
With club in hand I learned quite fast,

To defend from long-gone dangers past,
With thirst for blood and taste for flesh,
I killed for food, and hid the rest.

—*Joe Haan*

From his earliest days, Joe was dogmatically anti-religious. Even so, he always seemed to have an innate spiritual sense that gave him insights into the natural world about him—the stars and galaxies, the very universe itself, plants and living creatures, as well as ancient prehistoric people that populated the world thousands of years ago. In his heart, Joe was a Neanderthal poet—a cultural intermediary—which is why he was attracted to Native American people and married a beautiful and trusting woman from the Choctaw Nation in Oklahoma.

Darwin was Joe's god and he tried throughout his life to differentiate between false man-made religion and the true spiritual quality of nature, which was available and free to everyone through observation. Joe believed the demise of religion was a Darwinian inevitability as people freed themselves from the shackles of humankind's myth-filled past through emancipating knowledge, especially science.

To express his deepest feelings, Joe wrote poetry. He loved to recite his poems, play his guitar and harmonica, and show off his talents in many fields. He believed that to protect the species of life as we know it on this planet, people must understand the origins of life, and that meant understanding evolution through constant struggle and strife—survival of the fittest. In a preface to his poems, Joe wrote the following "Acknowledgment."

To Whom It May Concern:

The general theme of this work reflects chronic skepticism. Of that, I plead guilty. I owe one apology only, and that is to the devil, for lacking the ability to be more severe in my criticism of all organized religion. I wish to extend a very special thanks to all the world's deceiving and hypocritical leaders who play a vital role in the lives of some who suffer from honest doubt. They contribute much to my iconoclastic disposition. Also, I must never forget the majority of my contemporaries who, being grossly misinformed, caused me to walk on forbidden paths and find fraudulence and hoax at every turn. It is clear to me the majority is almost always wrong.

—Joe Haan

P.S. My advice for the next generation—when all else fails, try common sense.

People would wonder and stand in awe of Joe—some said he was a colossus, and all who knew him said he was incomparable. Deep down, however, Joe knew he was terribly scarred emotionally—beginning with the early death of his mother; a flinching experience in an unloving orphanage; eight years as an indentured farm servant, constantly beaten, little opportunity for education; riding the rails with hobos and criminals around the country during the Great Depression, homeless, young, and vulnerable; and violent combat experience in Europe during the war, which caused dreams that never faded. But human ignorance is what made Joe angry, and it seemed that he was always angry, especially when tempted with alcohol, and it never took much of the "juice" to get Joe going.

After the war, Joe married his lifetime partner, moved to Texas as a totally free man at last, and had two sons with Helen—Jack and James. For nearly forty years, Joe worked as a card-carrying union ironworker on the tallest structures of Houston's skyline where he was called "*el Tigre Chiquito.*" At home, he built and harbored vast collections of fossils, rocks, stuffed animals, and countless works of taxidermy art in his garage laboratory. One of Joe's good friends, Tim Carlson, recalled:

> *Joe had turned his garage into a taxidermy shop and would mount well over a hundred deer heads after hunting season. He told everyone the meat was tainted during the taxidermy process, but he skinned the heads and put the meat in his freezer. I think we had venison chili about once a week when I stayed there. Helen made it with lots of hot peppers, and Joe would show off by eating raw jalapeno peppers straight from his garden . . . I spent several months sleeping on a cot in Joe's living room. One night, when I couldn't fall asleep, I started counting the skins and heads of animals that were mounted on the walls, or hides draped over furniture, or small animals mounted on shelves. I got as far as counting 137 before I fell asleep, and it was a very small house.*

Over the years, Joe especially enjoyed the company of young people, nephews, and friends. They tramped Civil War battlefields together, or spent a day or a month or two with Joe in Houston—"the only white man in a sea of black," he would say. They listened to his unending stories and songs; admired his latest taxidermy work and immaculate tropical garden in the backyard; met dozens of his eccentric friends as

Joe recited poetry, sang his songs, and played the guitar and harmonica; and visited tough, local honkytonks where Joe was well-known, sipping Lone Star, Budweiser, or the Sauterne he learned to drink in France during the war. And after a few beers, Joe would invariably recite the "Mess Song" of the Lafayette Escadrille, an American World War I volunteer flying squadron in France—words he learned shortly before some of the heaviest fighting of the war in late 1944:

> *Hold your glasses steady boys,*
> *For this life, it's a pack of lies.*
> *Drink to the dead already, boys, and*
> *"Hurrah!" for the next man that dies.*

On his first payday after landing in France three months earlier, Joe got drunk in Metz just before the Battle of the Bulge and was transferred into the infantry as a "grunt" rifleman from the relatively safe artillery. He had toasted "Here's to the dead already, boys . . ." once too often after slugging the First Sergeant and hitting one of the officers, and they certainly did not appreciate his last refrain: "'Hurrah!' for the next man that dies."

For Joe, the war never really ended, but it wasn't just World War II that he continued to fight—Joe's war was against prejudice, injustice, eternal ignorance, superstition, manmade gods, pretentious people, and man's incredible inhumanity toward his fellow man and other living creatures. That's what he deplored, lashed out at, and sought to change through his actions and words. Joe was angry at many things, but his anger was tempered by love of the natural world and the earth's ancient, unchanging origins found in its soil and rock structures—what Joe called the soul of the earth. Above all, Joe was angry at man's stupidity and proclivity toward violence. He said he had tried understanding and kindness early on but they often didn't work, though he would always extend a hand of friendship to the down and out.

To Joe, the insanity of the twentieth century's bloody wars that killed countless millions from 1914 to 1945, and his experiences in the orphanage and on the farm in the 1930s, were proof that humankind had learned little or nothing from its violent past. It was condemned to repeat the errors of its ways because of man's continued ignorance.

Joe understood that for most of human history our species had lived in small hunter-gatherer bands and the species had evolved, but was still quite primitive when it came to fundamentals. Survivors had adapted to changing environments and evolved by developing capabilities that were passed down genetically to succeeding generations. New circumstances activated varying genetic potential, causing individual behavior to respond differently from one time to another. People adapted to new information and gradually adjusted their ancient genetic reflexes with new human experience.

Joe was a classical survivor, a "disciple of experience," and he scoffed at man's religious myths. A letter Joe wrote to his friend Tim Carlson illustrates his thinking and humor.

December 1988

Tim —

Kurt Vonnegut's Bluebeard *follows my own autobiography to the last paragraph, just like my poems. Vonnegut should be required reading for all students of philosophy and metaphysics to truly enlighten them. But I was quite disappointed for his reluctance to give us the unadulterated truth about Lazarus, brother of Mary and Martha.*

I am one of the few hominoids on this biological penal colony of the galaxy that knows the true fate of Lazarus. Seven days after the Great Samaritan brought him back to this cruel plain of disease and pain, with all his birth defects including blindness, he staggered up against a double-humped Bedouin camel who was trained to dislike Jews and Gentiles. Alas, poor Lazarus was struck by both hind feet simultaneously, doing irreparable damage to his cerebral hemisphere. Runners were sent immediately to attempt to find a first aid man. As the fates would have it, the only medico in Jerusalem was a man called Jesus. He was located, at last, extremely intoxicated on wild desert fig wine in the local house of ill fame, so was rendered incompetent to provide any aid, and so poor Lazarus passed on to his promised reward.

So now, my communicators, I know you're curious about the fate of the camel, and this is the most shocking part of this Biblical tale. The camel was born with a very distinctive birthmark, which took the form of the Star of David. It was located six inches below its anal opening inside the left femur and so was considered divinely sacred and was spared the fate of Lazarus. It is said the camel lived to be 900 years old according to the legend of the meticulous Methuselah, who everyone knows lived to be 969 years and three hours old.

—Joe Haan

Joe's poetry is often stark and gut-wrenching, but it's Joe who is talking and it's self-revealing. In his writings, Joe tried to tell the truth as he saw it and understood it, based on self-education and bitter experience growing up poor in St. Paul in the 1920s, the desperate 1930s, and war-ravaged 1940s. What follows are fifty or so of Joe's surviving poems, stories, and songs he wrote over the years, from about 1938 to 1990, as well as some autobiographical commentary. In Joe's last letter to his niece Wendy Haan in 1990, he signed it, "god's angry man," which was meant to be a descriptive epitaph.

September 11, 1990

Wendy,

I received the [typewritten] poems and wish to extend my sincere gratitude for the consideration you have given my humble work. I am enclosing the poem "High Steel" which I wrote at noon break, the last day in the iron patch. "Pickett's Charge" I wrote on the Gettysburg Battlefield in 1938—I spent the night walking on that hallowed ground. The preceding day I walked from Chambersburg, a distance of 28 miles west of Gettysburg, Adams County, down that same road Lee advanced on Meade's forces, 70,000 Confederate soldiers and only Buford's cavalry, one regiment, to stem the tide.

In regard to your question as to why I frequently use the word "god," [it] is to impress my small-minded contemporary audience in love with a myth. If you read between the lines of my work, and not misinterpret it, you will detect sheer unadulterated skepticism and also criticism to expose the mad vanity of all religion, the basic cause of war that served no ultimate purpose. The Thirty Years War is an example—1618 to 1648; the adversaries were Catholics versus Protestant. In the two world wars this century, every private soldat *in the German Army had inscribed on their field buckle the words "Gott Mit Uns"—"God With Us."*

Gott Mit Uns

Under the roots of trees,
Dead ages lie down,
To cover this false promise
On rusting buckles:
"Gott Mit Uns."
So many Gods, so many creeds,
So many ways that wind and wind.
What the world needs is
More men that can be kind,
To cultivate more true creativeness,
And far less destructiveness.

Wendy, I am writing a thesis on organic evolution, minus divine assistance, quite lengthy. I will send you a copy when complete, if you wish.

SUBJECT: ANTHROPOLOGY

The chimpanzee-orangutan and gorilla have precisely the same anatomical structural build as homosapien man—206 major bones. We, in a time past, also had a tail that was discontinued in our evolution due to lack of use; the very arm and shoulder structure is similar. The bicipital muscle comes from our common ancestors who used it for swinging from branches of trees in the endless hunt for food. They were herbivorous for they had not the claw or fang to tear flesh. They added meat to their diet only after becoming semi-civilized. And now modern man has an inheritance, a holy sacred ritual called communion. The recipient of the rite is on his knees in his Sunday's best, with mouth open and mind dead. The Christian Sachem places a thin white cracker in said mouth and utters these words: "Take ye all of this for this is the God that died for you." Stamped upon this magic cracker are these words, "Jesus of Naz-a-reth - Rex Judora." This rite evolved from ancient judicial systems. The victim condemned was cast to the mob that crucified him and then ate him as a vicarious God, to gain for self the strength of him. From this ages old system so evolved modern communion.

—God's angry man,
Joe Haan

II

"Fish (Fly-Replete in Depth of June . . .)"

All who knew Joe called him a "*survivalist.*" He learned what he had to know out of necessity, starting when he was very young, still in single digits. Joe first learned to fish, trap, and hunt on the hated farm in southern Minnesota. He always loved living out-of-doors, for it was his temple where he worshipped. He became an expert shot with a rifle and virtually lived outdoors for over seventeen years from 1928 to 1945—on the farm, on the road, in a CCC camp in the Minnesota North Woods, and with Patton's Army in Europe during some of the toughest fighting of World War II.

Joe loved wildlife of all types, but especially fish—primeval creatures of the dark and deep. Maybe that's what attracted him to Rupert Brooke's poem, "Heaven—Fish (fly-replete, in depth of June . . .)," a statement pitting life and all existence against the inevitability and chance constantly facing every creature trying to survive on the planet.

Joe developed a well-trained eye for finding rare stones, agates, and fossils, and he collected Indian arrowheads and artifacts throughout his life. He started collecting on the farm as he walked alone many hours behind a horse-drawn plow, turning over the spring soil and picking up glistening gems from the soul of the earth. Where ancient wisdom came from, he did not know, but it always seemed to Joe there was much wisdom in the earth, in ancient cultures, and with the living creatures of the wild. Joe never owned a watch until he joined the Civilian Conservation Corps (CCC) in 1940, but he was good at observing time from the sun, moon, and stars, and he always enjoyed staring at the night sky, tracing the constellations and watching the planets wander across the emptiness of space and time.

Joe probably came across Rupert Brooke's poetry in CCC camp or from one of the Little Blue Books he often carried when he was riding the rails—he could buy them for a nickel during the Great Depression. There was a Little Blue Book for nearly every piece of classical literature ever written, and Joe was especially attracted to poems and essays on evolution and paleontology. Joe recited Rupert Brooke's poetry at CCC camp and in the Army because Brooke was known for idealistic war sonnets the troops liked so well.

The Little Blue Books appealed to Joe because of his love of history that went back to his earliest days. They reminded him of his lonely, solitary days struggling at the orphanage and on the farm when the only freedom possible for a young orphaned boy—an indentured ward of the state and lowly farm servant—was talking to himself. As he walked alone like primeval man, he discovered the natural rhythm and rhyming of words; wandered the fields and wooded hills; trapped chicken hawks, foxes, weasels, muskrats, skunks, and beaver; snared pheasants, prairie chickens, and rabbits; shot gophers, squirrels, sitting ducks, and other small game with a homemade slingshot; and fished in the local stream with a handmade willow pole and homespun lures. All the while, he wondered about life, and what lies beyond—about fish and other ancient creatures—as he would dawdle away a "wat'ry noon." Later in the day, he would gaze at a moon so close, yet far away, and the beckoning evening stars. "Heaven" was a poem Joe used to recite a lot.

Heaven

Rupert Brooke, English poet (1887–1915)

Fish (fly-replete, in depth of June,
Dawdling away their wat'ry noon)
Ponder deep wisdom, dark or clear,
Each secret fishy hope or fear.

Fish say, they have their Stream and Pond;
But is there anything Beyond?
This life cannot be All, they swear,
For how unpleasant, if it were!
One may not doubt that, somehow, Good

Shall come of Water and of Mud;
And, sure, the reverent eye must see
A Purpose in Liquidity.
We darkly know, by Faith we cry,
The future is not Wholly Dry.

Mud unto mud!—Death eddies near—
Not here the appointed End, not here!
But somewhere, beyond Space and Time.
Is wetter water, slimier slime!
And there (they trust) there swimmeth One

Who swam ere rivers were begun,
Immense, of fishy form and mind,

Squamous, omnipotent, and kind;
And under that Almighty Fin,
The littlest fish may enter in.

Oh! never fly conceals a hook,
Fish say, in the Eternal Brook,
But more than mundane weeds are there,
And mud, celestially fair;
Fat caterpillars drift around,

And Paradisal grubs are found;
Unfading moths, immortal flies,
And the worm that never dies.
And in that Heaven of all their wish,
There shall be no more land, say fish.

Two of Joe's other favorite poems he learned to recite on the road were "The First Idealist" by Grant Allen ("A Jellyfish Swam in a Tropical Sea") and Langdon Smith's "Evolution" ("When you were a tadpole and I was a fish"). Joe said he found them in public libraries and in the Little Blue Books he purchased when he was on the road in the 1930s, "riding the rails."

Joe memorized them because he said he could then own them forever—for nothing—and they appealed to his belief in evolution, love of nature, sense of justice, humanity, compassion, and his overall view of life. Both poems help set the stage for a better understanding of Joe's poetry and philosophy, and for his preference for the world of the great unknown as opposed to the world of manmade gods.

The First Idealist

"A Jellyfish Swam in a Tropical Sea"

Grant Allen (1848–1899)

A Jellyfish swam in a tropical sea,
And he said,

"This world, it consists of Me!
There's nothing above and nothing below
That a Jellyfish can ever possibly know,
Since we've got no sight, or hearing, or smell,
Beyond what our single sense can tell.

Now, all that I learn from my sense of touch
Is the fact of feelings, viewed as such,
But to think they have an external cause,
Is an inference clean, against logical laws.

Again to suppose, as I've hitherto done,
There are other Jellyfish under the sun,
Is a pure assumption that can't be backed
By a jot of proof—or a single fact.

In short, like Hume, I very much doubt
If there's anything else at all without,
So I come, at last, to the plain conclusion,
When the subject is fairly free from confusion:
That the universe centers solely of Me,
And if I were not, then nothing would be!"

That minute, a shark was strolling by,
Just gulped him down in the twink of an eye;
And he died with a few convulsive twists,
But somehow, the universe still exists.

Evolution

Langdon Smith (1858–1908)
American journalist, writer and poet

When you were a tadpole and I was a fish
In the Paleozoic time,
And side by side on the ebbing tide
We sprawled through the ooze and slime,

Or skittered with many a caudal flip
Through the depths of the Cambrian fen,
My heart was rife with the joy of life,
For I loved you even then.

Mindless we lived and mindless we loved
And mindless at last we died;
And deep in the rift of the Caradoc drift
We slumbered side by side.

The world turned on in the lathe of time,
The hot lands heaved amain,
Till we caught our breath from the womb of death
And crept into light again.

We were amphibians, scaled and tailed,
And drab as a dead man's hand;
We coiled at ease 'neath the dripping trees
Or trailed through the mud and sand.

Croaking and blind, with our three-clawed feet
Writing a language dumb,
With never a spark in the empty dark
To hint at a life to come.

Yet happy we lived and happy we loved,
And happy we died once more;
Our forms were rolled in the clinging mold
Of a Neocomian shore.

The eons came and the eons fled
And the sleep that wrapped us fast
Was riven away in a newer day
And the night of death was past.

Then light and swift through the jungle trees
We swung in our airy flights,
Or breathed in the balms of the fronded palms
In the hush of the moonless nights;

And, oh! what beautiful years were there
When our hearts clung each to each;
When life was filled and our senses thrilled
In the first faint dawn of speech.

Thus life by life and love by love
We passed through the cycles strange,
And breath by breath and death by death
We followed the chain of change.

Till there came a time in the law of life
When over the nursing side
The shadows broke and soul awoke
In a strange, dim dream of God.

I was thewed like an Auruch bull
And tusked like the great cave bear;
And you, my sweet, from head to feet
Were gowned in your glorious hair.

Deep in the gloom of a fireless cave,
When the night fell o'er the plain
And the moon hung red o'er the river bed
We mumbled the bones of the slain.

I flaked a flint to a cutting edge
And shaped it with brutish craft;
I broke a shank from the woodland lank
And fitted it, head and haft;

Then I hid me close to the reedy tarn,
Where the mammoth came to drink;
Through the brawn and bone I drove the stone
And slew him upon the brink.

Loud I howled through the moonlit wastes,
Loud answered our kith and kin;
From west and east to the crimson feast
The clan came tramping in.

O'er joint and gristle and padded hoof
We fought and clawed and tore,
And cheek by jowl with many a growl
We talked the marvel o'er.

I carved that fight on a reindeer bone
With rude and hairy hand;
I pictured his fall on the cavern wall
That men might understand.

For we lived by blood and the right of might
Ere human laws were drawn,
And the age of sin did not begin
Till our brutal tush were gone.

And that was a million years ago
In a time that no man knows;
Yet here tonight in the mellow light
We sit at Delmonico's.

Your eyes are deep as the Devon springs,
Your hair is dark as jet,
Your years are few, your life is new,
Your soul untried, and yet—

Our trail is on the Kimmeridge clay
And the scarp of the Purbeck flags;
We have left our bones in the Bagshot stones
And deep in the Coralline crags;

Our love is old, our lives are old,
And death shall come amain;
Should it come today, what man may say
We shall not live again?

God wrought our souls from the Tremadoc beds
And furnished them wings to fly;
We sowed our spawn in the world's dim dawn,
And I know that it shall not die,

Though cities have sprung above the graves
Where the crook-bone men make war
And the oxwain creaks o'er the buried caves
Where the mummied mammoths are.

Then as we linger at luncheon here
O'er many a dainty dish,
Let us drink anew to the time when you
Were a tadpole and I was a fish.

III

The Last Iconoclast

"I have sworn upon the altar of god, eternal hostility against every form of tyranny over the mind of man."

—Thomas Jefferson to Dr. Benjamin Rush
Sept. 23, 1800

Joe's friends called him the "last iconoclast" because of his unique, inextinguishable spark of life and inimitable myth-shattering personality. But it was his undying hostility to all types of tyranny that caused Joe to describe himself as "god's angry man." What epitomizes him best are the words of Thomas Jefferson written to his friend, Dr. Benjamin Rush: "I have sworn . . . eternal hostility against every form of tyranny over the mind of man."

Formally, Joe had less than an eighth-grade country school education, but over the course of his life he accumulated vast knowledge—the equivalent of a PhD or two in wisdom and understanding of complex subjects. People came to recognize his skills and background in taxidermy, geology, evolution, paleontology, prehistoric fossils, poetry, ironwork, and American history. He was almost totally self-taught and had to figure everything out by himself, especially during his formative years on a lonely, desolate, and loveless farm from age ten until his escape to freedom at eighteen. Except for training courses in the Army and a few specialty courses in drawing and taxidermy after the war, the only formal education Joe received was during the two years he was consigned to the orphanage from 1926–1928, from age eight to ten, followed by haphazard country school attendance while on the farm. In the final analysis, Joe was his own teacher.

In late 1928, Joe was indentured to a hard and cruel German farmer in southern Minnesota, and his fitful classroom education was interrupted two years later when he was expelled from school for continual fighting. By this time, Joe was well on his way to become "god's angry man."

As a child, he was always small for his age, and as an adult he measured little more than 5 feet, 6 inches in height, and weighed 125 pounds. He was very lithe, strong, wiry, and quick in everything he did, which was a typical Haan trait. He had blue eyes and light, thin brown hair that reflected his Dutch genes. His hands were gnarled from long years of hard work, but they were artistic-looking hands, supple and deft—strong, sensitive, and expressive hands. They could easily kill an enemy soldier silently from behind, but also shape and mold clay and etch works of art, creatively and with care. Joe's "dress-up" clothes were always army-style khakis, wherever he went—khaki shirt and pants with a matching khaki-colored hat and never any underwear, ever. That quirk went back to his days at the orphanage when he learned to despise underwear and vowed never to wear it again. People who knew him over the years have told stories that drew the image of a fiercely independent, self-made twentieth century poet-philosopher. He was molded and shaped by hardship, adversity, and personal struggle for survival as an orphaned child, Great Depression nomad, and World War II soldier—"god's angry man."

- An alcoholic father and premature death of an angelic mother
- Two years of institutionalized living, imprisoned within the walls of a drab and loveless orphanage overseen by a stern, bleak-eyed matron
- Harsh cruelty suffered as an indentured teenage farmhand for eight years—a slave to ignorance on a small, remote Minnesota farm
- Lack of love, thirst for knowledge, little or no formal education
- Escape from beatings and brutality on the farm to ride freight trains around the country with depression-era tramps and hobos, working at odd jobs
- Security in Roosevelt's Civilian Conservation Corps (CCC) camp in the great North Woods of northern Minnesota
- Violently savage World War II experience as a private soldier in Patton's Third Army:
  - Conflicting emotions while sharing a foxhole with a dead German soldier for three days in Alsace-Lorraine, France, October 1944
  - Awarded Bronze Star Medal for heroism behind German lines during the Battle of the Bulge when American forces suffered 80,000 casualties
  - Wounded in hand-to-hand combat in Germany in 1945 and decorated with the Military Order of the Purple Heart

To those who knew him, these events turned Joe into the "last iconoclast"—a myth-shattering giant who was forcefully independent, deeply sensitive, and constantly challenged by the meaning of life. He was one who struggled with the inherent incongruity of cruel, manmade gods and ruthless people who corrupted their human souls for power and money in the name of religion and greed. Joe said he would prefer the Greek gods, if he had to accept any god at all, because they were tolerant, willing to negotiate, and amusing.

Joe would tell the story Protagoras related to Socrates, a skeptic of democracy, of how Zeus taught men the art of politics and in the process left mankind free to rule themselves. In developing the principles of democracy to protect society and secure the newly established Greek city-states, Zeus asked his messenger Hermes to deliver two gifts to mankind—a concern for the opinion of others and respect for the rights of others. Hermes asked Zeus if he should deliver these gifts to a select few or give them to everyone. Zeus said to give them to everyone—let all the people have their say in governing—and thus did Zeus give democracy to the ancient, squabbling Greeks. Protagoras finished his story by telling Socrates that in Athens, on the general question of government, everyone participated because of the gifts of Zeus. Joe thought this was the way for gods to act, especially when compared with divine rights of medieval Christian kings a thousand years later, or modern theocratic Muslim dictators in the Middle East—and all militant fundamentalists.

From his earliest days, Joe was a sensitive person—someone who was expressive, musical, and poetic—and his poetry and writings spoke to the harsh experience of his formative years. Joe was an avid reader and wrote throughout his life—essays and iconoclastic workingman's poetry that scoffed at man's ignorance, follies, and anthropomorphic gods. He also wrote songs he would frequently sing accompanied by his guitar and harmonica, and he liked it when people said he reminded them of Woody Guthrie.

Joe's entire life was a struggle for the survival of the fittest based on events that molded him from early childhood through the war, buttressed with a fervent belief in Darwin's evolution of the species. Joe noted that Freud had said people are forever changed by the traumas of their youth, and that was certainly true in Joe's case. Another truism Joe picked up in France during the war was a statement that embodied his struggle for survival on the hated farm: "Poor soil makes poor people, and poor people make poor soil worse."

In the Army, Joe had a constant problem accepting discipline, and as a high steel Houston ironworker, friends and fellow ironworkers called him *"el Tigre Chiquito"*—the little tiger—because of his fierce independence. He took great pride in the name.

Joe's poem, "Shadow of the Past—the Ghost," represents the struggle for survival he lived every day of his life, for as far back as he could remember. Survival of the fittest became a fundamental part of Joe's belief system from his earliest years and was reinforced year after year through constant struggle. The poem is fundamentally autobiographical, which is why he signed it, *"This creature were I = JBH."*

Shadow of the Past—the Ghost

Joe Haan (Notebook II, misc)

I was spawned of the Tree of Life,
And ate the fruit with little strife,
I knew not then who I were—
(With so simple of mind, I did not care)
I roamed the forest, roamed the plain,
Knew not whence, or where I came.

As time passed by, I stood upright,
Learned to hunt, to kill, and to fight;
With club in hand I learned quite fast,
To defend from long-gone dangers past,
With thirst for blood and taste for flesh,
I killed for food, and hid the rest.

Plainsman I was, a wandering beast,
Prelithic and strong, to say the least;
I knew not yet, to flake a flint,
So cold the night that came and went,
No gods had I—I had no time,
To nourish thoughts, along that line.

Thus, how I lived until one day,
A saber tooth—he spied my way,
A shadow spotted upon the ground,
From high above he sprang, no sound,
Hit me hard as I turned round,
I lost my club, he took me down.

I rolled afast upon my feet,
Frightened and shaken, not yet beat,
Unharmed and desperate, I looked around,
Spied a rock upon the ground,
Fetched the stone as well I could,
And faced the cat—right there, I stood.

Heartfelt fear, a fear to taste,
When seeing cold death, face-to-face,
Afraid were I, there is no doubt,
But there I stood, to give him clout.
A puzzled cat—I did not run,
As other prey might well have done.

We circled round, with slowing grace,
This cat and I stayed face-to-face,
A beast of terror—filled with dread,
I slowly raised my stone o'er head,
He made his move, I faced him there,
He leaped, I caught him in mid-air.

With all my strength, I drove the stone,
With crashing blows, crushed skin and bone,
Like a beast gone mad, I mashed his head
Again and again and the beast lay dead;
Slowly I stood—clawed, bleeding and weak,
And cast that stone not far from my feet.

Though beknown not to me, or even realize,
That cat had been crippled with broken thigh,
Had he not been old and with broken tusk,
It would have been me who lay in the dusk.
As I stood there in silence collecting my wits,
I soon noticed the stone, fragmented in bits.

Why it broke, it's now obvious to all,
Upon a larger stone, it chanced to fall,
So I took my club and sat me down,
To rest, as I pondered shards on the ground;
A simple thought then crept to mind,
As I mused the wealth of this, my find.

With nary a thought nor hardly a hint
That the broken stone would be called "flint."
The years have gone on since that day,
I'm now flaking flint, needless to say,
I've lost some hair, not much, I propound,
But colder it gets as winter rolls round.

Eolithic Man am I, now exploring the land,
And braver I be, with stone axe in hand,
The flint I'm now chipping, but must learn still,
How to scrape and cure the hides of my kill;
Fast, though I'm learning, short days now grow cold,
I envy furs of all beasts, ever so bold.

How warm it must be, in a mammoth's fur hide,
The great cave bear's fur keeps harsh cold outside.
Winters drift by, fine summers then came,
Armed with spear and an axe, I searched for my game,
I learned to make tools—a good hunting tooth,
In primitive ways, parts roughly made smooth.

Now I gather the grass that's already dry,
To make a soft bed where I then can lie.
But while chipping my flint in my cave one day,
Occasional sparks fell upon the hay,
Quickly, I learn what sparks provoke,
Soon I see trickles of simmering smoke.

And much to my very great surprise,
A fire did blaze before my eyes.
A thought came to mind while observing this,
I can make fire anytime I wish—
Quickly, I learned to make fire my slave,
To cook my food and so warm my cave.

Mesolithic, I'm bound, along life's way,
I've long since shed my old paleo day.
As I follow the trail of Neanderthal Man,
I've nursed no thought of a godly plan,
I've yet no reason to look to the sky,
To plea to the gods and ask, "Why am I?"

Though I've learned to enjoy the stars at night,
And wondered how and why they are so bright,
Then I turn me away with a shrug of shoulder,
For survival's my thought, as I grow older.
Never yet have I turned my face from the sod,
And wondered if ever there was a god.

I've learned already, midst summer winds,
How to dry and scrape all my good skins.
I've learned to take ash from my cold fire,
And with my fingers, paint all I desire,
Colorful clays beckon my call,
As primitive paintings appear on the wall.

And I knew, though why, as yet I cannot say,
That some day soon, I'll be working clay.
A newer age in my life, as I use my good stone,
My first try to carve on wood and bone,
To portray things I see, that live and must die,
Never once looking godward to cry, "Who am I?"

Yes, a newer age comes, as I gaze 'cross the land,
I'm not as shaggy now as Neanderthal Man.
Each morn that I rise from the same old bed,
Far then, I wander from my small homestead;
One day while resting, not thinking a lot,
I toyed with some hide, and tied my first knot!

I leaped on my feet, shouted with glee,
Many things can be done with this, I can see.
Lashing sticks for a drag
Or leads covered with reed,
Quickly I learned to make ties—
So well, indeed.

I'm working my clay, doing much more,
Polish my weapon, smooth every pore,
My paintings improve along with time,
I'm working the ore, so yellow and fine,
Pretty rocks that sparkle, as I pass by,
Attract me now and catch my eye.

But I've had little thought, of so little mind,
To create a god in this primitive time,
Till upon one dark and starry night,
I saw a bright trailing streak of light,
With a shrug of my back, I gave it naught,
No concern to me, or so I thought.

For ere I've seen a falling star,
I knew not how or why, or cared so far.
I returned to my cave with naught to say,
For what can be said, in this primitive day,
But the next few nights I've thought things out,
I've learned from error, there is no doubt.

I've advanced thus far on ingenuity,
And learned much more from curiosity,
I've painted and carved big bears and things,
Awed by rivers and mountains, birds with wings,
But I've never trembled in unholy fear,
Or fell to my knees, as lightning struck near.

I've yet to cross myself in a volcano's wake,
Or pray for deliverance as earthlands quake,
I've had little thought of primitive mind,
To create a god, or to be so blind
As to sacrifice virgins to demons unseen,
Or make burnt offerings to please some fiend.

I've not gone far with my thinking mind,
But I'll do more in the space of time,
I'll learn soon, there is no doubt,
To focus my mind and reason things out.
For you can now see, as long as my birth,
Gods have not trod upon this earth.

This creature were I = JBH

IV

Growing Up Poor in St. Paul

1918–1925

Joe read Thomas Gray's "Elegy Written in a Country Churchyard" when he was in his teens, indentured on the southern Minnesota farm. Like Lincoln, Joe said Gray's characterization of "the short and simple annals of the poor" perfectly described the Haan family growing up poor in St. Paul in the 1920s. Joe's elegy, "The Vagabond Road," casts a forlorn and mournful tone of a desperate young boy living in utter poverty with a drunken father, the pulsing daily pangs of hunger, and the piercing loss of a dearly beloved mother.

Joe's story centers on his early formative years from 1918–1945 and begins with the Haan family—his father, mother, brothers, and sisters—when they lived in St. Paul during the first two decades of the twentieth century. Joe was born in St. Paul in 1918 and, along with his two older sisters, Rose and Cecilia, was consigned to an orphanage by the Ramsey County Court in St. Paul following the untimely death of their forty-five-year-old mother in September 1925. The court made the three children wards of the state of Minnesota.

Their institutionalized orphanage experience, coupled with indentured service following release from the orphanage, left permanent and indelible marks on all three—scarred and repressive memories of a loveless and harshly disciplinarian institution. The orphanage was not unlike a prison in its daily routine of rising at 6:00 a.m. marching to breakfast, chores, marching to school, more chores, marching to dinner and back, more chores, and lights out by 7:30 p.m. All the while, they were guarded by a stern, bleak, beady-eyed, and unloving matron.

The Haan Family

There were five Haan children—Danny, Kenny, Rose ("Sis"), Cecilia ("Bub"), and Joe ("Honey" or "Little Joe"). There was also a half-brother, Harold Carmody, who lived with their maternal uncle and aunt. Harold was the only child from their mother's first marriage to Edward W. Carmody and was the eldest of their mother's six children. The court records refer to Joe's mother, Marie, as "Mrs. Carmody."

The children were all quite young and in school when she died unexpectedly in 1925. To make matters worse, their father, Daniel Frederick Haan, was a hapless alcoholic, unable to care for his family. At the urging of Aunt Sadie, their mother's sister and dearest aunt, the Juvenile Court in St. Paul placed Rose, Cecilia, and Joe—the three youngest children—temporarily in the St. Paul Protestant Orphan Asylum in 1926.

The following year, they were placed in the State School Orphanage in Owatonna, officially named the *State Public School for Dependent and Neglected Children*. The children would have preferred to live with Aunt Sadie, but she was a widow with one child, Charles, and did not have the means to take them into her home.

The oldest Haan boys—Danny and Kenny—were placed in the custody of their maternal uncle, Joe Hadley and his wife Maude in North St. Paul, and were able to get jobs, look out for themselves, and even help the younger children with food, clothing, books, money, and moral support.

The sad story of the plight of the young Haan children is contained in the Ramsey County Juvenile Court and State School Orphanage files, as well as in unopened letters contained in the files—letters written to and by the children when they were consigned to the Owatonna Orphanage.

Later in life, but still as relatively young adults, both Rose and Cecilia died of ovarian cancer. A dangerous cancer gene lurked in the Haan family, especially its female members, and it's quite possible their mother also died from ovarian cancer, as well as an aunt and a niece. Was there also an alcoholic gene?

Oblivion

Joe Haan (Book II, #3)

Time had no womb to enter in,
For eternal time has always been,
Count the tides and count the suns,
Count lives of men whose course has run.

Organic things within the sea,
Do they dream of things to be?
Ferocious sharks go gliding by,
Little fishes then will die.

Men rush madly to their chore,
To a job they abhor.
The sands of time erode away,
The value of their task today.

Like little fishes in the pond,
They too, dream of things beyond.
When all your atoms have finally fled,
Then you have found an eternal bed.

The Roaring Twenties

It seems fitting that Joe was born in 1918, shortly before the last violent months of the First World War, because war was to have such a huge impact on his life while serving on the same fields of battle a quarter of a century later. The Haan kids grew up in St. Paul during the "Roaring Twenties" and prohibition era—a period marked by economic prosperity, political corruption, jazz music, feminist flappers, and stylish art deco architecture.

When Prohibition became law in 1920 by amending the federal constitution, the nation's breweries and distilleries were shut down, creating a demand for "bootlegged" beer, whiskey, and gin. Smuggling, gambling, prostitution, extortion, robbery, and murder thrived. Corrupt city officials and police in St. Paul protected notorious gangsters. Every kid loved to hear stories about John Dillinger, "Baby Face" Nelson, "Machine Gun" Kelly, Alvin Karpis, and the Barker Gang, whose unlawful activities included robbing banks, mail trucks, and trains; kidnapping; and ransom.

What we know from history is that the Roaring Twenties was a period of economic prosperity and a booming stock market that rose higher and higher every day until the inevitable crash in 1929. Automobiles, radio, and the movies brought people and events closer together than ever before in history.

But the good times bypassed the struggling and impoverished Haan family. Judging from the five addresses listed in the Juvenile Court records, the Haan family moved frequently from rented home to rented home, some without running water or indoor toilet. As their father's abusive alcoholism progressed and their mother faced an early death, the family moved frequently from one house to another.

HAAN FAMILY ST. PAUL RESIDENCES 1918–1926

544 Rice St.	1918–1923
Gaultier, near Edmund	1923–1925
2013 Hudson Road	Summer 1925
1786 E. Minnehaha	September 1925 *(residence at the death of Joe's mother)*
271 Edmund Street	October 1925–1926

The Ramsey County Juvenile Court records reveal that the dwelling at 1786 E. Minnehaha, where the Haan family lived when their mother died in 1925, was a one-story frame house where five persons resided. Rent was $20.00 per month, and there was "no bath or toilet. Sewer being put in." The next residence at 271 Edmund Street was considered "clean, four rooms and bath, $25 per month rent," according to the welfare worker's report.

The records show that St. Paul social agencies were well acquainted with the Haan family beginning as early as 1909, with various court entries in 1912, 1914, and 1915, followed by multiple entries in the 1920s, culminating in lengthy court deliberations in 1925–1926 regarding the Haan children. The father, Daniel Haan senior, had police records of three prior run-ins with the law—petty larceny in 1912, disorderly conduct in 1913, and failure to support three dependent children in 1914. These were all related to alcohol abuse, which became increasingly severe over the years.

As a result, the decade of the Roaring Twenties roared right past the Haan family because of their father's alcoholic drinking, inability to hold a steady job, death of his common-law wife of seventeen years, and utter neglect of his five dependent children. Three years after the Juvenile Court Order declared the children wards of the State of Minnesota and placed them in the Owatonna Orphanage, the 1929 stock market crashed, bringing an abrupt and bitter end to a post-war era of national hedonistic excess.

A new era called the Great Depression set in across the country, and like a giant vise in the clutches of a great reaper, the Depression gripped hardest at the poorest and neediest across the land. This was the climate Joe emerged from at the age of seven, following the death of his mother and coming of age during the tribulations and hardships that followed.

An Alcoholic Father

Joe never talked about his mother and father because it was too painful. His father was born in Groningen, Midwolda Province, Holland, on September 2, 1877, and died in West St. Paul, Minnesota, in September 1943. His full name was Daniel Frederick Haan and he is buried in Ramsey County, where he spent most of his American years. His plot lies in Oak Hill Cemetery, 310 Park Lane in South St. Paul. Joe did not know or even care if there was a marker on his father's grave. As far as Joe was concerned, Daniel Haan returned his ashes to the earth, where everyone returns—to ultimate oblivion.

Joe was in the Army when his father died and missed the funeral by five hours, even though the Army had granted emergency leave. After his mother died, and because of the pain he experienced at her funeral, Joe swore he would never go to another funeral in his life—not for anyone. Though he saw many men blasted away into oblivion when he was in Europe during the war, only once, he said, would his hands ever rest upon a coffin. Never again would he ever attend a funeral, not even his father's or his dearest sister's.

According to court records, Daniel Frederick Haan was never formally married to Joe's mother, Marie Mamie Hlavac (Hadley) Carmody. They were considered a common-law couple under Minnesota law. Joe's mother had three sisters and two brothers. She was born in Iowa in 1880 to parents who had recently emigrated from the province of Bohemia in Czechoslovakia, precisely where Joe wound up with Patton's Army at the end of World War II.

Trying to fully integrate into American society when they enlisted in the Army during World War I, Joe's maternal uncles, Joe and Albert Hlavac, anglicized the family name in 1918 by changing it to "Hadley." When Joe's mother died in St. Paul on September 22, 1925, she was buried with the other Hlavac family members in Calvary Cemetery at 763 Front Street in St. Paul. The family plots have a large "Hlavac" stone marker, as well as markers for the "Hadley" brothers, but there is no gravestone for their mother, so neither Joe's mother or father have any markers as memorials. Joe sometimes wondered if a granite stone would ever mark his grave, and he often said, "That's the way it is, nature's way—ashes to ashes, dust to dust, then oblivion."

Many stories have been passed down about Joe's father, Daniel Frederick Haan. Over the years, Joe may have grown to appreciate his father's perspective on life a little better, but he never forgave him for the way he neglected and abused his children and their mother. Joe's father was very intelligent and had a charming Dutch accent that sounded nearly Irish, which is why he called himself "Dan McCann." He was an exceptional speaker and storyteller, so good that people said he could sell ice to Eskimos.

Sis's husband, Leonard Quist, owned a potato truck during the Great Depression. He frequently brought Dan along as a helper because everywhere they went, people liked Dan McCann's stories and gift of gab. Dan was such a good salesman that he once sold an entire truckload of potatoes to a bar owner in southern Minnesota, telling everyone in the packed bar that the bar owner couldn't sell one sack of McCann's Minnesota Red River spuds, let alone an entire truckload. Standing behind the bar in front of his patrons, the bar owner's pride got the best of him and he bought the entire truckload. Dan McCann spent the remainder of the afternoon telling jokes and stories over many rounds of drinks.

He was good at telling jokes and getting people to buy him drinks in the bars where he sold his hundred-pound sacks of potatoes from the truck. Bent down with age, wiry, slightly built, and graying, he would typically enter a bar with a hundred-pound sack over his shoulder. Shouting out in his delightful accent, "Dan McCann's back with the best spuds in the state," he would then open the sack packed with the prize potatoes on top. He would put half a dozen of the largest spuds on the bar, betting anyone within earshot to show him better ones. This routine worked every time and repeat business rarely suffered because of Dan McCann's charm, even from proud bar owners goaded into buying an entire truckload.

But he couldn't keep a job and times were not good during the Depression for the charming Dutchman. Writing to his daughter in April 1939, Dan McCann requested assistance from his children:

Dear Cecilia—

I got a letter from Rose last week and she said Kenny is going to college, but she did not give me his address and she did not mention Joseph. What is Joe doing, is he in St. Paul? Am still on relief which is no good of course. I need clothes awful bad. I got a pair of lumberjack pants last fall and it looks now like a gunnysack. The coat I got from Len two years ago is nothing but a rag. I got two heavy work shirts last fall, and got one suit of heavy underwear. It is getting too warm to wear this goods. So I made up my mind to ask you to ask Kenny to help me. He sure could get me a second-hand suit, they're so cheap at the Goodwill Store. And maybe he has some underwear and shirts to spare, it's awful to be without clothes and look like a tramp. So please talk to him and see what can be done. In case you get something for me, address me as Dan McCann, am known only by that name.

Hope this reaches you in good health,
With love and best wishes,
Your Father,
Address Gateway Hotel #220,
near Washington and Hennepin

P.S. I hope Kenny will soften his heart and help his old Dad.

His children helped him out with a new suit of clothes, food, and money. But over time, Dan McCann's love of drink turned him into a hard-core, though fun-loving, alcoholic. Sadly, he was unable to take care of his family as times got tougher for him in the 1920s, and alcohol began to take its final toll on his life. He eventually died from alcohol—letters to and from his children at the orphanage list his address at skid row hotels on Washington Avenue in downtown Minneapolis, where he lived in the 1930s. The only surviving pictures of Dan Haan senior were taken shortly before his death in 1943.

The Mermaid

Joe Haan (Book II, #30)

At ebb tide in a small lagoon,
A mermaid frolics under tropical moon.
Her head is covered with silver hair,
An iridescent body, scaled so fair.

Shoreline sands, laid down in time,
Organically fertile from ancient slime.
A perfect, rustic, verdant scene,
Varied flowers bloom, for mermaid queen.

Beyond the lagoon, a reef does rise,
A natural groin of nature's disguise.
No shallow water, or peace is there,
For great white shark, has there his lair.

Venture not, beyond the lagoon,
Unwary swimmers meet their doom.
For hungry shark must constantly eat,
So caudal flippers not cease to beat.

The trusting mermaid, swimming then,
Approached the watery killer's den;
The sea came red with bubbled froth,
A beautiful mermaid, forever lost.

Death of a Sainted Mother

When Joe's mother died in 1925, it cut the heart out of him—searing and branding him with pain he felt his entire life. Up to that time, she was his greatest comfort, calling him "Honey" and "Little Joe" because he was so small. The five Haan children were aged seven to sixteen when she died—left to care for themselves due to lack of support from their alcoholic father.

The three oldest boys—Harold Carmody, Danny, and Kenny—were teenagers living with the Hadleys, old enough to find jobs and bring food and clothing to the younger siblings. Rose ("Sis") was the next oldest at twelve when their mother died, and she took care of Joe, the youngest at seven, and their sister Cecilia ("Bub"), who was ten. Kenny remembered Joe crying as the family followed the hearse bearing their mother's body, saying, "Where is my mother? Where has she gone?" Joe could not believe her tenderness, especially toward him, was gone forever. No more milk and graham crackers when she trudged home from her cleaning job, the young kids waiting anxiously for the little food she might bring home after her hard day's work.

Dan McCann would show up at home from time to time, long enough to stay ahead of the landlord's demand for back rent. He moved his hapless family from place to place throughout poorer and poorer parts of St. Paul, staying a few weeks ahead of the past-due rent check. The wanderings of the disintegrating Haan family around St. Paul are easily traced in the court documents on file at the State History Center in St. Paul. They were part of the State School Orphanage records because the Ramsey County welfare authorities finally caught up with Dan McCann, revealing a story of rampant alcohol abuse and severely neglected and abused children.

The 1926 Court Order that placed the Haan children in the Owatonna Orphanage recounted the October 1925 visit of a policewoman and social worker to the Haan residence two weeks after their mother died:

> *Mrs. Hessian [policewoman who accompanied Mr. Paulson, the welfare worker] reported that the mother died two weeks previous; that the father is a habitual drunkard; that the children are alone in the home at the corner of White Bear Avenue and Minnehaha Street. Mrs. Hessian further stated that the house was fairly clean, that the only stove in the house, and from which it was heated, was a small gas stove. There was half a loaf of bread, some milk, and a few doughnuts for the entire family.*
>
> *The children were in school when the visitor called on October 7th 1925 . . . Rose told the court that she and the younger sister kept house. She said that their mother died September 22nd 1925. On October 10th 1925, Probation Officer called at 1768 E. Minnehaha Street and found that the family had moved on the previous day . . . former landlady refused to tell where the family had moved . . . to tell the court and welfare workers to mind their own business; that they had made enough for poor Mr. Haan.*

On October 24, 1925, Joe's father appeared in court and the representative of United Charities in St. Paul made a favorable report on the new home conditions at 271 Edmund Street. The father stated for the record that he had lived with Mrs. Carmody (Marie Hlavac Hadley Carmody) for seventeen years and that they had never been married. By February 9, 1926, the same charity reported that the father was not working and the referee appointed by the court stated:

> *. . . that she heard he [Mr. Haan] was lying in bed all day . . . that she expected him to go to work and provide for the children, or the children would be brought back to court and taken away from him . . . that he was drinking very hard; that Reverend Grant . . . had given him a roast for the children; that Mr. Haan sold the roast for liquor.*

The Juvenile Court Order, "In the Matter of the Neglect of Rose Marie, Cecilia, and Joseph Haan," concluded on August 7, 1926, that the Haan children:

> *. . . are neglected and dependent and proper subjects of the State's guardianship, education, care, and control. It is therefore ordered, adjudged, and decreed that the said Rose Marie, Cecilia, and Joseph Haan be and they are hereby committed to the State Public School at Owatonna, Minnesota, according to law.*
>
> *Grier M. Orr, Judge of the Juvenile Court*

Joe found the shock and loneliness of being motherless and torn from his siblings through the Court Order overwhelming. The death of his mother was a frightening and terrifying experience that haunted him throughout his life. It was one that came back to haunt him again in 1959 when his beloved "Sis," Rose Marie, died of ovarian cancer at the age of forty-six, nearly the same age as their mother, and likely from the same disease.

Stunted by poor diet and frequently facing what he later learned were the numbing pangs of constant hunger, Joe wrote "The Vagabond Road." It speaks of the bitter agony of a seven-year-old boy's "Small Frail Hands on a Coffin Gray," an agony that was to remain with him through the orphanage, indentured farm service, and down a lonesome "Vagabond Road."

The Vagabond Road

"Small Frail Hands on a Coffin Gray"

Joe Haan (Notebook I, misc)

In the year of our Lord 1925,
Like any other year,
Many human tragedies occurred,
For certainly the whole pudding of life
Is well-seasoned with such.

So quite early in the morning,
We find an undersized seven-year-old boy
Clutching the side of a cheap, gray coffin
Within the confines of a third-rate mortuary,
In the seedy slum of a large Minnesota city.

Streetcars, horse teams, primitive autos
Of all sorts flowed by the door
In a constant sluggish stream.
All day till late in the evening he stood,
His small frail hands
Clutched to the edge of the cheap gray coffin.

Inside reposed the Mother,
Who had been his source
Of nourishment and security,
A thin and slightly graying creature
Who departed to oblivion
In the darkness of death.

In later years he remembered
Being wracked by sorrow,
But rather, the pain was from
The pit of the body,
The pain recognized as hunger.

The Mother was a scrub woman,
One who worked for pennies per day,
Plus streetcar fare;
Six children she bore, in dire poverty,
He being the youngest.

In the pre-school age, he accompanied his Mother
To the homes of the affluent and wealthy,
To clean their mansions,
Wash their clothes of worldly grime,
On a washboard, by hand.

What he would look forward to,
With anticipation and anxiety,
Would be the hour of noon,
For some of the owners
Of these sumptuous mansions
Might provide a meal.

But others would deny that privilege,
So he learned at a very early age to steal—
When no noon meal was forthcoming,
He crept stealthily into their pantries
And took what was available.

The finality of death
Is a terrible shock to the human ego,
For we never pass this way again,

A message constantly transmitted to us
At every conscious moment of existence—

The lettered men of physics and chemistry,
Without serious gaps in their education,
Know beyond a reasonable doubt
That only the lowly atom
Will survive without dissolution.

Atoms without emotions, reason,
Personality, consciousness, or sentimentality,
For the atom alone is godly—
The reason for everything that exists—

For even if god existed,
That god would be
As emotionless as the atom.

And so, most become nameless martyrs
In anonymous death,
Only those principals
In which they reverently believed,
We hope shall survive,
And become infinitely better.

As man marches down
The endless corridor of time,
To an unpredictable future,
He shall either walk in the sun,
Or return to the primitive darkness
That was his past.

Were it not for the William Cunninghams,
That darkness would have
Partially descended
On the stage of civilization;

For the average man,
With his narrow egotistical concept of
Who he is, why he is, where he is going,
Lacks the fortitude and intellect
To pay the price.

V

The Orphanage

1926–1928

After their mother died, Aunt Sadie Kjeldtsen, their favorite aunt, went before the Ramsey County Juvenile Court. She urged the authorities to formally examine the deplorable family situation, described by her in the court records as "bad." Aunt Sadie—gentle, nice-looking, grandmotherly—loved the Haan kids, but she was a widow with one son on limited income and lacked the means to support the Haan children.

Aunt Sadie was one of the few rocks of stability in the turbulent lives of the Haan children, and they loved her very much. Although Joe rarely talked about it, he had a deep, affectionate regard for Aunt Sadie and thought about her a lot when he was on the road or crouched in a foxhole with German 88s exploding around him, even praying a time or two out of primal instinct and fear.

Trying to remain a step ahead of landlords, social workers, and Juvenile Court authorities, Dan Haan senior moved his children from house to house. A kindly Lutheran minister befriended the family and gave them food, but the

1926 court records reveal that Dan Haan promptly traded a beef roast he had received from the church for liquor. Then he paid the minister to baptize the children as Lutherans (their mother was Catholic) so he could place Sis, Bub, and Joe, the three youngest, in the Protestant Orphan Asylum in St. Paul, with a pledge that he would pay for their room and board. Predictably, he did not pay and he was soon back in court.

The orphanage contacted the Juvenile Court, who took formal action to place the three children in the State School Orphanage in Owatonna as legal wards of the State of Minnesota until they reached the age of eighteen. The Court Order was final and irreversible, like a prison sentence with no appeal.

At eleven, Bub was three years older than Joe when they were placed in the Owatonna Orphanage following the Court Order. Due to problems with a temporary foster family, Sis remained in the Protestant Orphanage Asylum in St. Paul until January 1928 when she followed Joe and Cecilia to Owatonna.

Though lonely and frightening, their orphanage experience seemed to have made the Haan children stronger and more adaptable than many of their contemporaries. But all three suffered significant tradeoffs, emotionally and physically, as scarred and damaged children.

The older boys fared better. As soon as he was eighteen, Danny joined the Army and escaped to a new and better life. With Kenny, he avoided the orphanage because they were the oldest and found a home with their maternal uncle and aunt. Another maternal aunt, Mrs. Arthur G. Walters, raised Harold Carmody, the older half-brother. Harold was seventeen when their mother died, and he later had two daughters who grew up in St. Paul and lived there as adults. Though the court records referred to their mother as "Mrs.

Carmody," the five children carried the name "Haan" on their birth certificates, and that is how they were recorded in the court records and orphanage files.

The Owatonna Orphanage—the Minnesota State Public School for Dependent and Neglected Children—was established in Owatonna, Minnesota in 1886 and per-manently closed in 1945. The State of Minnesota provided a home for orphaned and abused children under the age of sixteen until a Minnesota family could be found to take them under an adoption, foster, or indenture contract. This contract provided room, board, clothing, access to education, and the opportunity to learn an employable skill.[1] In the 1920s, the Owatonna Orphanage was the third largest orphanage in the United States, with about five hundred children ranging from infants to teenagers. More than 10,000 children were enrolled in the Owatonna Orphanage from 1886 to 1945, when it finally closed.

In the 1930s, the ratio of boys to girls was about 3:1. Due to overcrowding, the orphanage served as a temporary holding facility for children to be placed with a permanent foster family until they turned eighteen and were no longer wards of the State.

As a result, most children stayed at the orphanage less than a year but studies have verified that two-thirds of the children did not do well the first time they were placed with a foster family. Adoption was rare, and the much abused Minnesota Indenture Contract became the primary method of moving children into private homes to make room for new arrivals. And because there were so many more boys than girls and so many people lived on farms in the 1930s, boys were typically indentured to Minnesota farmers. Girls often

1. The Minnesota State Public School for Dependent and Neglected Children—the Owatonna Orphanage—has been restored and preserved as a museum that tells the sad story of orphaned and indentured Minnesota children. http://www.orphanagemuseum.com/home.php.

fared better, depending on the home, and there were far fewer girls to place.

Joe first learned about farming and hard work at the orphanage, which raised its own food and livestock and was totally self-sufficient with a large farm, garden, granary, greenhouse, icehouse, nursery, hospital, carpentry shop, school, gymnasium, swimming pool, laundry, and employee housing complex. The orphanage grounds consisted of several hundred acres of farmland and a campus that had an array of buildings with sixteen cottages (two-story brick dormitories) for the children, 25–35 children per cottage. Why they called them "cottages," Joe didn't know. His memory was of a frightening brick building and hardnosed, unattractive matron. The boys feared her because of her stern rules and frequent punishment.

Over the years, nearly two hundred children were buried in the children's cemetery at the orphanage, many with gravesites that only listed their orphanage file number for identification. There was not even a name to go with the grave—ashes to ashes, dust to dust, and then oblivion, as Joe would note. Children were reminded that they would wind up in the nameless children's cemetery if they didn't follow the rules or misbehaved. Stories told by former orphaned children and documented in the orphanage records in the State History Center in St. Paul are exceptionally sad.

What is especially revealing in the Haan files are letters from various people who had written to or about the Haan children—letters from their brothers and other relatives who sent some money along from time to time. Joe's 1928 Indenture Contract placed him with a German immigrant family near Wells, Minnesota. The selection process at the orphanage was like bidding on an animal at a farm sale or on a slave at an antebellum Southern slave market. Frightened children were lined up in a large room in front of potential foster families who asked prying questions and looked them over carefully, checking the "merchandise." The children were abruptly dismissed without any word regarding their status for several days. Joe's matron eventually told him he would be leaving soon and was lucky to be able to go to a farm where he would have good food, learn useful skills, and attend school.

But with the exception of some hard lessons in farming and a little school, Joe never received the items legally required under his Indenture Contract. Critics called it the "ancient, inflexible, and much abused Indenture Contract" and in 1936, shortly after he ran away from the farm for the last time, Minnesota abolished the Indenture Contract system. It was too late for Joe's benefit. In his book of reminiscences of the Owatonna Orphanage, fellow "state-schooler" Harvey Ronglien concluded in *A Boy from C-11:*

> *Although the environment made us physically strong, it left many of us emotionally deficient. Emotional starvation is inseparable from institutional life . . . individual attention was minimal . . . the children suffered from lack of attention, appreciation, recognition, and love needed for a healthy childhood. For many, it left scars that would last a lifetime . . . the legacy of the [orphanage] is that . . . a large institution is not conducive to raising emotionally healthy children. Those of us who grew up there have faced lifelong challenges . . . our social order was very importantly governed by unwritten rules, similar to those observed by prison inmates. May this book forever serve as . . . a remembrance for . . . their struggle to overcome the scars left by this institution.*
>
> *—Harvey Ronglien*
> *Ward of the State 1932–1945*

Like many other state-schoolers from the Owatonna Orphanage, Harvey Ronglien went on to serve in the Army during World War II where twenty-five orphanage comrades paid the final price for serving their country, listed as killed in action. How many more state-schoolers served during World War II and were wounded in action and decorated for bravery is not known. Harvey Ronglien has planned a veteran's section in the Owatonna Orphanage Museum to pay tribute to the many orphanage veterans who served their country from 1886 to 1945.

For Joe, life at the orphanage was a real change, especially the plentiful food. Another big surprise was all the kids, numbering nearly five hundred when he arrived in 1926. But the first thing he experienced was separation from his sister Bub, which was very upsetting, and then they washed his hair with kerosene to kill possible lice. The new arrivals received clean clothes and plenty to eat, the first time in Joe's life, but it was hard adjusting to cottage life with twenty-eight other boys. They got up early in the morning and marched everywhere just like the army, and they all had regular jobs. In addition to their jobs, they had chores at their cottage, where they made their beds, scrubbed floors, and washed windows. Being put in with a bunch of rowdy boys Joe didn't know, and being separated from his sisters and brothers, made him more anxious, frightened, and lonelier than ever.

The three Haan children were split up for the last time in 1928 when Joe was indentured to the German family near the town of Wells in Faribault County. Sis, who had turned fifteen in April of that year, was indentured to the Pinkham family in the city of Faribault, leaving thirteen-year-old Bub still at the orphanage. Except for the fact that children at the orphanage lived in an institutionalized setting and deeply sensed a lack of love and attention, the system worked reasonably well for Joe's sisters.

Sis was indentured to Reverend Victor E. Pinkham and his family at the St. James School for Boys in Faribault from 1928 to 1933. And when Bub turned seventeen in 1932, she was indentured to a St. Paul family, following a bad experience with a farm family. Bub later attended St. Joseph's Academy, the oldest Catholic school in Minnesota, located at 355 Marshall Avenue on Cathedral Hill in St. Paul. Writing to Kenny in the fall of 1932, Bub told of a recent visit by their father and the problem of censorship:

> *October 28, 1931*
>
> *Owatonna, Minnesota*
> *State School*
> *Dearest Ken,*
>
> *When I came home from school last night they called me over to the office and Pa was over there. He said he had been in Wisconsin working but the job was finished and he didn't have anything to do. So he is going to Chicago and see his brother Fred. He was in Faribault yesterday too and saw Sis. He talked with her for a while, but she had to go to school so he couldn't stay very long. I felt so sorry for him; he didn't have much money and he was dirty looking. He wants you to write to General Delivery, Minneapolis. He said we should write to Danny, have him write to Pa too. He said that when Danny got out of the Army he wished he would go with him, but Danny won't, I know that much . . .*
>
> *Be a dear and do something for me. We are having a party and I need some money for a new pair of slippers for the dance. I had enough money to get some stamps so I wrote and mailed this letter myself cause* they always read our mail. *So when*

you write back don't let on that I asked for money and they won't even know the diff. Lots of kids do it. You don't need to tell Aunt Sadie or she might think I'm getting bad, but I always have been. Just think, I'll be seventeen in June and then just one more year. Boy I could jump for joy to think I'll get out of this hole. . . .

—Bub

Sis was five years older than Joe and had taken care of Joe and Cecilia after the death of their mother in 1925 and before going into the orphanage. Joe and his two sisters remained close over the years—Sis was like a mother to him and he frequently lived with Bub after she got married. Having lost his mother at such a young age, Joe's relationship with his sisters was the closest thing to maternal love he would experience as a child. He only occasionally revealed that feeling, but it remained with him and tugged at him throughout his life.

Sis was fortunate when she was placed in the custody of Reverend Pinkham, who was an instructor in history at Seabury Divinity School in Faribault. Reverend Pinkham and his wife and daughter lived with Mrs. Pinkham's father, Frederick E. Jenkins, who was Headmaster of St. James School for Boys in Faribault. Reverend Pinkham later became a history professor at Carleton College in Northfield, and Sis remained in contact with the Pinkhams throughout her life. In return for room, board, and clothing, Sis took care of the Jenkins household and the Pinkham's only child, Winfried Elaine, a 1948 graduate of Carleton. The Pinkham–Jenkins household was full of books and they placed a high priority on education, especially history.

Sis was a good student, rapidly making up for lost time and completing high school and Normal School Teacher's

College in Faribault. Following school, she became a grade school teacher in Millersburg, Minnesota, where she met and married Leonard Quist. The love of history she received from the Pinkhams was passed on to Joe and her children. Joe remembered being interested in history from an early age, especially the American Civil War, because Sis knew many Civil War songs. She would sing these songs to Joe when he was very young and later to her children, telling sad stories of the soldiers in blue and gray.

But Joe's anger and internal rage grew with each passing day at the orphanage, especially when Sis was taken away to live with the Pinkhams and Joe was left motherless once again. Joe remembered one summer afternoon when the orphanage children were herded into the steam tunnel in the basement of their cottage to seek protection from a tornado. As the winds howled and blew outside and the sky blackened, Joe asked questions about god when the matron made the children pray, "Dear Jesus, protect us from the cruel wrath of god's storm."

Joe wondered out loud, "What is wrath? Why would a god full of cruel wrath send a storm to kill small children?"

But when he asked the matron what a tornado was, and if the cruel and wrathful god would let the children die, a hard knock against his left ear was all he received. His anger began to rage, first at everyone around him, and then at god for being senseless and cruel.

Later, that same year, Joe screamed in anger when he learned in Bible class that god had let his only begotten son die a horrible death, nailed to a cross. Joe wondered at the insane cruelty of a god who would do such a thing to his own son. He asked himself, "How could that be?" And when one of the kids in Bible class told him that grown-up Christians ate the body of Jesus and drank his blood in church, he threw up in class. He was nine at the time.

Besides Bible class, the children were made to attend chapel every Sunday morning. It was a boring service that seemed like it would never end as the sermon droned on and on, seemingly forever. Some of the other boys in Joe's cottage felt like he did, but Joe was the only one to speak out and ask questions about god. He soon learned to keep them to himself, especially in Bible class at school.

Equality Dead

Joe Haan (Book II, #18)

Of gods and kings, and noble men,
Who dwell in castles, grand,
At sumptuous feast, you gorge yourself,
Produced by slavery's hand.

The wine you crave is from the grave,
Of those who've gone before,
From grapes of wrath, you take your bath,
And forever close the door.

On frozen ground, lie derelict men,
Whose time has finally run,
They grow the grape, fill the vine,
From which the wine was spun.

Blood is wine—wine is blood,
Shed by serfdom's kind,
For haughty, wealthy, selfish men,
To opiate the troubled mind.

VI

A Cruel German Farmer

1928–1936

Under the terms of the Indenture Contract with the State of Minnesota, Joe was transferred from the State School Orphanage in Owatonna to the legal custody of a cruel farmer. The farm was about fifty miles southwest of Owatonna near the town of Wells. The farmer was the son of German immigrants, and he turned out to be a stern and insensitive master. Joe's situation on the German farm turned out to be far less fortunate than that of his two sisters, for Joe was to become a virtual slave in twentieth century America. His childhood had ended.

As he looked back as an adult, Joe said life with the German family was like a tale from a bleak and dreary Dickens novel. He lived on a remote, desolate, poverty-stricken farm during the Great Depression, with little food. He worked constantly from sunrise to sunset, seven days a week. The farmer and his wife grew up speaking German and the first thing they told Joe in gruff German accents was that the farmer's name in the German Bible meant "god's strong man," and in other places it meant "angel of death." Joe was young, only ten, and very impressionable. The farmer demanded that Joe learn what he called the "German Orphan's Prayer:"

> *Thanks to god, I will never forget I am a poor orphan. The trials and tribulations of life will better my state here on earth and after death, so I must be faithful and humble in serving my master and those who feed me and keep me clothed and fed.*

This was Joe's introduction to the German farmer during his initial beating in the woodshed, where he was told kids needed to be taught lessons about their place with grown-ups, and that kids needed to be toughened up with a leather strap so they could handle the hardness of life. For eight years, the German farmer treated Joe like a farm animal. Joe came to look upon the farmer as the cruel and unjust god he had first learned about at the orphanage.

The farmer had inherited a small, poor farm from his immigrant father. Across the road were the larger farms of his two German uncles, each with 120 acres, where Joe helped during slack time. The German farmer was in his early thirties, big and powerful, with strong hands and brawny arms like an all-powerful god. Joe was small for his age—well under a hundred pounds in the early 1930s. The German farmer had farmed all his life, and that was all he knew. His only interest was in taking care of the animals and the crops. He looked on Joe as a servant and unpaid hired hand that he fed, grudgingly.

According to Joe, the German's wife, his "Frau," was little better and always took the farmer's side in everything. If the Frau would see Joe crying or moping from a beating and holding his throbbing left ear, she would grab him by the back of his neck and tell him it would be worse next time.

Starting with the day of his arrival at the farm, the German farmer beat Joe in the same woodshed where the farmer's father had beaten him. He began a pattern of feeding Joe cold leftovers in a lonely corner of the kitchen, away from the rest of the family. He made Joe sleep alone in a cold, sparse, windowless and unfinished attic room, and refused to let Joe attend school regularly after a fitful first try. He never gave Joe a birthday or Christmas gift and never said a kind word or offered any encouragement. He robbed Joe of his youth and taught him to hate the German farmer and his god, in that order, and he made Joe so angry he wanted to kill him. If he could have killed him, Joe said he would have done it in a minute, without regret. But he was too scared, so he raged silently in anger.

One day during the first summer on the farm, a fierce thunderstorm rose up in the west and everyone went into the basement of the farmhouse for protection. Lightning, thunder, and strong swirling winds made it seem the house would lift off its foundation, and the German farmer prayed loudly on and on over the howling storm, beseeching god they would not be struck down by lightning. Joe remembered the storm at the orphanage, and he secretly prayed that the German farmer would be the one struck down by the wrath of his own cruel god, but the farmer's prayer prevailed and everyone was safe.

There was no end of work on the German farm, where drudgery was never done—getting up before dawn, working until dark, winter and summer, seven days a week, every day of the year. The cows had to be brought in from the pasture, fed and milked twice a day. Cow and horse mangers were filled morning and night, and horses curried, shod, and harnessed. Stalls had to be cleaned and manure shoveled and spread in the fields. Pigs were fed their daily corn and slop morning and night; chickens and ducks had to be fed and cooped up at night, eggs picked daily.

And in the spring and summer, there were fields to be plowed, dragged, planted, and tilled—endless hours in the fields behind horse-drawn equipment. Hay had to be cut, raked, loaded, and hauled to the haymow in the barn, two cuttings a year. And when harvest time came, winter wheat, oats, and barley had to be cut, shocked, and threshed—a big event on the farm when the threshing crew arrived during hot and humid late summer "fish-fly" days.

In the fall, there was corn to be picked, shelled, bagged, and stored. Wagons and machinery needed constant repair. There were wooden forks, scythe handles, and wagon-wheel spokes to fashion and fix. Wood had to be cut and chopped for the daily needs of the kitchen stove and never-ending winter stash. Hogs were slaughtered in late fall, as it got cold, to make blood sausage for winter. Lye soap was made from wood ash and hog-fat lard, mixed and boiled for hours in a large kettle over an outdoor fire. From time to time, dead calves and pigs had to be buried. Before winter set in, crocks of stinking sauerkraut were stowed away, rutabagas, potatoes, and squash stored in the root cellar for leaner days. In his spare time, Joe helped brew homemade beer, dig potatoes, strain milk, churn butter, make cheese, and on the sly, occasionally taste the homemade German beer.

In winter, they would cut endless blocks of ice from nearby Cobb Creek and drag them by sled over the snow to the ice shed surrounding the milk-house. The ice shed was a wattle-work of sticks and wands, dank, sour-smelling, and double-walled, where milk and cream could cool year-round. At the age of twelve, Joe dug a deep new hole for the foul-smelling two-seat outhouse filled with rotting excrement, wishing all the while it was the farmer's grave he was digging.

This was the work the German farmer demanded, and even more, from the age of ten to eighteen—all for no wages, little school, no love, no affection, no books, no radio, no music, no news, no joy, no sense of belonging. His only gift was oppression and cruelty that bred hate, and meager food. Manure smells from horses, pigs, and cows were part of the everyday life on the farm Joe grew to hate so much, and these clinging odors permeated his memory of farm life forever. Once experienced, they could never be released, like the clinging smell of a dead and putrid animal.

Sometime later, when Joe was in Germany during the war, he would demonstrate no compunction or hesitation in killing a cow in a stinking manure-filled barn when his unit was bivouacked outside a small German village. Joe was on an infantry patrol when two German civilians approached and motioned for him to follow. They led Joe to a foul-smelling barn where a solitary old cow was kept in a stall that had not been cleaned for months. The barn brought back memories of the hated Minnesota farm and the German civilians gestured to Joe how hungry they were, asking if Joe would please shoot the cow for them. Without a second thought, Joe shot the cow between the eyes and in a few minutes there was no trace of it to be seen, not even the blood. Shooting the cow was like a tonic, for when Joe left the farm, he said he would never milk a cow or get manure on his boots again. The smell of the barn brought back memories of the hated German farm, and killing the cow was like symbolically shooting the hated farmer.

As a youngster, Joe had asked why the farmer's cruel god bound the animals to the farm and why Joe in turn was bound to him, and for that he received a hard whack on his bad left ear. And when Joe asked, "If there is a god, why would he send me here, unloved and unfree?" Another thump on the ear. Joe's only freedom would come on rainy days or a snowy winter afternoon when he might steal away to hunt, trap, and dream—if he could contrive an excuse, or during that rare time when the family might go to town for the day.

The unfinished attic room was not only cold in winter, but it was oppressively hot in summer, with no windows and no fresh air. So Joe started sleeping in the barn and outside under the stars when it got really warm. Joe loved the stars. His favorite time was on a clear night when he would fall asleep counting and naming the stars overhead. And he started to collect everything around him—snakes, grasshoppers, ants, bees, berries, wild honey. It was fun to skin and dissect snakes, and he even learned to smoke the meat and make tasty snake jerky.

One time, Sis came down from Faribault with an Audubon book containing pictures of birds, and another book with pictures of animals. She also brought the *Old Mother West Wind* series by Thornton W. Burgess, which depicted animal characters like Peter Rabbit, Jimmy Skunk, Sammy Jay, Bobby Raccoon, Little Joe Otter, Grandfather Frog, Billy Mink, Jerry Muskrat, Spotty the Turtle, and Old Mother West Wind and her Merry Little Breezes. There were lots of pictures in the *Old Mother West Wind* books, and Joe started to draw virtually everything he would see around the farm—birds, squirrels, rats, mice, moles, gophers, foxes, rabbits, beaver, raccoon, muskrats, weasels, turtles, and skunks. He was also interested in every type of insect—ants, butterflies, grasshoppers, mosquitoes, and beetles that he collected in bottles, along with houseflies and horseflies that he mounted on old sticky flypaper so he could study their skeletons when they dried. Beehives and anthills were especially interesting—entire communities that seemed to be guided only by instinct. Nothing seemed voluntary about bees and ants. There was no free will—each one seemed to have an appointed role to play in the grand order of things.

But how about people? What was the grand order of things for people? Were people guided by instinct like ants and forced to work as slaves, or did they have the ability to choose freely in the "cosmic shooting gallery of life?"

Joe remembered the David and Goliath story from Bible class at the orphanage, and he determined to make a leather sling like David's, which he proceeded to do. He dreamed of hurling a stone at the German farmer. Instead, Joe became good at using his slingshot on small birds and animals. And he taught himself to make leather writing strips and clothes he had seen Indians wear in picture books his older brother Kenny and Sis gave him.

Rabbits were the most plentiful game on the farm and about the easiest to catch, and he learned to tan their hides. He was also good at hitting striped gophers with his slingshot. They would stand up straight in the pasture, and if he moved silently, he could get close enough to hit them with a small, smooth stone from the creek. He learned the value of decoys by taking a dead gopher and propping it up with a stick so it appeared to be on lookout. This invariably brought out other gophers that became easy to hit. What fun!

Joe began to live for his daily explorations down to Cobb Creek, which ran around the farms a short distance away. Joe's friends became birds, insects, animals, and all of nature. He made daily notes of his observations and he hurried to finish his work each day so he could explore nature and wildlife around the farm and along Cobb Creek. The German farmer told Joe he was a pretty good worker if he would just follow orders. But Joe simply wanted to get the work finished in a hurry so he could do the exploring he had planned the night before, lying in bed.

Farm work was hard, hot, and heavy during the summer harvest season. Joe liked the late fall and winter best because there was more free time to observe nature and draw pictures of insects, animals, reptiles, birds, and trees, and he kept his observation notes every day of the year.

Notes on the Farm

—Joe Haan, 1933

- **Farm work**—Bring the cows in from pasture, milk cows, haul manure, strain milk; slop pigs, pick up eggs; plow, disc, and rake the fields; plant corn, oats, flax, and winter wheat; cut, bundle, shock, and thresh grain; cut and shell corn; cut, rake, and haul hay to haymow in barn; plant potatoes in the spring, haul bushel baskets of potatoes to the root cellar in the fall; repair machinery, barn, and sheds.

- **Reptiles & Animals**—Bull snakes, garter snakes, salamanders, toads, frogs, mud turtles, snapping turtles, mink, badger, bobcats, cougar, lynx, muskrat, rats, mice, foxes, rabbits, moles, beaver, baby raccoon, muskrat, weasels, pet ferrets, skunks, gray squirrels, red squirrels, chipmunks, striped gophers, pocket gophers, vole, shrew, wolverines—studied mating habits and skeletons, tanned hides—snakes, rabbits, and squirrels made good smoked jerky.

- **Insects**—Butterflies, crickets, grasshoppers, moths, ants, honey bees, wasps, yellow jackets, mosquitoes, beetles—collected house flies and horseflies on fly paper, studied insect skeletons, made drawings.

- **Fish**—Minnows, shiners, suckers, carp, buffalo, catfish, and bullheads from Cobb Creek; pickerel, Northern pike, perch, dogfish, large mouth and small mouth bass, rock bass, walleye, crappies, sunfish, trout—made drawings of fish types—smoked carp was a winter specialty.

- **Trees & Plants**—Cedar, pine, jack pine, spruce, elm, ash, linden (stringy linden bark made good rope), birch, black walnut, sugar maple, white oak, red oak, black oak, wild flowers, ferns, water lilies, nettles, poison ivy, milk plants, grasses—collected seeds and leaves in the fall, made drawings of various trees and leaves.

- **Fruits & Berries**—Gooseberries, red currants, strawberries, raspberries, plums, apples, and wild grapes—berry juice made good ink for writing on hides.

- **Birds**—Robins, bats, orioles, woodpeckers (several types), crows, blackbirds, grackles, hummingbirds, cardinals, blue jays, barn swallows, sparrows, Canadian geese, mallard ducks, teal ducks, loons, pheasants, chicken hawks, Hungarian partridge, prairie chickens, swans—learned mating sounds, drew shapes and colors of birds.

- **Bird Drawings**
    1. **Kite**: hawk-like bird with long pointed wings and a forked tail
    2. **Killdeer**: North American Ring Plover, common in Mississippi valley
    3. **Kingfisher**: straight, deeply cleft bill with smooth edges
    4. **Bluebird**: thrush family
    5. **Bob-o-link**: thrush family, Reed–Rice–Butter bird, Skunk blackbird
    6. **Cat Bird**: thrush family
    7. **Cow Bird**: builds no nest, lays eggs in nests of other birds
    8. **Brant**: small wild goose
    9. **Buzzard**: American vulture, feeds on dead animals
    10. **Owl**: many varieties
    11. **Domesticated fowl**: chickens, ducks, geese

12. **Crested Grebe**: (billed, web-footed)
13. **Bunting**: related to the finches, resembling the sparrow
14. **Eider Duck**: sea duck of the North, white plumage
15. **Coot**: web-footed bird of the rail family, Scoter or Surf Duck
16. **Purple Heron**
17. **White Egret**: heron family
18. **Bittern**: small, pale, buff, spotted Heron
19. **Bat**: short, furred, winged animal
20. **Falcon**: small hawk
21. **Goshawk**: short-winged
22. **Purple Grackle**
23. **Humming Bird**
24. **Grosbeak**
25. **Dove**
26. **Curlew**: shore bird of large size
27. **Awk**: short-winged, web-footed diving bird of the North Atlantic
28. **Albatross**: long-winged, web-footed bird of the sea
29. **Condor**: Vulture of the high Andes, California Condor similar
30. **Cockatoo**: crested parrot, handsome plumage

When Joe was about eleven and started reading schoolbooks Kenny and Sis would bring, he discovered in the haymow of the barn an old and faded farmer's almanac someone had purchased and discarded years before. The almanac told Joe things he had never heard before and he carefully memorized every word, line by line, a practice he followed throughout his life when he would encounter something new that attracted his attention and interest. This early knowledge from an old and humble farmer's almanac with dirty, torn pages stimulated Joe's interest in plants and animals, as well as rock formations and locations of the stars he retained throughout his life. Joe even made a calendar so he could track when the moon would rise and when to expect a full moon, and he learned about trapping and skinning animals.

One spring, based on his recent knowledge from the old farmer's almanac, Joe started laying wire rabbit snares along the ditches of the small cow pasture behind the barn, and to his excitement, he successfully snared several rabbits as they came there to eat milk-thistle throughout the summer. He skinned them, removed the meat for smoked jerky, and left the hides to dry, but the skins soon hardened and cracked because Joe had not yet learned the tricks of tanning. He soon discovered the effects of salt, water, and animal fat. Later, he added boric acid and wood ash used in making homemade soap. This made the leather softer and it was easier to remove the hair. He also learned to tan hides by smoking them like the Indians did, and he smoked fish he caught in the creek and made lots of smoked rabbit and snake jerky.

That same summer when he was eleven, the German Frau asked him to get rid of some moles in her garden. Joe quickly learned how to set traps. He was soon good at trapping, and that kept him going, especially in winter when he would set trap lines along the creek. In addition to wildlife, Joe was attracted to wild flowers, every type of berry, and the different trees and grasses. And when he discovered a nearby Indian mound with arrowheads and other trinkets buried in the ground, he was overjoyed with excitement at his discovery. He spent the next eight years digging and excavating his private Indian burial site.

Joe remembered being so very lonely, sitting along the bank of Cobb Creek and the adjacent meadow looking for four-leaf clovers. But in his solitude, he discovered the spiritual quality of wildlife and nature itself. Because he was so lonely, the surrounding nature and wildlife seemed to make up for his loneliness. They became his friends and companions, and he soon felt spiritually at home in the wild as a naturalist. That discovery made a big impact on Joe. For the first time in his life, he had something to be thankful for, and that made him happy.

For the rest of his life, wherever he was—riding a freight train, hunting in the wilderness, cold and shivering in the trenches of France, or on a steel I-beam high above Houston in the wind—Joe was thankful for nature and life surrounding him. That made him happy and grateful to be alive before entering man's inevitable oblivion. Joe remembered John Muir's words, "Come to the woods, for here is to rest, there is no repose like that of the green, deep wood."

But at the farm Joe's anger frequently surged. Once, when he read about milk thistle in the old almanac, and saw the rabbits eat it, he decided it must be good for other living creatures. But this conclusion, even if it was right, failed to open a door to the pursuit of happiness.

> *Milk-Thistle or Ladies Thistle,* Carduus marianus, *Latin. An indigenous plant, growing on ditch-banks, road-sides, the borders of cornfields, and on rubbish; it flowers in the month of August. Though often a very troublesome weed in pasture and other lands, the milk-thistle may be eaten in the spring as a salad and the tender stalks, if peeled and soaked in water to extract their bitterness, afford a delicious dish; the scales of the flower-cup may be used as a substitute for artichokes; and the roots, as well as the leaves, while young, are wholesome food. Rabbits, likewise, are exceedingly fond of the leaves and stalks of the milk-thistle, which tend*

to preserve their health, especially when kept in a domestic state.

—The Old Farmer's Almanac, 1891

Joe also read about milk-vetch and milk-weed in the Almanac and when he suggested milk plants might be good for cows and people to eat, as they were said to be, he received a hard pounding on his bad ear. The German farmer told Joe only a "dumb orphan" could have learned such stupidity.

Milk-Vetch, or Astragalus, *Latin. A genus of indigenous, perennial plants, consisting of 80 species, the principal of which is the glycyphyllos, Common or Sweet Milk-vetch, Liquorice-vetch, Wild-liquorice, or Liquorice Cock's-head; it grows in meadows, pastures, and on ditch-banks, where it flowers in the months of June and July. This plant will thrive with uncommon luxuriance in poor barren soils and yield an abundance of tender and succulent herbage. Its cultivation has, therefore, been strongly recommended as an excellent winter-fodder for cattle, which devour it with avidity. Cows depastured on this plant are said to yield an abundance of rich milk from which circumstance it has received its most proper English name.*

Milk-Weed, the Marsh, Wild Parsley, or Wild Milky Parsley, Selinum palustre, *Latin. An indigenous perennial plant, growing in damp and marshy situations, where its stalk attains the height of three or four feet; and flowering in the month of June or July. Every part of this vegetable, on cutting it, exudes a milky juice; its aromatic root may serve as a substitute for exotic spices in medicine, and for culinary purposes; the Russians use it instead of ginger and the Laplanders chew it in the same manner as tobacco is chewed.*

Milk-Wort, the common, or Polygala vulgaris, *Latin. An indigenous perennial plant, thriving on heaths and dry pastures, flowering in the months of June and July. This herb is eaten by cows, the milk of which it remarkably increases, also by goats and sheep, but is refused by hogs. Its roots possess an extremely bitter taste, together with all the virtues of the American rattlesnake-root. According to expert knowledge, it is given with success in pleuritic cases, operating as a purgative, emetic, and diuretic. A spoonful of the decoction, made by boiling an ounce of the herb in a pint of water, till one half be evaporated, sensibly promotes perspiration as well as expectoration, and has therefore been used with advantage in catarrhal fevers and defluxions on the lungs; three spoonfuls of this medicine, taken every hour, have sometimes afforded considerable relief in dropsical cases.*

—The Old Farmer's Almanac, 1891

What Joe had learned, and what he had come to understand through observation, was that the fruit and seeds of milk thistle plants were beneficial to living creatures. What he did not know was that they had been used for more than 2,000 years going back to ancient China and the Romans as a treatment for disorders of the liver, bile ducts, and gallbladder. The medicinal ingredient found in milk thistle is silymarin, an extract of milk thistle seeds, an antioxidant that protects against cell damage. [2]

2. The University of Minnesota Masonic Cancer Center has recently verified the medicinal benefits of milk thistle and its variants. http://www.cancer.umn.edu/cancerinfo/NCI/CDR466216.html (accessed August 2010).

Within a short time, Joe's frustration over his bewildering lack of knowledge and inability to do anything about his situation—the utter hopelessness of his condition with no one to turn to or even talk with—made him boil with rage when he came in contact with people. Joe was okay when he was outdoors and all alone, but he was angry all the time when around the family and other people. On the fourth of July 1934, Kenny drove down from St. Paul with Sis and Bub to see Joe on the farm. Joe's latent anger shows in a photograph taken that day of a surly sixteen-year-old Joe and his three closest siblings.

Kenny, Sis, and Bub were important to Joe, but he had come to know there was no escape from the farm until he turned eighteen in February 1936. Joe had also learned that the 1928 Indenture Contract between the State Public School in Owatonna and the German farmer was a travesty and total farce. The farmer did not abide by its written terms and the State Agent charged with the responsibility of checking up on Joe simply did little or nothing. Later, in 1946, Joe found out there were only three state agents to cover the entire state of Minnesota, an impossible task. This is what the orphanage records reveal and what Joe came to understand.

Except for a brief period shortly after his arrival on the farm, Joe attended school irregularly during the eight years he lived on the German farm. And because of the remoteness of the farm, State School officials visited infrequently, if ever at all, to check up on his living conditions with the German family. It was a violation of the Minnesota Indenture Contract.

For all practical purposes, Joe was forgotten by the system, never interviewed or questioned by a State Agent, and his State School Orphanage records confirm this conclusion. At a bare minimum, the terms of the Indenture Contract required the following:

The Agreement requires that the child shall be kindly treated as a member of the family, attend public school, trained in some useful occupation, attend church and Sunday school, and receive, at the age of 18, a small sum of money [$100.00 specified in the contract] or reasonable wages. It also gives the applicant a term of trial, usually three months, during which time he may return the child, if, for any reason, its return is advisable. The purpose is to provide a permanent home for the child.

Joe remembered his matron at the orphanage telling him about the Indenture Contract and how lucky he was to be selected to live on a farm with a regular family and go to school. But that didn't happen. Until Kenny and Sis brought Joe some books, the only reading material in the German household was an old worn out family Bible in German. Joe could barely read at first, and most of the words made little sense because they were in old German script.

He tried to learn German, but he came to hate the farmer, his German Bible, and his cruel god, and he scoffed when the Frau told Joe he would burn in hell if he blasphemed the lord by not saying his prayers at night. Joe had already concluded there could be no god. Prayers like, "Now I lay me down to sleep, I pray the lord my soul to keep," made no sense, especially the part that said, "If I should die before I wake, I pray the lord my soul to take." Joe asked and implored, "Why would a kindly, friendly, loving god let me 'die before I wake?'" Between beatings in the woodshed, Joe appealed to a deaf heaven, and cried, "Why is there no one to hear me, no one to love me, no one to care for me, anywhere in this cruel world?"

Although the German Frau forwarded Joe's letters to Kenny, his letters sent via the orphanage to Sis were unanswered and marked, "Return to Writer, Unclaimed." Sis's letters to Joe were withheld by the German family and returned to the Owatonna Orphanage where they were permanently placed in Joe's file, forever unopened during his lifetime.

The following letter is an example, dated November 17, 1928, and written to Joe from his fifteen-year-old sister, Sis, when he was a lonely ten-year-old orphan on the remote farm. Joe never saw it. The precious letter was returned to the State School Orphanage in Owatonna, unopened and permanently placed, along with other unopened letters written to Joe over the years, in his orphanage file. This letter and others from his brothers and sisters are still in the Haan file at the State School Orphanage archives, unopened until now and never seen by Joe at the time or returned to the writers during their lives:

November 17, 1928

Miss Rose [Sis] Marie Haan
Seabury Campus
Saint James School
Faribault, Minnesota (Care of Mrs. V. E. Pinkham)
Dear Brother Joe:

Honey, why don't you write to me? I suppose you don't know my address, but I'll give it to you in this letter. You know I'm not at the State School [in Owatonna] any more either. I'm out to a home in Faribault. Even if you can't write very well you can at least try.

Don't you get the letters I write to you? I hope you like your home for I'm sure if you're good, the people will be very good to you. Have someone help you write a letter if you can't write it by yourself.

Well, Joe, I've been gone [from the orphanage] a month now. I haven't heard from Aunt Sadie yet. She knows her dear little Joe is gone [from the orphanage], but she's glad because she wants you to have a nice home. If Aunt Sadie ever comes to see me, we will probably come to see you. Wouldn't that be nice?

Are you in the country? In Waseca? Do you go to school? Well, Joe, I hope you'll get this letter. Cecilia is over in Cottage 10 now [at the orphanage]. She took my place.

Well, Sweetheart, I must close now. Be a good boy and remember everything. Be sure to write to me and tell me how you are, won't you?

Well, Goodbye Darling
Your Loving Sister,
Rose Marie Haan,
Much love

Rose was a careful writer and knew from experience that her letters, as well as Bub's and Joe's, would be censored by orphanage officials, going and coming. Any criticism of the orphanage or its officials, or of the foster homes, meant the letters would not be mailed, so the children quickly learned to use coded language and say the opposite of what they meant. Writing from the Pinkham household in Faribault to her brother Kenny in St. Paul on August 9, 1929, Rose complained that she had received a letter from Bub at the Owatonna Orphanage, only fifteen miles away, but the letter was censored and Joe's address was erased, once again:

Dearest Brother,

I wrote to Bub, and heard from her. She sent me Honey's address again, but it was erased [again].

You know I'm expecting our Aunts to come down pretty soon before winter sets in. If they come, I'll see Bub then and I can get Honey's address. Bub says he has a nice home and the people are awfully nice, but if I don't hear from him soon, I'll go crazy. Bub, I guess, is a little Happy-Go-Lucky too, but how I wish I was with her. Write anything you please when you write to me [here] because no one reads my letters. Thank Goodness! Bub is in seventh grade this year and Joe is in fourth or fifth, I don't know which it is. When you referred to the "old man," did you mean "Pa?" I feel sorry for him but he can't care much about us kids or he would write to one of us. The last time I heard from him was last March. He was in Minneapolis then.

Best wishes and Good Luck to you.
Your Loving Sister,
Rose Marie Haan—
Or rather my real name (Sis)

The officials at the orphanage censored the children's letters and deliberately withheld some of them, forever unopened. The Owatonna State School Orphanage and the State Agents charged with inspecting the living conditions in the farm home where Joe lived for eight years totally failed in their responsibilities to Joe, the Haan family, and the people of the state of Minnesota to ensure that Joe was properly cared for by enforcing the terms of the Indenture Contract.

Unfortunately, failures like Joe's case were not uncommon. This was especially so for children residing in remote, hard-to-reach areas like the German farm, which was two hours by sleigh from the nearest town in winter.

Because of the way Joe was treated by the German family, and because of so many bitter disappointments in his early years, Joe raged resentfully every day at people around him and at the world, defied authority, and asked throughout his life:

> *Why, if there is a god, does he treat small children so horribly? Why are people so hard on the animals, and why is god so hard on the people?*

Joe suffered terribly during his first two years on the farm—physically, emotionally, and spiritually—and had become virtually uncontrollable at the local one-room country school as a result. This is especially clear in a 1930 letter to the German family from Joe's teacher.

> *March 28, 1930*
>
> *Wells, Minnesota*
>
> *Dear Mr. and Mrs. ______,*
>
> *I'm sorry that it has become necessary for me to inform you concerning Joseph's behavior before and after school and at recess periods. He has been fighting almost every day he has been in school. His fighting did not bother, though, until Joe Stenzel's children came here. Since those children are here, he thinks of nothing, but fighting. He just needs to open the school door and then he starts a fight before he gets his coat off. He can't go home at night unless he beats up someone first before he goes.*
>
> *I have warned him plenty of times and now he tries to get his revenge through telling the Stenzel boys to do his fighting. These boys do so because they know Joseph will harm them if they don't do*

as he says. All of this causes nothing but trouble all day long.

Joseph treats the little children much too roughly. He has also caused a division of the children into two groups. He has the three Stenzel boys on his side and all day long, he leads them into trouble with one another. Such conditions are very unpleasant. Joseph's anger becomes so terrible that he has no control over his speech and he says very unpleasant things not only to the children, but also to me.

Will you kindly speak to Joseph regarding his fighting? It will not only be for the good of the school, but also for his own good.

I thank you very kindly for your cooperation in this matter.

Sincerely yours,
Miss _______[3]

But there was nothing that could be done to restrain Joe's anger, so the German farmer simply removed Joe from school. The only thing that would serve to channel Joe's anger was kindness, books, and being alone outdoors. By the time he was eleven, Kenny and Sis had located Joe at the farm, and over the years they brought him clothes, food, money, and most importantly, books and writing materials. During the summer of 1931, Joe's maternal aunts arranged to drive Sis and Bub down to the farm for their first reunion with Joe after leaving the Owatonna Orphanage. In a letter to Kenny after the visit, Rose recounted the events of the day:

3. On Joe's last trip to Minnesota in the 1960s, he stopped by the German farm and went through the Rose Hill Protestant Cemetery in Wells where the surnames of the German farmer's family and the teacher are etched on several granite tombstones.

July 12,1931

Dearest Ken,

Your letter was the first letter I've gotten since I came back and maybe you think I wasn't glad to get it! Gee, it was lonesome here after I came back . . . Bub says she was lonesome too. Honey sure is a cute little kid. He looks just like he always did, to me. He's taller, of course, and maybe a bit cuter. He was so bashful at first, but he soon got used to me and got over his bashfulness. He milked the cows for us, and took us into the granary and showed us the different feed, naming each kind. He's a regular little farmer now. We didn't bring him anything, but Bub and I and Dot gave him a little money. He had a knife and said he got it from his teacher for being the smartest kid in school—but he hates Arithmetic. Gee, Ken, you ought to go down and see him sometime, even if you do have to take the bus. Honey remembered all the old kids we used to know and asked us about them. He almost cried when I told him Aunt Maud had died. He asked about her. I didn't think he remembered her . . . Well, . . . I'll close with lots of love to you.

—Just Sis

Over the years, Kenny kept in touch with Joe. In 1933, Joe was overjoyed when he received a rifle from Kenny for Christmas, and in four surviving letters to Kenny, starting in December 1933 and continuing through January 1936, Joe expressed his gratitude and hopes for the future to his older brother:

[December 17, 1933, age fifteen] They said if I behaved myself I could go up to the Cities for

Christmas, but if I didn't I would have to stay home. And if you would come and get me because I would probably get lost if I went on a bus or train alone because I never rode on one before by myself. I am busy studying for our Christmas program in school.

[March 9, 1934, age sixteen] I got the book that you sent me. It surely is a good story. I never went to school today . . . I had to stay home and do chores. I sure had a lot of fun hunting with the rifle you gave me for Christmas. I shot 7 rabbits—2 jacks and 5 cottontails. There is a lot of rabbits around here. About a month ago, I shot a blackbird over in the neighbor's grove. One day there was a flock of prairie chickens back of the house in the alfalfa field . . . couldn't seem to get them. We are going to have a Declamatory Contest here . . . the name of my piece is The Cat Came Back. *It is quite long but I already have it learnt. I was in 3 other times and I took first place each time. I killed 2 big rats today under the corn stack. The other day there were three pheasant roosters by our driveway . . . just when we were ready to shoot at them they flew up so we didn't get their meat. Last Saturday I seen a flock of wild ducks.*

[October 7, 1934, age sixteen] The pheasant crop around here isn't quite as thick as it was last year because of the dirt storm that we had last spring. A lot of the [pheasant] eggs were covered with dirt and were destroyed. But anyway, I think that there is enough for you to come and hunt whenever you wish. The law is only open in the afternoons for 16 days, but in that time I think there will be plenty pheasants slain. Tonight when

I brought the cows home I heard pheasants crowing all over, ork, ork, ork. The clock is ready to strike nine and that is bedtime. Your brother, JBH

[January 12, 1936, nearly eighteen] I wish to thank you a few dozen times for the presents you sent. Did you get the pair of spats I sent you? I have been hunting quite a bit this winter. I shot 11 rabbits. I caught a weasel a couple of weeks ago and shipped its hide to the Olleg Fur Company in Iowa. I don't know what I will get for it. I got a present from Aunt Sadie. She sent me a necktie. P.S. I was going to tell you about the chicken hawks that I caught. I set some traps out in the field with chicken meat on it. I caught five that way and I shot one in the grove with the rifle. I nailed them all up on the corn crib with their wings spread out. They look purtty nice. Joe

Graduating from Faribault High School and Normal School Teacher's College where she received her teaching degree and certificate, Sis had access to elementary school textbooks. She also brought Joe art paper, charcoal, soft lead pencils, and crayons for drawing animals. She even purchased books on astronomy and geology that piqued his interests, as well as astronomical charts with the names and locations of the planets and night stars—and even a current Farmer's Almanac that he learned to treasure for its common sense lore, ready-made for a lonely farm boy interested in everything.

Joe rapidly became a good reader, self-taught from his earliest days, and his older sister made certain that he learned to write. Joe's letters from that time were sparse, though Sis gave him stamps, and only four letters have survived. Joe tended to print later in life, but his handwriting in his surviving letters was good. His spelling was self-taught and strictly phonetic.

Shortly after she graduated from high school, Sis and Kenny tried to get Joe released from the farm and into their custody. The Owatonna Orphanage stood firm in rejecting their request, saying that the Indenture Contract was a legal and binding contract between the State of Minnesota and the German farmer, and that it must remain in effect until Joe's eighteenth birthday. Unless he could escape, Joe was destined to remain imprisoned on the German farm as a legally indentured slave.

The only clothes the farmer provided were hand-me-down farm overalls and worn-out boots. Joe hated the boots because they always hurt his feet, so for half the year he went barefoot. The first new shoes and boots Joe ever owned were issued to him when he enlisted in the Civilian Conservation Corps (CCC) in 1940.

When he was about thirteen or fourteen he had learned enough about tanning hides that he made a pair of Indian breeches and a leather shirt. He sewed them together with a needle made from bone, like the Indians. Joe even learned to tan hides so smooth they were like ancient vellum. He would write on them using homemade inks from wild grapes, blueberries, and raspberries. He often wondered what language ancient cavemen might have used and how they talked, and he eventually created a language called XOTÄNEF, based on his intuition and insights into early man and their need to communicate.

Sis also gave him a precious harmonica. He taught himself to play the songs that he wrote, but the ocean-like roar in his increasingly deaf left ear always caused problems.

Tragically, Joe wasn't the only ward of the State of Minnesota to be treated inhumanely and suffer degradations of physical and emotional violence. In *Boy from C-11,* Harvey

Ronglien, who was consigned to the orphanage shortly after Joe arrived, cites a case nearly identical to Joe's experience on the German farm. It is about a young boy from the Owatonna Orphanage who was indentured to a brutal and sadistic farmer near Caledonia, Minnesota. Ronglien writes:

> *The man forced the boy to do most of the farm work, berated him, isolated him, and tried to make him quit school. When he was 17 . . . [he] escaped after a severe beating . . .*

A former state-schooler himself, Ronglien told of other firsthand stories of indentured children from the Owatonna Orphanage who suffered cruel and humiliating treatment nearly identical to Joe. Kids were forced to live in the barn and eat alone in the kitchen while the family ate in the dining room or at the kitchen table. They were given endless reminders they were "bad" orphans. There were frequent beatings, constant berating, and little or no supervision from the State Agents who were required to make annual inspections.

The sense of loss and utter loneliness on the German farm—bereft of family, suffering constant beatings, no friends, no books at first, no one even to talk with—caused Joe to explode in anger, inside and out, virtually every day. When the farmer tried to crack down with discipline it almost always backfired and produced the opposite effect. So Joe sought the out-of-doors and other tonics as refuge.

Joe remembered one day, shortly before Prohibition was repealed by President Roosevelt, when the Watkins salesman stopped at the farm and was showing some of his products in the house. Joe stole into the back of the salesman's Model "A" Ford panel truck and took a large container of "tonic." The quart bottle contained what Joe later learned was bootlegged whiskey, illegal to sell in the early 1930s during Prohibition but widely available from a variety of sources. After tasting its bitter contents, Joe hid the bottle in the haymow. On the first rainy day, he ran off to nearby Cobb Creek to fish and try some more of the "tonic." It made him sick, and when he came back to the barn later in the day the farmer asked Joe why he looked so pale.

Joe also learned to tap into the farmer's homemade German beer in the cool milk-house. Joe said he hated the taste but liked the effect. He had good reasons to be in the milk-house every day—straining milk, separating cream, churning butter—and quickly learned that a swig of brew from the farmer's crock made him feel good. It also made him angry, a trait that would follow Joe throughout his life whenever tempted by alcohol.

Several of Joe's friends remember his "butter story." On the farm, Joe had to get up early to feed the animals and milk the cows, and Joe would usually come in for breakfast as the farmer's children were getting up. At night, after dinner, the children would play around the kitchen table while Joe washed dishes and cleaned up from the evening meal before going back to the barn to finish the daily chores and get away from the farmer. One of Joe's household chores was to put perishable food safely away. Because there was no electricity, the milk, cheese, and butter were stored overnight in a cool root cellar under the house. The homemade butter was placed in a two-gallon crock in the cellar and covered with a large pie tin weighted down with a heavy rock.

The Frau came upstairs one morning and complained to her husband that Joe must have forgotten to place the heavy rock properly on the cover because rats had pushed off the lid and started to eat the butter. For punishment, "so he wouldn't forget," the farmer made Joe eat the entire crock of butter before he could leave the basement storage room. It took Joe two days to dispose of the remaining two-gallon crock of butter, and he never ate another speck of butter for the rest of his life. Joe's wife, Helen, was forbidden to ever put butter on the Haan table in Houston—only margarine. In CCC camp and Army mess halls, Joe amused his comrades with the butter story—but angered them with demands that butter be removed from the table.

When asked, Joe often said to friends that most of his farm recollections were too painful to tell—like the frequent beatings. Or when the carnival would come to Wells, the nearest town, or when the county fair was held in Blue Earth—and everyone in the family would go to town except Joe. He would remain on the farm to feed and milk the cows and do the other farm chores that had to be done day and night. The German farmer and his Frau would constantly tell Joe before each woodshed beating:

> *You are being punished, orphan boy, for god allows no mockery. The Good Book says you will eat your bread by the sweat of your brow, for dust you are, and to dust you shall return.*

Joe was never to forgot those German words, repeated to him by his wardens on the hated farm nearly every day and before his routine woodshed beatings.

Farm life in the 1930s was difficult for everyone, not just Joe, and economic conditions throughout the country made hard times far worse. What Joe came to learn after he left the farm was that capitalism seemed to have gone haywire through disruptions caused by a recurring boom-and-bust economy.

Millions of people were out of work in the 1930s—unemployment was well over fifty percent in rural Faribault County near the German farm. Families didn't have much food either because it cost more to raise pigs and cows than what they could earn selling them. Crop prices had fallen by sixty percent after 1929, and other commodity prices also plunged. People had severe losses in the stock market—their entire life savings—and were forced to cut back on spending because they didn't have any money. Self-perpetuating deflation caused falling farm prices to drop further and farmers suffered even more. Until the banking system was finally stabilized in 1934 with federal deposit insurance, five years after the stock market crashed, bank panics were an almost daily occurrence during the Great Depression. Hard-working people, whose deposits represented their life's savings, suddenly lost all they had through no fault of their own. They had put money in their local banks for safekeeping and thought it was safe until they wanted to draw it out, but when their banks failed, the money disappeared into a black hole and was gone forever.

No one seemed to have any money in the 1930s, and this was especially true on the German farm. Joe remembered when he saw his first fifty-cent piece and couldn't believe the words "In God We Trust" written on the coin. And then he learned it was on all American coins and on all the paper money too. Later, during the war, Joe mused when he came across an old World War I German belt buckle with the inscription, "Gott Mit Uns." He laughed at man's brash stupidity about whose side god is on and pondered the finality and oblivion of death.

While the entire country was suffering economic hardship, a severe drought ravaged the agricultural heartland beginning in the summer of 1930 when Joe was twelve. The infamous Dust Bowl emerged and lasted until 1936 when he turned eighteen and finally fled the dreaded German farm. Immense dust storms—"Black Blizzards"—frequently reduced visibility to a few feet. They caused the largest migration of people in American history from farms in the Midwest, Texas, and Oklahoma—people often referred to as

"Okies" and immortalized in John Steinbeck's *The Grapes of Wrath.*

The German farmer's Indenture Contract with the Owatonna Orphanage terminated on Joe's eighteenth birthday, February 27, 1936. In reply to a letter from Mr. Vevle, the superintendant of the Owatonna State School Orphanage, the farmer attempted to explain why he had not remitted the $100 he owed under the terms of the contract. He never once mentioned Joe by name—referring to Joe only in third person throughout the letter:

February 24, 1936

Wells, Minnesota
Dear Mr. Vevle:

Received your letter some time ago, but on account of our bad roads here, we are unable to get out. We don't get any mail or can't mail anything unless we go to Wells, which is 2 hrs drive one way, with the team [horses]. Have been snow bound for over a month, never had the car out. On account of these road conditions, we were unable to have a truck come out after some hogs so we couldn't get $100.00. But as soon as they open up the roads we will get a truck to haul them off and will either send or bring the money. We asked him and tried to talk things over in a good way, what his plans were for the future, but like always, slam[m]ed the door for us and said, "It wasn't any of your business." We told him, that we were to send the money to you and he could get it from there whenever he was in need of it. The answer we got then, "I'll never go near that dump of a town and [even] if I don't get a penny."

You have no idea what kind of a temper he has for his age. He can't be beat for working if we let him do things the way he wants to, but if we want it done this or that way or try to teach him easier ways, then he loses control of himself, and it's hard to get along with him, when you always have to keep still and let him be boss. So, I don't see why we should try and make a home for him, when we can't be our own boss and have things done the way we want them. So, I wonder if you'll come and talk to him or get him when the roads open? Because if we mention going to Owatonna there will be war again. We offered him if he'd better himself he could stay but things don't seem to change.

Yours truly, _________

P.S. We asked him whether he planned on staying with us. He said he didn't know, so that's all the satisfaction we can get. We don't even know what we're at.

Within a month of the first letter, the German farmer apparently sold enough livestock to raise the $100 needed to fulfill the final terms of the Indenture Contract and on March 27, 1936, the State School in Owatonna received the following letter from the German farmer's Frau:

Wells, Minnesota
Dear Sirs:

Enclosed find check for Joseph Haan. We thought you would come and see after things so we could have sent it a few weeks ago. Joseph got one of his mad streaks again yesterday. He started tearing boards off from the barn and throwing them at Mr._____. So he told him to pack up and go. He left yesterday. Mr.____ wanted to take him to town *but he wouldn't ride. He started afoot. We wrote out a check for $5.00 and handed it to him. He took that and tore it to pieces and threw it ahead our feet. So whether he'll come after the $100.00 from [there] we don't know.*

Mrs. ________

Joe's version of what happened that day was a little more vivid and violent. The German farmer and Joe had a dispute about Joe's repair work on the north side of the barn and there was an ensuing scuffle. When the farmer hit Joe severely on his bad left ear with his fist for the last time, Joe got so mad he hit the farmer squarely on the back of his head with a two-by-four. Joe took off running toward Wells with only the clothes on his back, not knowing or caring how seriously he might have injured the detested farmer. Joe never looked back, but on his last trip to Minnesota in the early 1960s, with Helen and his two teenage sons in tow, Joe detoured from the main highway. He found the old German farm, where he had a friendly talk with one of the farmer's sons.

Some years later, shortly after leaving the Army, Joe filed a lawsuit charging the State of Minnesota with selling him into slavery to the German farmer under the terms of the Indenture Contract that were not fulfilled. The case was dismissed when the Ramsey County Court ruled that the statute of limitations had made Joe's claim invalid.

Joe left the hated farm a month after his eighteenth birthday. Shortly after President Roosevelt established the CCC camps, he was big and strong enough to finally defend himself against the hated "Angel of Death" and run away on the nearest freight train. After riding the rails with thousands of other down-and-out teenagers and Depression-era tramps and hobos from mid 1936 to the end of 1939, Joe joined the CCC in January 1940. He was assigned to a camp in the far northern Minnesota wilderness near the remote and isolated community of Isabella, not far from the Canadian border.

From there, Joe enlisted in the Army on January 17, 1942, five weeks after Pearl Harbor and America's declaration of war against Japan and Germany. Facing enemy German soldiers for the first time, Joe's conflicted feelings toward the German people were highlighted in his poem, "Memories of Death"—revealing a direct connection to his indentured experience on the German farm, memories of their treatment of him, their German ancestry, their rigid German ways, and the German accents Joe had learned to hate.

Paradise Disorganized

Joe Haan (Book II, #27)
By Father fa-nang-ler, Ex Soul Trapper

I just returned from paradise,
What I observed shocked my eyes.
No method or manner have they there,
And no one really seems to care.

I asked the keeper of the gate,
"What's the population rate?"
"My good man, god only knows,
We have them stacked, unnumbered rows."

I then inquired whether a quota be,
He raised his staff for me to see,
"You see there, high up in the sky—
Room enough for all to die."

Sir, may I enter the glittering room,
And see the precious golden throne?"
"Oh, no! And never, earthly friend,
That's reserved for haloed men."

So, what fools we mortals be,
To be snared in a heavenly sea.
Do not take that scripture bait,
Avoid a boring, endless fate.

VII

Riding the Rails
1936–1939

At the height of the Great Depression, more than a quarter million teenagers like Joe were on the road. They illegally hopped freight trains as they crossed the country back and forth, "riding the rails." They hit the road because they wanted adventure, wished to see the world, wanted to escape unhappiness at home. Sometimes it was because destitute fathers had too many mouths to feed, or as in Joe's case, it was because there were no jobs and nowhere else to go.

It was an exciting time for an imprisoned and untraveled teenager like Joe to be set free for the first time in his life, and especially for someone who was so inquisitive but who knew so little of the world except for his observations on the farm. Joe had been dreaming of escape for nearly a decade. Every night after prayers in the orphanage in Owatonna, the boys in C-11, Joe's cottage, would secretly plot their escapes, as though they were big-time prisoners at the Minnesota State Prison in Stillwater. The nearby train tracks were always the means of escape—beckoning rails that led the way to freedom like the Underground Railroad in *Uncle Tom's Cabin* and other Civil War stories he learned from Sis. The boys dreamed of hopping the nearest freight train and many tried their hand at it, but nearly all attempts were unsuccessful and they were quickly brought back to Owatonna.

So when Joe had his chance the day he decked the German farmer on the head with a two-by-four, he headed straight for the railroad tracks that ran through the nearest town, about ten miles from the farm. Joe never looked back when he ran away, nor did he care which direction he took to escape from southern Minnesota. Nor did he ever receive the $100 and two suits of clothes he was owed by the Owatonna Orphanage and State of Minnesota.

The town of Wells was a good jumping off point for a teenager to hit the rails. Wells had been platted in 1869 by a precursor to the Milwaukee Road—the Chicago, Milwaukee, St. Paul, and Pacific Railroads. As the town grew, it became a railroad junction, with one rail line running east and west between Milwaukee and Sioux Falls and a second running north and south between the Twin Cities, Des Moines, and Kansas City. The Milwaukee Road had innovations such as the famous high-speed Hiawatha *Rocket* passenger trains that reached speeds of 100 mph and more during the 1930s. It was forced to file for bankruptcy in 1935, just a year before Joe challenged the railroad bulls for the first time in Wells.

The 1930s were hard times for almost all Americans. For thousands of American teenagers, times were really tough "on the bum"—walking, hitch-hiking, hopping freight trains—riding the rails on the Milwaukee Road, Great Northern, Santa Fe, or Southern. Without money and half-starved, Joe and his companions suffered hardships and danger as they looked for odd jobs that were tough to find. They became inventive out of necessity. Riding the rails became an education about living on little food and dealing with cold nights, rough railroad bulls, panhandling, social banishment, arrest, jail, and being killed or injured hopping on and off moving trains.

Al Kussmaul from Mt. Hope, Wisconsin, wrote of his travels around the United States in his book, *Life on the Bum in the Early 1930s*. He summed up what it was like on the road in those days:

> *I was able to visit 37 states at an average cost of $1 per state, besides being in Canada. It is a tale of police blockades, big fat egg sandwiches, dust storms and floods, heat so hot it burned my back through my shirt, and cold that kept me up all night tending a fire. I accepted rides from a prizefighter and a wrestler . . . a cotton picker, a barber and a teacher and many more . . . I saw museums and monuments, mountains and plains, swamps and deserts. I worked as a babysitter, night watchman, fruit picker, and driver. I fished and hunted. I rode in trucks, cars of all types, a motorcycle, a train, a buckboard, and more Model Ts than Henry Ford. I was given help and directions from little old ladies, truck drivers, uncles and aunts, Cajuns, Mexicans, Darkeys, Texans, and a US Senator. I found a country crippled by the depression, split apart by prohibition and segregation, but working together, helping each other and struggling, not down and out. I found people from all over on the roads. Okies wanted to pick peaches in California, poor whites from the south wanted to build cars in Detroit, Darkeys from Mississippi wanted to go up North and work in the factories or textile mills, and Swedes from Wisconsin going to work in the oil fields of Texas. Everyone thought it was going to be*

better someplace else. It was the American way and I was in the middle of it.

Odd jobs were critical for survival and of all the different odd jobs Joe experienced, his favorite was with the circus or carnival where he would frequently land a roustabout laborer's job with the Ringling Brothers, Barnum & Bailey Circus, or one of the many traveling carnivals.

One day in the 1980s, Joe took Tim Carlson to the Houston Natural History Museum. There in a glass case was the skull of the famed 1930s circus elephant, Dumbo. It prompted Joe to tell his Dumbo story. In the 1930s, Dumbo was billed as the mightiest elephant in the world and, though the circus had suffered during the Great Depression, it had managed to stay in business. It happened that the circus was setting up in St. Louis just as Joe came riding into town on the rails in 1938. Everywhere the circus stopped, they hired locals for feeding and watering the animals. Joe got a job, along with some young fool who wanted to see what would happen if he stuck the lighted end of a cigarette in the elephant's trunk. When he did just that, Dumbo screeched in pain and promptly picked the young man up, threw him to the ground, and stomped on him, killing him in an instant. The City of St. Louis, in its divine wisdom, passed a law that read, "Any animal that willfully causes the death of a human . . . must be put on trial, like anyone else."

There is no record of what the Judge deemed to be "peers," or if Dumbo was represented by an attorney, but the trial was quick and the death sentence was carried out in a few days. The Sheriff asked for volunteers and about 150 men turned out at dawn. Dumbo was tied to a heavy stake, and the men lined up in a semi-circle with their hunting rifles. It was mercifully quick. Dumbo's skull looked like it had smallpox, with hundreds of nicks in the skull. Tim remembered Joe standing in front of the museum display case and saying, "Where was Clarence Darrow when Dumbo needed him?"

Joe's hobo years riding the rails were often frightening and even painful. Infamous railroad detectives—yard bulls—were armed with guns and clubs and they used them frequently. Joe was hit more than once by the yard bulls and he recalled jumping into a boxcar one day as a bullet hit the wall just a foot from his head. Joe's training on the German farm was good preparation for the hazards of the road, but he was young, uneducated, and inexperienced, as well as small and youthful-looking for his age.

Joe's fellow hobos liked him and took to him because he was entertaining, and many of them felt sorry for Joe because he looked so young. They showed Joe the ropes and how to catch a train. Joe showed them how smart and self-sufficient he had become, growing up alone on the farm, handy with his hands and tools. He was helpful to them with his resourceful, clever way of preparing rabbits he snared and other food he found growing along the countryside. Fights and violent encounters with other hobos over scarce food were frequent, especially when cooking a succulent hobo delicacy like one of Joe's favorite meals called "Hobo Cabbage:"

> *You take a head of cabbage and some onions from a local garden (unnoticed), split it three quarters' the way through and into four sections, split mostly but not all the way, opening the center enough for some cooking oil or lard (never butter) and four small onions. Wrap it tightly in corn husks and put it in the coals of a smouldering fire. Wait about an hour, or as long as you can hold out when you're hungry, and you have a feast for a hobo. You need a little salt to do it justice—try it sometime.*
>
> *—Joe Haan*

Except for the East Coast Civil War battlefields, Joe stayed away from the Deep South because of its reputation for injustice. But hobos and tramps liked California because it was warm and there was always fresh food available for the taking, often lying on the ground—like fruit that had fallen from trees surrounding large gardens and truck farms. And San Francisco was delightful for someone like Joe because it was a hotbed of ideas and radical thought, with outdoor lectures about social commentary, causes of the Great Depression, society in general, and Joe's favorite topics—evolution, religion, and survival of the fittest.

San Francisco also provided Joe with his first opportunity to explore museums and see the remains of prehistoric animals. Every day, Union Square was filled with panhandlers and soapbox orators of every political and religious persuasion surrounded by hundreds of pigeons. Soapbox orators supported their pet causes, mostly progressive, and they frequently talked about the suffering of the American people and how something terribly wrong had happened to the country.

Joe didn't pay attention to all of this because times had always been tough for him and he didn't have the same political view as most of the speakers. Many focused on the need for a social conscience and spoke out for free speech, social and economic injustice, against racism and teaching of religion in public schools, against war and weapons, and all of this Joe supported. Many of them were social anarchists who hated capitalism because it was exploitative. They protested low wages and unsafe working conditions, which made sense to Joe, but they also spoke against war and even against monogamy, which didn't seem to hold up to the scrutiny of nature's ways.

Joe remembered picking up a copy of Jack Reed's book, *The Ten Days that Shook the World,* about the 1917 Russian

Bolshevik Revolution. The anarchist newspapers said workers should be united as a class, the wage system should be abolished, that what was needed was grassroots democracy and a real working man's radical subculture. Some of this was pretty stirring and appealed to him at the time, but a lot of it also sounded wacky and crackpot. The more time Joe spent in museums and read about evolution, the more he came to concentrate his thoughts on ancient man and the struggle for survival without the shackles of manmade gods.

Portland, Oregon, was also a hotbed of radical thought, and word was out that the local police had ordered an end to all public speaking except at religious meetings. But atheists insisted they were "religious speakers," which was all right with Joe. Many local activists were arrested by the police and charged with disorderly conduct. Joe nearly avoided this fate, but he got caught up in a widespread police net and was arrested for distributing "obscene, lewd, or lascivious" materials. The promoters were supposed to pay him a dollar for handing out stacks of handbills, but Joe never got paid. The police let them out of jail the next day without a fine and Joe got a free meal and place to sleep for his trouble.

In Portland, the local Communist Party had organized "unemployment councils" that people could join by signing up for "political change" in solidarity with employed workers. Portland had several thousand registered members at the time and one of the benefits was that the city agreed to provide free shelter for over a thousand unemployed working people. Joe thought it was a good deal, but there was no work and too many panhandlers in Portland, so he headed back to northern California.

While traveling to San Francisco in 1937, Joe heard of John Dos Passos and the Sacco and Vanzetti case about the two young men who were wrongly convicted and executed. John Dos Passos visited them when they were in prison in the 1920s and wrote a book, *Facing the Chair*. The book fascinated Joe and had a big impact on his attitude against capital punishment.

Reading about Clarence Darrow's 1924 defense of murderers Nathan Leopold and Richard Loeb also fascinated Joe, especially Darrow's impassioned twelve-hour plea to save his young clients' lives. The following year Darrow volunteered to defend John Scopes' right to teach evolution in the Dayton, Tennessee, public high school. Clarence Darrow had already reached the top of his profession at the time, and the Scopes trial, featuring William Jennings Bryan as prosecutor, brought him even greater notoriety. Joe admired Darrow's courtroom plea to the jury:

> *If today you can take a thing like evolution and make it a crime to teach it in the public school, tomorrow you can make it a crime to teach it in the private schools, and the next year you can make it a crime to teach it to the hustings or in the church. At the next session you may ban books and the newspapers. Soon you may set Catholic against Protestant and Protestant against Protestant, and try to foist your own religion upon the minds of men. If you can do one you can do the other. Ignorance and fanaticism is ever busy and needs feeding. Always it is feeding and gloating for more. Today it is the public school teachers, tomorrow the private. The next day the preachers and the lectures, the magazines, the books, the newspapers. After while, your honor, it is the setting of man against man and creed against creed until with flying banners and beating drums we are marching backward to the glorious ages of the sixteenth century when bigots lighted fagots to burn the men who dared to bring*

> *any intelligence and enlightenment and culture to the human mind.*[6]
>
> —*Clarence Darrow*

And Darrow's iconoclasm appealed to Joe, especially his highly publicized statements on religion:

> *I do not believe in God because I do not believe in Mother Goose. I am an agnostic—I do not pretend to know what many ignorant men are sure of. Some of you say religion makes people happy—well, so does laughing gas. The origin of the absurd idea of immortal life is easy to discover—it is kept alive by hope and fear, by childish faith, and by cowardice.*
>
> —*Clarence Darrow*

Joe had a life-long fascination with the American Civil War, going back to the haunting songs and stories of the Civil War he first heard as a child from his sister Rose. Joe's years on the road riding the rails from 1936 to 1940 gave him the opportunity to become acutely aware of the insanity and futility of war—especially Americans killing other Americans. He was also able to study the history of the Civil War by tramping days on end through its bloody East Coast battlefields on many travels throughout the United States in the late 1930s. He would do this again with friends and relatives in the decades following World War II. The insanity of war consumed Joe as a constant theme and was expressed in his poem, "Pickett's Charge," written on the Gettysburg battlefield in April 1938, a couple of years before he joined the CCC camp in the North Woods of Minnesota.

---

6. Douglas Linder, University of Missouri-Kansas City (UMKC) School of Law, Clarence Seward Darrow, 1857-1938. http://www.law.umkc.edu/faculty/projects/ftrials/Darrow.htm (accessed August 2010).

Pickett's Charge—July 3, 1863

Joe Haan, Gettysburg, Pennsylvania, April 15, 1938

As I gaze on Gettysburg's rolling hills,
My heart with much emotion fills;
I see the soldiers, blue and gray
Who died upon that July day.

Young Pickett's heart with courage beat,
As he led the charge that sought defeat;
The flower of many youth did die,
When federal guns, they did defy.

Confederate ranks did swerve and sway,
As they charged against a leaden spray.
Their path was marked with trails of dead,
Scattered on a grassy bed.

On they came, through shot and shell,
Not seeing their comrades as they fell,
Up the Cemetery Ridge they came,
Where they so gained immortal fame.

At last, the Union men they met,
To be repulsed by bayonet;
Then they turned, did not retreat,
But knew deep down they were beat.

Their common names will be forgot,
As flesh and bones soon will rot.
But these men who fought in sixty-three,
Time now records their gallantry.

During his Civil War travels, Joe learned all the stanzas of the elegy, "The Bivouac of the Dead," and he would often recite them in his twangy eloquence while tramping with friends and nephews through Civil War battlefields and cemeteries—Vicksburg, Shiloh, Pea Ridge, Gettysburg, Antietam, Chancellorsville, Manassas, Arlington, and others.

"The Bivouac of the Dead" was written by Theodore O'Hara in memory of Kentucky troops killed in the Mexican War. O'Hara was born in Danville, Kentucky, on February 11, 1820, died June 6, 1867, witnessed combat in the Mexican War (1846–48) as a captain and brevet-major, and served as a colonel commanding the 12th Alabama Regiment during the Civil War (1861–1865).

Joe came across the poem when he was riding the rails in the late 1930s and walked alone through virtually every Civil War battlefield along the East Coast. He first read "The Bivouac of the Dead" on the McClellan Gate and metal placards in Arlington Cemetery across the Potomac from Washington, DC. He recited all of the stanzas by heart as he walked solemnly through Arlington Cemetery with his nephew in 1974.

The Bivouac of the Dead

Theodore O'Hara (1820–1867)

The muffled drum's sad roll has beat
*The soldier's last tattoo;**
No more on life's parade shall meet
That brave and fallen few.

On Fame's eternal camping-ground
Their silent tents are spread,
And Glory guards, with solemn round,
The bivouac of the dead.

No rumor of the foe's advance
Now swells upon the wind;
Nor troubled thought at midnight haunts
Of loved ones left behind;

No vision of the morrow's strife
The warrior's dream alarms;
No braying horn nor screaming fife
At dawn shall call to arms.

Their shriveled swords are red with rust,
Their plumed heads are bowed,
Their haughty banner, trailed in dust,
Is now their martial shroud.

And plenteous funeral tears have washed
The red stains from each brow,
And the proud forms, by battle gashed,
Are free from anguish now.

The neighing troop, the flashing blade,
The bugle's stirring blast,
The charge, the dreadful cannonade,
The din and shout, are past;

Nor war's wild note nor glory's peal
Shall thrill with fierce delight
Those breasts that nevermore may feel
The rapture of the fight.

Like the fierce northern hurricane
That sweeps the great plateau,
Flushed with the triumph yet to gain,
Came down the serried foe,

Who heard the thunder of the fray
Break o'er the field beneath,
Knew well the watchword of that day
Was "Victory or death!"

Long had the doubtful conflict raged
O'er all that stricken plain,
For never fiercer fight had waged
The vengeful blood of Spain;

And still the storm of battle blew,
Still swelled the gory tide;
Not long, our stout old chieftain knew,
Such odds his strength could bide.

T'was in that hour his stern command
Called to a martyr's grave
The flower of his beloved land,
The nation's flag to save.

By rivers of their father's gore
His first-born laurels grew,
And well he deemed the sons would pour
Their lives for glory too.

For many a mother's breath has swept
O'er Angostura's plain—
And long the pitying sky has wept
Above its moldered slain.

The raven's scream, or eagle's flight,
Or shepherd's pensive lay,
Alone awakes each sullen height
That frowned o'er that dread fray.

Sons of the Dark and Bloody Ground
Ye must not slumber there,
Where stranger steps and tongues resound
Along the heedless air.

Your own proud land's heroic soil
Shall be your fitter grave;
She claims from war his richest spoil—
The ashes of her brave.

Thus 'neath their parent turf they rest,
Far from the gory field,
Borne to a Spartan mother's breast
On many a bloody shield;

The sunshine of their native sky
Smiles sadly on them here,
And kindred eyes and hearts watch by
The heroes sepulcher.

Rest on embalmed and sainted dead!
Dear as the blood ye gave;
No impious footstep shall here tread
The herbage of your grave;

Nor shall your glory be forgot
While fame her records keeps,
Or Honor points the hallowed spot
Where Valor proudly sleeps.

Yon marble minstrel's voiceless stone
In deathless song shall tell,
When many a vanquished ago has flown,
The story how ye fell;

Nor wreck, nor change, nor winter's blight,
Nor Time's remorseless doom,
Shall dim one ray of glory's light
That gilds your deathless tomb.

* "Tattoo"—a bugle or drum call that tells soldiers to return to their quarters in the evening.

Joe crisscrossed the country several times as he rode the rails in the late 1930s. He was aware of the winds of war blowing from Europe and found that by frequenting small-town libraries, he could keep up with the news and often befriend local citizens who would lend him a hand. He found that he could also avoid hobo competition when "bumming" a meal or finding an odd job or two for a few days' room and board. People tended to feel sorry for Joe because he was small and looked so young.

He liked the free access to books, magazines, and newspapers as well as the kindness, congeniality, and peaceful quiet of public libraries in nearly every community. This is where Joe would go to study, write, memorize favorite passages, and learn from books while he was on the road. That's how it was for an uneducated but inventive young nomad in the late 1930s.

Joe picked up copies of Emmanuel Haldeman-Julius' Little Blue Books that had their heyday in the 1920s and 1930s and sold for a nickel. The Little Blue Books were a series of small, staple-bound books that reprinted virtually all of the classics. They were designed to "bring education to the masses" and "strike a blow" for the freedom of the human mind. That philosophy appealed to Joe, and the books were cheap and could easily fit into your back pocket.

Joe found poems on evolution especially fascinating, and the Little Blue Books were his source for favorites like, "Heaven—Fish-fly Replete in the Depth of June;" "The

First Idealist—A Jellyfish Swam in a Tropical Sea;" and "Evolution—When You Were a Tadpole and I Was a Fish." Joe also cherished his Little Blue Books collection of Clarence Darrow's debates and essays:

- *Environment vs. Heredity.* A Debate between Clarence Darrow and Albert Edward Wiggam.
- *Can the Individual Control His Conduct? Is Man a Free Agent or Is He the Slave of His Biological Equipment?* A Debate between Clarence Darrow and Dr. Thomas V. Smith.
- *Are We Machines: Is Life Mechanical or Is It Something Else?* A Debate between Clarence Darrow and Will Durant.
- *Is the US Immigration Law Beneficial?* A Debate between Clarence Darrow and Lothrop Stoddard.
- *Is the Human Race Getting Anywhere?* A Debate between Frederick Starr and Clarence Darrow.
- *Facing Life Fearlessly: The Pessimistic versus the Optimistic View of Life* by Clarence Darrow.
- *The Ordeal of Prohibition* by Clarence Darrow.
- *The Skeleton in the Closet* by Clarence Darrow.

Joe remembered one day finding a library book that made a big impact at the time. It was a series of lectures by a renowned nineteenth century defender of agnosticism—*The Lectures of Colonel Robert G. Ingersoll: Including His Answers to the Clergy and His Oration at His Brother's Grave.*

> *Ladies and Gentlemen:*
>
> *An honest god is the noblest work of man. Each nation has created a god, and the god has always resembled his creators. He hated and loved what they hated and loved, and he was invariably found on the side of those in power. Each god was intensely*

patriotic, and detested all nations but his own. All these gods demanded praise, flattery, and worship. Most of them were pleased with sacrifice, and the smell of innocent blood has ever been considered a divine perfume. All these gods have insisted upon having a vast number of priests, and the priests have always insisted upon being supported by the people, and the principal business of these priests has been to boast about their god, and to insist that he could easily vanquish all the other gods put together. These gods have been manufactured after numberless models, and according to the most grotesque fashions. Some have a thousand arms, some a hundred heads, some are adorned with necklaces of living snakes, some are armed with clubs, some with sword and shield, some with bucklers, and some with wings as a cherub; some were invisible, some would show themselves entire, and some would only show their backs; some were jealous, some were foolish, some turned themselves into men, some into swans, some into bulls, some into doves, and some into holy ghosts, and made love to the beautiful daughters of men. Some were married—all ought to have been—and some were considered as old bachelors from all eternity. Some had children, and the children were turned into gods and worshiped as their fathers had been. Most of these gods were revengeful, savage, lustful, and ignorant; as they generally depended upon their priests for information, their ignorance can hardly excite our astonishment.

Joe said he spent the entire day reading the Ingersoll lectures and they made a big impression on him because that was exactly the way Joe summed up man's fickle and pagan gods in his own mind. And he recalled looking down at the last nickel in his pocket that day and laughing to himself as he read the inscription, "In God We Trust," on the front of it.

There was lots for Joe to read in the libraries—Jack London's *To Build a Fire* and *The Call of the Wild*; Robert Service's "The Cremation of Sam McGee" and "The Shooting of Dan McGrew;" Sherwood Anderson's *Puzzled America;* Nathan Asch's *The Road: In Search of America;* Edmund Wilson's *The American Jitters;* James Rorty's W*here Life Is Better: An Unsentimental American Journey;* Theodore Dreiser's *Tragic America;* Louis Adamic's *My America;* and John Dos Passos's *In All Countries.*

Joe also read about Henri Bergson's *Creative Evolution* and Erskine Caldwell, who wrote about creating social change through literature. He heard about Stewart Holbrook, a lumberjack and workingman's writer and historian from Portland. Holbrook was popular and influential with social criticism, like Mark Twain and Will Rogers.

Great plays by Clifford Odets and Eugene O'Neill hit a chord in Joe's soul as he read their words and speeches aloud in open freight cars, dead broke and hungry, racing along lonely tracks to nowhere.

Meanwhile, Joe's buddies on the road and people back in Minnesota told him about the good deal in the CCC camps around the country. He heard that if he joined the CCC program in Minnesota he might be able to get assigned to the North Woods where he could hunt and fish, so he decided to put his name on the waiting list after swinging through St. Paul in the summer of 1939.

Fido's Fate

Joe Haan (Book II, #5)

My polytheism dictates to me,
A God, in every galaxy.
For man must have his Gods and Dogs,
As down life's road he slowly plods.

Both are words made by man,
In a lifetime, they too soon will span.
Oh, will my Fido be with me,
In my waited trip through eternity?

Will the carrier of rabid bite,
Too, find heaven in its flight?
But backward spell the word of Dog —
You also have the word called God!

VIII

Northwoods CCC Camp

1940–1941

After spending Christmas of 1939 with Kenny, his sisters, and their families near St. Paul, Joe enlisted in the Civilian Conservation Corps on January 10, 1940, for the first of three six-month terms. He was assigned to Isabella, Minnesota, which was located within the Superior National Forest in the remote Boundary Waters Area in Lake County. It was called the "Superior Roadless Area" at the time. In 1940, Isabella was about as remote and isolated as you could get in the Upper Midwest. The Canadian border was about thirty miles away, and there were no roads across the swampy, forested wilderness in Stony River Township.

The nearest communities to Isabella were Ely, forty miles to the northwest, and Finland, fifteen miles southeast. The small village of Silver Bay on Lake Superior was ten miles beyond Finland.

Isabella straddles the Arctic Watershed, or Northern Divide—where rivers flow north to the Hudson Bay and Arctic Ocean or south from that point to the Gulf of Mexico. At nearly 2000 feet above sea level, Isabella is Minnesota's second highest point. It has remained a true wilderness, with moose, deer, timber wolves, lynx, black bear, grouse, and partridge, and exceptional fishing in the many streams and lakes.

The CCC program was part of President Roosevelt's 1933 New Deal legislation. It was a public works relief effort for unemployed young men precisely like Joe, with a focus on natural resource preservation, especially forest and soil conservation. The CCC program relieved high unemployment caused by the Great Depression and was designed to carry out a broad natural resource conservation program on federal, state, and municipal lands. Except for the Army-style approach to daily life, it was right up Joe's alley. Tasks included building roads and trails and remote wilderness logging, with time to hunt and fish in primeval splendor. Joe was in his element, and better yet, he was getting paid more money than he had ever earned in his life.

The CCC program was limited to young men from eighteen to twenty-five whose fathers, like Joe's Dan McCann, were out of work and on relief. Average enrollees were just like Joe—poor, homeless, and in their late teens or early twenties. They were all paid $30 per month, which was more than a private in the Army at the time, and far more than there was to spend in the wilderness. The rules required that everyone had to send $25 back home to their families each month, which Joe remitted to Bub for safekeeping in a savings account. For many families around the country, twenty-five dollars a month in CCC money was a major source of income.

As soon as Roosevelt's legislation was signed into law on March 31, 1933, the CCC program became one of the most popular New Deal initiatives. Joe said the Civilian Conservation Corps was like being in the Army, only a little less rigid. The Army imprint was immediately present throughout the CCC camps. General Douglas MacArthur headed the Army at the time and appointed General George C. Marshall to organize the CCC. During World War II, General Marshall became the Chief of Staff of the US Army. Later, he became Secretary of State under President Truman, and created the Marshall Plan for the post-war economic recovery of Western Europe.

Joe was assigned to Company 3703, F-54. His serial number was CC7-272557. His discharge paper, dated June 25, 1941, listed his features: "blue eyes, brown hair, medium complexion, 5 feet, 6 inches tall, 120 pounds." According to Margaret A. Haapoja, writing in *Forest Magazine,* Summer 2009:

> *From 1933 to 1942, when the last camp closed, Minnesota had 148 CCC camps with 77,000 enrollees. The Chippewa National Forest had twenty-three camps, and the Superior National Forest had thirty.*

Recruits signed up for six-month enlistments and could extend for two additional terms, which Joe did. He served at Isabella from January 1940 until June 1941. There was a waiting list to get in, and by the time the CCC program disbanded at the start of World War II, over three and a half million young men had joined and were assigned to nearly three thousand camps located in all forty-eight states. One of the CCC newsletters at the time stated:

> *This is a training station, and we're going to be morally and physically fit to lick Old Man Depression.*

Joe's Isabella pictures show Army-style wooden barracks with a couple dozen men assigned to double-decked wooden bunks along each side of the one-story barracks. The mess hall was a long barracks building with twenty wooden tables and a kitchen at one end, but no electricity or running water. There was also a tool shed, blacksmith repair shop, supply building, and a barracks building for the company headquarters. CCC troops got up early and went to bed early—6:00 a.m. bugle call in the morning and lights out with taps at 10:30 at night. They learned to take orders, but that was a little hard for Joe. Two US Army lieutenants were in charge of Joe's company. There were "leaders" for each barracks and the daily work crews, much like NCOs in the Army. The latrine, sinks, and gravity shower were in a separate building, and everyone remembered the cold walk on winter mornings to clean up and shave.

Following reveille at 6:00 a.m., the troops would fall out in front of the flagpole and stand at attention while the flag was raised. At 7:00, they would march in step to the mess hall for breakfast and then back to the barracks for 7:45 inspection, followed by work duty in the wilderness from 8:00 to 5:00. They rotated KP duty (kitchen police), but some, like Joe, got it more often than others for mouthing off.

For lunch each day, they were issued a brown paper bag containing one baloney and one peanut butter sandwich. At 6:00 p.m., they stood retreat in front of the flagpole, followed by a big dinner in the mess hall at 7:00 and free time until lights out. Everyone thought the food was great. The only place to spend money was in a little canteen that sold pop, candy, and tobacco for rolling cigarettes or chewing.

In her *Forest Magazine* article, Margaret A. Haapoja quoted Lowell Laager of Calumet, Minnesota. Laager joined the CCC in 1940 and remembered the following:

> *We had very good food . . . We lined up outside the mess hall in orderly fashion until the mess cook opened the door . . . We were seated at the same table, same place every meal. You waited until the cook gave the order to eat. There was no smoking in the mess hall, no loud talking . . . It was a real good learning experience for me for when I went into the Navy because it was the same routine there.*

One evening during a winter thaw at the beginning of his first enlistment, Joe and a friend tried to walk out of camp to the nearest wilderness saloon, which was several miles away. Unfortunately, they broke through the ice and got soaking wet up to their armpits. They struggled to walk back to camp in freezing weather. Joe was laid up for several months with pneumonia, nearly dying from exposure. He was released to the care of his sisters for several weeks but was soon back in camp in time to help put out a raging forest fire. The camp newsletter posted the following article:

> *On May 24th at 12:40 p.m., twenty-two men from Company 3703 left for forest fighting at Camp 11. When this initial crew reached the burning area, about 35 acres were on fire. At 1:40 p.m. another crew of ten men left camp. Detachments from the Spruce Lake CCC and Gogoka CCC camps were also assigned to this fire. The fire started near a lumber camp and spread rapidly to cause destruction of cedar, jackpine, and spruce timber in the area. The last crew of men returning from the fire arrived in camp on May 26th. Needless to say, all the men were dog-tired and welcomed the chance to crawl into their temporarily unused bunks.*

Each CCC camp was large enough to support a "company" that consisted of about two hundred young men. There was always more than enough to eat and plenty of exciting friends the same age who lived together in wilderness camps under quasi-military discipline. Joe said that his eighteen months in CCC camp were the happiest of his life up to that time, and he was even putting money in the bank. Joe had new shoes and boots, clean work clothes during the day, and an Army-style uniform for dress—better than anything he had ever owned. The breakfasts consisted of all he had ever wanted to eat—plus pancakes, bacon, and eggs every day. Most young men were malnourished and poorly clothed when they entered the CCC program, but they soon put on weight and rapidly became physically fit. For Joe, the routine was a breeze—threshing and putting up hay on the German farm in August were much tougher than CCC camp or Army basic training. The only hard part now was taking orders.

Joe genuinely liked the CCC program and its military camaraderie, even though strict military discipline threatened KP or even dishonorable discharge. Joe often pushed the limit when a leader tried to "lord himself" over Joe or one of his buddies.

Few of the men in Joe's company had even a year of high school and fewer still had any work experience beyond odd jobs. So Joe fit right in, and his lack of formal education was compensated by his esoteric library studies he picked up on the road. With eight years of hard, independent farm work behind him as experience, plus what he had learned traveling around the country, Joe found that small as he was—five feet six and 120 pounds—he could wield an axe or saw better than most of his CCC camp buddies. He could also handle himself in a fight and was smarter and tougher than the average "Joe."

They were outdoors every day, even when it was thirty below zero in January. Joe loved every minute of it, especially the chance to fish, hunt, and trap on weekends. The fishing and wildlife were incredible in the northern Minnesota wilderness. Although he found others who shared his love of nature, Joe was never really happy unless he was alone outdoors, so he generally fished and hunted by himself. When Joe left the CCC program after his third enlistment, his company's June 18, 1941, newsletter, the *Baptism Blade,* ran the following news flash:

> *Barrack 8 was filled to the gills Sunday night with pickerel fried by "Chef" Seals, thanks to Joe Haan.*

Posted in the Minnesota Historical Society's *Greatest Generation* online series, nineteen-year-old Michael T. Sanchelli of St. Paul summarized his CCC experience when he was assigned to CCC Camp No. 1721 near Isabella in northeastern Minnesota in the 1930s:

> *There were four of us boys in camp 1721 near Isabella, Minnesota from the old neighborhood known today as Railroad Island . . . up at 5 a.m., breakfast at 6 a.m. and into the woods. I had quite an interesting job, I was measuring pulp logs for average diameter in a one-cord rack. I had a crew of four other boys with tapes; two would measure the diameter and the other two would measure the length of each log. The logs already had the bark removed. I would mark the circumference and the length down on a sheet of paper. All week the talk was of going to Ely, Minn. on a weekend pass, and it had reached a high pitch. Everybody was waiting for quitting time . . . We were not going to eat supper*

in camp because we wanted a change of menu from the government's Army-type food. It would be about a two-hour drive between our camp and Ely over the bumpy clay and gravel road covering the 50 miles. When we came to camp in April from Ely, it took us 4 hours to get through the mud of the thawing road, which is now Highway 1 of Minnesota—we extended it to the North Shore.

Many of the young men in my day didn't go [into the CCC] because they thought it was too military. We wore army khaki . . . stood reveille and retreat, and we were governed under army regulations. We ate army style, we slept in barracks, and we even had leaders as in the service they had noncoms. The two regular army officers were the Captain and the Doctor, the rest were all civilians, and if a person didn't like it he could just leave it. Many of the young men of the CCC were more than prepared when they were called for service in World War II, physically and mentally. I never regretted going to the CCCs. The $25 a month that went home to my mother was sufficient to keep our family eating right, and the $5 that was left to me at camp was more than enough to keep me in cigarettes and beer.

At night, Joe played his guitar and harmonica, listened to stories from his buddies and told his own, composed poems and sad love songs for everyone's amusement, and read a variety of books and magazines. Whenever he found a poem he liked, or something special on evolution, Joe memorized what he had read. He loved to recite his collection of poetry and stories in the barracks or outside when sitting around a roaring camp fire.

In short, the CCC program was made for Joe, and Joe was made for the CCC. It helped him come of age. Joe had started memorizing poems on the German farm from the schoolbooks Sis brought him, and by the time he landed in the Isabella CCC camp, Joe had a wealth of stories, songs, and poems gathered from books and public libraries around the country. His self-esteem soared when he sang and recited poetry, much of it already laced with the iconoclasm that suited his view of the survival of the fittest in a cruel and godless world. With little else to do at night in a remote logging camp in far northern Minnesota along the Canadian border, Joe became the camp entertainer with his guitar, harmonica, and wealth of recitations.

Joe loved to quote the opening lines of "On the Nature of Things" ("De Rerum Natura") by Lucretius, and never forgot it. Lucretius was a Roman philosopher and poet who lived about 100 BC and is known for his six-part poem, "On the Nature of Things." It was especially appealing to Joe because Lucretius argued that gods might exist but they have no influence on humans—the universe was not designed by gods but was the result of random natural events. Like Joe, Lucretius believed human unhappiness came from fear of the gods and fear of death. Quotations from Lucretius that especially appealed to Joe included:

> *"Nature does all things spontaneously, by herself, without the meddling of the gods."*
> *"Such evil deeds could religion prompt."*
> *"Fear is the mother of all gods."*

On the Nature of Things

Titus Lucretius Carus (c.99–55 BC)

No single thing abides; but all things flow.
Fragment to fragment clings—the things thus grow
Until we know and name them. By degrees
They melt, and are no more the things we know.

Globed from the atoms falling slow or swift
I see the suns, I see the systems lift
Their forms; and even the systems and the suns
Shall go back slowly to the eternal drift.

You too, oh earth—your empires, lands, and seas—
Least with your stars, of all the galaxies,
Globed from the drift like these, like these you too
Shalt go. You are going, hour by hour, like these.

Nothing abides. The seas in delicate haze
Go off; those mooned sands forsake their place;
And where they are, shall other seas in turn
Mow with their scythes of whiteness other bays.

The seeds that once were, we take flight and fly,
Winnowed to earth, or whirled along the sky,
Not lost but disunited. Life lives on.
It is the lives, the lives, the lives, that die.

They go beyond recapture and recall,
Lost in the all-indissoluble All:
Gone like the rainbow from the fountain's foam,
Gone like the spindrift shuddering down the squall.

Flakes of the water, on the waters cease!
Soul of the body, melt and sleep like these.
Atoms to atoms—weariness to rest—
Ashes to ashes—hopes and fears to peace!

Science, lift aloud your voice that stills
The pulse of fear, through the conscience thrills—
Thrills through conscience with news of peace—
How beautiful your feet are on the hills!

The CCC program reduced its operation as unemployment eased and the Great Depression diminished. When Roosevelt initiated the military draft in 1940, fewer eligible young men were available for the CCC program. And as war raged in Europe in the late 1930s and early 1940s, the CCC program shifted its emphasis toward national defense. After Pearl Harbor, nearly all federal programs focused on the war effort and by then, Joe and most of his friends had joined the Army.

Joe received his Honorable Discharge from the CCC program on June 25, 1941, and returned to St. Paul to see Bub, Sis, and Kenny. By this time, Bub and Sis were married and had started their families. Pictures from that period show Joe as a happy, well-fed, good-looking twenty-three-year-old young man strumming his guitar for his young nephews. But before long, Joe and most of the CCC boys he knew were in the Army on the heels of America's declaration of war against Japan and Germany. Following the Japanese attack on Pearl Harbor, Sunday, December 7, 1941, President Roosevelt gave his historic speech on the radio:

> *Yesterday, December 7, 1941—a date which will live in infamy—the United States of America was suddenly and deliberately attacked by naval and*

> *air forces of the Empire of Japan . . . I ask that the Congress declare that since the unprovoked and dastardly attack by Japan on Sunday, December 7, 1941, a state of war has existed between the United States and the Japanese Empire.*

On December 11, Japan's allies, Germany and Italy, declared war on the United States, and Congress responded immediately by declaring war on each of them as well. The world was now at war, and another formative chapter in the life of the last iconoclast—"god's angry man"—was about to unfold.

War

Joe Haan (Book II, #38)

Man made thunder in my ears,
Tale of death is what one hears.
Lightning flash within my eye,
Giant guns light up the sky.

The earth is gashed, burned and torn,
Fearful soldiers cower and mourn.
So, unmerciful god, now do they pray,
"End this terrible, frightful fray."

All the enemy's prayers, they too,
Have one request for god to do:
"Help us win this holy war,
For infidels knock upon our door."

Oh, sainted mother, for you we die,
No sound minds to ever ask us, "Why?"
Tormented screams, from bodies torn,
From warrior men, forever worn.

What was once a forest land,
Are but limbless trunks that now stand.
Putrid odor be death's perfume,
Where human fools come, to meet their doom.

IX

Army Life

1942–1945

All three of the Haan brothers—Danny, Kenny, and Joe—served in the Army during World War II. Danny was already in the Army at the time of Pearl Harbor on December 7, 1941. Kenny had just graduated from Macalester College in St. Paul. Joe leaped at the chance to enlist with friends he had made at CCC camp.

Joe was more than ready to go to war with the Germans if for no other reason than to show the hated farmer who would survive in the final struggle for the survival of the fittest. Before Joe left the farm, he remembered the German farmer saying in his thick accent that Hitler's German master race would someday rule the world. When Joe killed a German sentry with his "sharp as a razor" combat knife on Christmas night 1944 during the Battle of the Bulge, he said he thought of the hated German farmer back in Minnesota.

Going from CCC camp into the Army was easy for Joe, and the draft was what the country needed at the time. From 1940, until it was abolished by President Nixon in 1973 following protests against the Vietnam War, an entire generation of young Americans like Joe had accepted the draft as a responsibility of citizenship. To Joe, the draft was as American as apple pie. In war and peace, Americans from different economic classes and ethnicities accepted compulsory military service and served together. They bonded and formed personal relationships that lasted a lifetime, even though they frequently had little else in common. And because of the common terror shared in combat, nearly everyone who served in World War II became bound together in a lasting fraternity of military service for the rest of their lives. The Haan boys were no exception.

Danny enlisted in the Army in the early 1930s and made the Army his career, serving first in the US 7th Regiment under Colonel George Marshall at Vancouver Barracks, Washington. Joe had little contact with Danny over the years, though they would write occasionally, and he had a chance to pop in on Danny a time or two in Vancouver when he was riding the rails out West in the late thirties. Joe looked up to his older brother and was fascinated by Danny's stories about Army life. People thought Danny looked like Humphrey Bogart, for he was lean and slightly built. Danny had a way of talking, drinking, and smoking cigarettes like Bogart, as well as the way he smiled and laughed. And like his father, he was a good story teller.

Danny served in the Pacific during World War II and in the Korean War during the American retreat from the Yalu River. He traveled the globe and rose to the rank of Chief Warrant Officer (W-4). He retired from the Army in the late 1950s and later worked for the US Post Office in Vancouver. Danny and Joe were last pictured with their father, Dan McCann, during a November 1942 visit with Sis and her family in Northfield. They were wearing their uniforms and fascinated their nephews by digging trenches and making grenade holes in Sis' victory garden while telling about Army life and their exciting experiences. During the visit, Bub wrote to Kenny:

Dear Kenny—

Joe is home on furlough and looks just grand. He weighs about 145 pounds and is as solid as a rock. He loves the Army and prays the Germans can hold out long enough in Africa so he can help whip them. I never saw anyone so anxious to get into a scrap. We are going down to Northfield tomorrow to see Sis. He has to be back in Camp Hood Wednesday. We were down to Aunt Sadie's yesterday and saw Uncle Charlie, also went to Uncle Joe's. We had a grand visit with all the relatives.

—Bub

Kenny served in counterintelligence in Iceland during World War II and was recalled to active duty as a captain during the Korean War. He worked his way through high school and Macalester College in St. Paul and attended Harvard University after the war. He retired as a lieutenant colonel from the Army Reserve in the 1970s. As a civilian, Kenny had a long and successful career in labor mediation with the US Department of Labor Relations. His wife Betty graduated from Macalester in 1943, a year behind Kenny. They had five children—Heidi, Heather, Peter, Wendy, and Chris. Kenny saved virtually everything over the course of his life, providing invaluable collections of pictures and letters to piece together the fragments of Joe's life.

After training with a tank destroyer battalion in Texas and the Southwest for two years, Joe shipped out to England and France during the summer of 1944. Landing in Normandy in August, he served as a private in Patton's Third Army. He saw some of the toughest fighting of the war during the Battle of the Bulge, where he was decorated with the Bronze Star Medal for heroism during a combat mission behind enemy lines on Christmas night 1944. Crossing into Germany, Joe was wounded in March 1945 during hand-to-hand combat and received the Military Order of the Purple Heart.

Shortly before heading for Europe, Joe was transferred from the tank destroyer battalion to a field artillery battalion, which increased his deafness significantly. He was reassigned as a "ground-pounder" rifleman in the 101st Infantry Regiment on December 15, 1944, just as the Battle of the Bulge was about to unfold. He told everyone when he was home on leave in 1942 that he wanted to transfer to the infantry and get into the paratroopers, so he finally got his wish. The reassignment from the relatively safe field artillery battalion to become front line infantry fodder was precipitated by Joe's continued insubordination, which was lubricated with a little of the Sauterne wine he had discovered and learned to savor in France. Joe's Army discharge records contain the following information:

Private First Class Joseph B. Haan, US Army, 17047734

- Born in St. Paul, Minnesota, February 26, 1918
- Enlisted as a Private at Fort Snelling, Minnesota, 17 January 1942
- Separated as Pfc, honorable discharge, Camp McCoy, Wisconsin 6 November 1945 Height 5'6"—Weight 126#
- Military Occupation Specialty: Rifleman 745: Expert Carbine, Expert .30 Cal.
- Company "A," 706th Tank Destroyer Battalion August 1942–April 1944
- Battery "A," 752nd Field Artillery Battalion, April–December 1944, US Third Army
- Headquarters Company "C," First Battalion, 101st

Infantry Regiment (rifleman), 26th Infantry Division ("Yankee Division"), US Third Army ("Patton's Own") December 1944–October 1945
- Combat Service: 16 months in Northern France, Rhineland, Ardennes, Central Europe
- Total Active Service: 3 years, 9 months, 20 days
- Awards and Decorations: Bronze Star Medal for Valor, Purple Heart, Europe–Africa–Middle East Theater Service Medal with Two Overseas Service Bars, Expert Combat Infantryman's Badge, Expert Carbine Badge, Expert .30 Caliber Machine Gun Badge
- 100% Veterans Administration (VA) disability, total deafness caused by artillery

Joe liked the Army and said he liked being a private. He hated it when he had more than one stripe and said privates deserved the right to mouth off because it came with the rank. He was promoted to corporal several times, even sergeant. He said it was nice to get the pay raise, but he wouldn't accept the responsibility that came with more rank. He usually got into a fight on payday and wound up losing his new stripes.

The Army wasn't all that different from CCC camp, and it was a snap when compared with work on the farm. He had good clothes, new shoes, and all the food he could eat. He loved the comradeship of the common soldiers he got to know, and he was paid in cash. But Joe could not imagine giving orders, and although he was frequently befriended by officers and sergeants who recognized his intelligence and abilities, he was incorrigible when it came to defending his beliefs and receiving inane orders.

Joe was at his best when he worked alone in the wilderness or with one or two others on a special mission, like the winter night he won his Bronze Star Medal a few miles south of Bastogne, Belgium. In combat, Joe was unquestionably one of Patton's best infantrymen. Give him a dangerous combat mission behind enemy lines and Joe could be depended upon to complete it, if left to his own devices—that's how Joe's comrades remembered him at their reunions after the war.

Joe's problem in CCC camp and the Army was that he could not stand to take orders from people he considered narrow-minded like the German farmer, or dumb like many sergeants, or brainwashed with religion like so many Southern officers he met. There were plenty of dumb sergeants and brainwashed officers in the Army.

Joe had shown his inability to accept discipline at the orphanage, and it got worse on the German farm. But in CCC camp and the Army, the rules were more strictly enforced. This was especially true in Patton's Third Army under combat conditions. No one screwed up or mouthed off and got away with it under Patton.

One of Joe's problems was when he took a drink of anything containing alcohol. After a few beers or a little French Sauterne wine, Joe was ready to take on the entire battalion staff or tear into his own sergeants for the slightest perceived offense. This is exactly what he did during his unit's much needed rest in Metz, France, shortly before the Battle of the Bulge. That's when Joe was demoted to Pfc for the last time and was reassigned from the artillery to the front lines of Patton's infantry.

Predictably, Joe left the Army in November 1945 with the same rank he had following boot camp—Private First Class (Pfc), with one chevron stripe on his sleeve. During nearly four years in the Army, Joe was promoted to Corporal (two stripes) at least three times. Some of his Army records are missing and he may have been promoted to Corporal four times, and even Sergeant (three stripes) for a short while. Even so, he was always busted back to his favorite rank of Pfc, mostly for fighting and insubordination. Joe left the

Army at the end of the war with sixteen months of combat service and nearly four years of active service as a highly decorated private soldier.

He remembered standing inspection in Germany toward the end of the war when the inspecting general saw the Purple Heart and Bronze Star Medal on Joe's chest, along with his other combat awards and medals for expert marksmanship. The general asked why Joe hadn't been promoted, and the captain said Joe was a better soldier as a private. The general looked at Joe and smiled. He understood.

Joe's buddies said he was a shining star that brightly illuminated their surroundings wherever he went with his songs and poetry. They also said Joe epitomized what was later called the "Greatest Generation"—World War II vets steeled and molded by the hardships of the Great Depression. In Joe's case, he was crafted by the orphanage, his lonely existence on the hated German farm, riding the rails, and working at the CCC camp.

Joe reached the front lines with Patton's Army in the fall of 1944. Goaded on by anti-German Army propaganda, he was ready to kill "Krauts" and all he could think of was the hated farmer and his German accent—until he spent three days in the same foxhole with the corpse of eighteen-year-old Corporal Friedrich Hofman and recognized the futility of war and common bonds of all humanity. The experience triggered Joe's poem, "Memories of Death."

The following narrative is based on Joe's journal and chronology of Army service, surviving military records, wartime letters, notes Joe kept while in the Army, and unit histories Joe received over the years from fellow veterans, compiled from war records for their reunions.

Private Joe Haan, a Soldier's Memoir

Joe enlisted in the Army at Fort Snelling, Minnesota, on January 17, 1942, shortly after the attack on Pearl Harbor. He had been out of CCC camp for six months and said he loved every minute of his Army adventure at Fort Snelling because he knew he could take whatever they might dish out. He was amused when an old drill sergeant told the recruits, "The Army can't make you do something, but it sure as hell can make you wish you did."

Following basic training for thirteen weeks, he was a buck private in the Army with no stripes. In 1942, privates were paid $21 per month, nine dollars less than the CCC. But by January 1943, monthly pay for a Pfc was raised to $54, minus $6.40 for life insurance (paid by allotment), plus $10 monthly overseas pay and an additional $10 in monthly combat pay. Everyone was paid in cash on the last day of the month, usually in the mess hall by one of the officers, but getting paid under combat conditions was irregular. Joe's first payday in Europe after leaving the US on July 2, 1944, was in Metz, France, in late November 1944, just before the Battle of the Bulge. Many soldiers, like Joe, would spend all their cash on payday and were constantly broke, so he set up a $25 monthly allotment to his sister Bub.

Following boot camp, Joe was assigned to Camp Chaffee, about five miles from Fort Smith, Arkansas, for initial tank destroyer training on April 4, 1942. He loved Oklahoma because he had his first chance to explore Indian artifacts and burial sites with the Native Americans he met near the Army Post. Joe's next assignment was Fort Sill near Lawton, Oklahoma, on June 30, 1942, when he was assigned to the 18th Field Artillery School and trained on the 105 mm howitzer that replaced old World War I French 75s. Joe met Helen Jessie and her family while stationed at Fort Sill, and they stayed in touch through the war. She was gentle and kind and told Joe about her life as an impoverished Native American Choctaw growing up in Oklahoma.

By early August, Joe transferred to Camp Hood near Killeen, Texas, where he was assigned to Company "A," 706th Tank Destroyer Battalion. He attended battalion-level Tank Destroyer Pioneer School, training on the Army's primary anti-tank weapon, a 3" (76 mm) gun towed by M3 half-tracks. Everyone wore the Tank Destroyer insignia, which displayed a black panther's jaws crushing a tank with the motto, "Seek, Strike, Destroy." Texas was hot and tank destroyer was tough duty for everyone, with constant cannon bombardment making Joe's ears ring day and night. He never told anyone in the Army about his bad left ear, but it seemed to him that nearly everyone was somewhat deaf from the constant roar of the big guns. Joe was promoted to Pfc and busted back to buck private while he was stationed at Camp Hood, calling it no big deal. In a letter to Bub dated September 2, 1942, Joe wrote:

> *Dear Sister—*
>
> *I am now stationed at Camp Hood, Texas. It is in the central part about forty miles from Waco, which is the nearest town. I will be here a few weeks to finish training. There are only Tank Destroyer Battalions stationed here. We are going through special advanced training, after which one Battalion of tank destroyers will be assigned to some Armored Division which will be ready to go into action. I received my first rating two weeks ago, from a buck Private to Pfc, private first class. It's only a five dollar raise with one stripe on my sleeve, the first step toward the long climb to the top. I would have made it long time ago if I would*

have behaved, but I was pretty wild when I first went in. But the Army makes you over regardless who you are or where you come from . . . I hope that I will be able to get a furlough sometime this fall. I can't find out a darn thing around here, the order changes every day, they told us we were going down to Louisiana and we land here in Texas.

Write soon, —Joe

In a letter to Kenny from Camp Hood, Texas, dated October 13, 1942, Joe wrote:

Hi Soldier—

Received your letter a few days ago after it traveled quite a ways, first to Camp Chaffee, then Leesville, Louisiana, and finally Camp Hood, Texas, where our Battalion is going through some rigid training. I'm enclosing an article out of the May Colliers*; it will give you some idea what type of training we are taking. As for me I think it is really the best possible training we could get. We ford rivers with our full field equipment, crawl through fifty yards of barbed wire entanglements with our nose rooting mighty close to Mother Earth, because machine gun slugs are zipping close to our heads; there are also land mines in the form of ¼ sticks of dynamite planted around the wire; all in all, when you get through that, you have less fear of gunfire and explosions. I took a retest on my IQ and made 120; I also passed the Mechanical aptitude*[7]*. I am glad to hear you made such a high grade. You*

7. The Army General Classification Test (AGCT) was administered to millions of young men during World War II. Joe's score of 120 placed him in the top 30% of all men taking the test. The median score through June 30, 1944 was 98.7. A score of 110 or higher was one of the prerequisites for officer candidate school.

should be a sure bet for OCS. I suppose by the time you get this letter you will be in a different outfit. I guess the Army can't teach you anything about the rifle, if you keep shooting the way you did the first time. I have qualified as gunner in the Anti-Aircraft; I had a rating [Pfc] but was busted for violation of the 11:30 curfew. However, I will attempt to keep my nose clean in the future and get back up to the top. I haven't heard from Dan for about a month, but got a letter from Bub a short time ago. Well, Ken, write when you find time. I don't know how long I am going to be here, but rumor has it, that we are going to California soon.

Write soon, —Brother at Arms, Private Joe Haan

In mid-November, Joe's tank destroyer battalion moved to the Army's military training center at Camp Bowie, two miles south of Brownwood, Texas, for advanced combat survival training maneuvers. Local attractions were dances, nightclubs, theaters, stores, and markets. Brownwood was fun, especially the dance halls and honkytonks, but Joe tended to stay in the barracks reading and writing poetry because he knew he would get into trouble if he went to town. He noted that he was, "still a buck private, not a bad place to be."

Preparing to face the German Army in North Africa, Joe's battalion moved into the California desert on January 9, 1943, about seventy miles southwest of Needles, California, for large-scale tank destroyer combat maneuvers. Joe remembered the cold, blowing sand in the winter desert near Needles and said it felt colder than Minnesota. Joe kept telling people of his desire to get into the infantry, especially the paratroopers. On May 31, 1943, Bub wrote to Kenny in Iceland from St. Paul.

Dear Soldier—

Today I was very happy when the postman left me your V-mail. I only wished that it had been a longer letter . . . Our dear brother Joseph is in Arizona on maneuvers. He has been in the desert since Christmas so he ought to be brown and healthy. His latest address is: Pvt. Joe Haan, Co. A. 706 Tank Destroyer Bn. Desert Maneuvers, C/O pm Los Angeles, Calif. In his last letter he said he was trying to get transferred to the paratroopers. Why? I can't imagine! He sent home some rattlesnake skins and stones he picked up in the desert. He certainly seems to be enjoying himself. Danny's latest address is Sgt. Dan Haan, Co. H. 321 Infantry. APO 81, C/O P.M. Nashville, Tenn. David speaks of you and Joe all the time . . . All my love, good luck,

—Bub

Joe's anti-tank battalion continued desert combat maneuver training near Yuma, Arizona, during the month of July. This was hot, tough, and hard duty in the blistering Arizona summer, with the immediate prospect of heading for North Africa. Without water, the desert heat frequently caused delusions and hallucinations. Joe experienced the fantasies of a mirage when he and a buddy tried to walk without water across a lonely stretch of rock and blowing sand in search of fossils and rare stones. They quickly learned how distances in the desert can deceive and how easy it is to underestimate the bleak and vast expanse of arid wasteland.

By August 1943, Joe was back in Texas, this time at Camp Maxey, eight miles north of Paris, Texas. Here, Joe's Company "A" of the 706th Tank Destroyer Battalion underwent six months of additional intensive combat training maneuvers.

With its artillery range, heavy shells, difficult obstacle and infiltration courses, and intense August heat, Joe called remote Camp Maxey "the hell-hole of the great state of Texas, a perfect Darwinian laboratory." On September 13, 1943, Rose wrote to Kenny in Iceland about their father's funeral:

Dear Kenny—

Wayne and I got your cards the other day and are glad to hear that you got that promotion. So it's Sergeant Kenneth Haan now. That sounds good. I guess the Army really appreciates and knows merit after all. It didn't take long for you to come up from buck private, did it? I suppose Bub had written to you about Pa. We gave him a nice funeral, and he passed away without having to suffer for one minute so I suppose it's all for the best. We were glad to be able to see Joe and Danny again. Joe spent a couple of days down here in Northfield. He had a 16-day furlough so he had quite a bit of time to get around and enjoy it . . . Lots of love from us all.

—Sis

P.S. Here's the obituary from the St. Paul paper: "Daniel Haan, 66, passed away suddenly Sept. 7th. The dear father of 1st Sgt. Daniel A. Haan, USA in Arizona; Sgt. Kenneth Haan, USA overseas; Pvt. Joseph Haan, Camp Maxey, Texas; Mrs. Leonard Quist (Rose) of Northfield, Minn. and Mrs. Ferris Mahmood (Cecilia) of White Bear, Minn. Also survived by five grandchildren. Funeral services at Klecatsky Mortuary, 611 W. 7th St. Saturday 2 pm Interment Oak Hill cemetery."

On October 1, 1943, Joe wrote to Kenny from Camp Maxey, Texas:

From: Private Joe Haan, Co. A. 706. T.D. Bn., Camp Maxey

Dear Ken—

I received your letter today, the 31 of Sept. I suppose I would have received it sooner had you put on the proper address. I left the California desert the 1st of July, from there went to Arizona but still stayed in the desert. However, I left there the 1st of August and came to Texas. Our camp is up in the extreme northeastern corner, ten miles from the Oklahoma border. I guess I have been in every camp in Texas. Dan's outfit came out to the desert and were stationed a few miles from us, but we came to Tex the same week they moved in. Undoubtedly you have heard by this time through our sisters of the death of our father the 7th of this month [September 1943]. I was granted a furlough to go to his funeral, but unfortunately, I did not get the telegram in time. I got to St. Paul five hours after the funeral was over. Dan was there, so I got a chance to see him anyway. How do you like it in Iceland? Do you think you will ever get into any action in the European theater? I think we might go some place this winter, as we have gone through some intensive training in the past few months.

I would like to tell you about our equipment and methods of stopping the enemy tanks, but I suppose it would be censored out. Do you get much practice with small arms? I have qualified as expert on the .30 caliber machine gun, and sharpshooter on the Springfield rifle, so I guess I could do all right on the Japs and Huns if I ever get a crack at them. Do you ever see any German aircraft? It seems to me I read where German bombers attacked bases on Iceland.

Dan is still in the desert maneuvers training with his unit. He is in the 81st Infantry Division. Well, must close for now, hope to hear from you soon.
—Brother Joe

Joe remained in North Texas until January 15, 1944, when his unit was transferred to Louisiana for sixty days of mass-scale training maneuvers and mock invasion exercises. Rumors were rampant about the imminent allied European invasion, and Joe expressed eagerness to get into action with the "big push" as soon as possible and kill Germans. As the maneuvers in the swamps of Louisiana drew to a close, Joe sent a letter to Ken in Iceland on March 9, 1944, and described his recent trip to Mexico:

From: Private Joe Haan, 17047784,
Somewhere in the swamps of Louisiana
Co.A, 706 T.D. Bn., APO 20—A, C/O Postmaster,
Shreveport, Louisiana
Dear Ken—

Received your card the other day and glad to hear from you. So you got a furlough. How did you like England? I have met several men that have been there, but they didn't think so much of it. I have a few friends over there who write to me occasionally. I took a trip to old Mexico in December. I went to the second largest city, which is Monterrey. It is two hundred miles south of Laredo, Texas. I had a ten day furlough so that gave me ample time to study the country and costumes, some of which are strange indeed—that is, in contrast to the way we US citizens live. One thing that seemed rather peculiar to me was the way they transport their domesticated animals, such as goats and chickens, on the same public carriers as the people ride on. I made the trip to Monterrey by bus, which was a ride I'll long remember. The bus itself was an obsolete affair, model of about 1930; every mile threatened to be its last. We had to cross a mountain range on a road which was hardly wide enough for two vehicles to pass. But the driver seemed to disregard this fact, for after we had gained the top of the mountain trail we came down the other side as fast as the old crate would coast.

I certainly wish I had more knowledge of the Spanish language. I would have had a much better time if I had. I was in a restaurant trying vainly to make the waiter understand I would like a steak dinner. After much incoherent jabbering and gesticulating on his part, I finally decided on the old method of hit and take; in other words, I closed my eyes and with my finger on the menu I played the game of tic-tac-toe. If I miss, I'll take this. It did not prove to be so successful, however, for after a few minutes wait, my man returned with one of the damnedest concoctions I ever tasted.

There is much poverty down there. I have never seen so many beggars and private peddlers. You can't walk on the sidewalk for them. That is, they use the walks for display windows. You can buy anything from soup to nuts without ever entering into any of the shops. There doesn't seem to be a middle class, only the very rich and the poor. Either you drive a limousine or lead a burro. It is a strange thing, indeed, that our own next door neighbors should be so backward. It certainly opened my eyes. A country that is as rich in natural resources as Mexico, with only a scant population of nineteen million, should have no excuse for poverty amongst its people. It's the old case where the many sweat and slave to enrich the few, not capital versus labor but labor enslaved and held in servitude by capital—that's Mexico. If they would oust the present day reactionaries for a more liberal form of government, they would indeed have a great little country. What do you think of me as a radical? That's the way you get hanging around bowerys, skid rows, and soapbox lectures.

Well, Ken, I am down here in the state of Louisiana on maneuvers and have been for two months. It certainly is a swampy hole. I am looking forward to going overseas sometime this spring. Would like to get in on the big push. Are there any women in Iceland? You fellows must really know what suppressed desires are. In this country you have to beat them off with a club.

Write soon,—Brother at Arms

Rumors persisted about shipping out to Europe for "the big one." Still trying to get into the infantry, Joe was disappointed when in early April he was reassigned to Battery A, 752 Field Artillery Battalion at Camp Bowie, Texas. This unit was organized and equipped to provide artillery support for an infantry regiment. After sixteen months of hard training, the artillery battalion had just received its alert orders for imminent departure overseas and all passes and furloughs were cancelled.

During the next eight weeks, equipment was carefully checked, packed, and rechecked, and duffle bags were stuffed for a long train ride—three days and four nights to Boston, Massachusetts. Knowing that four days would typically be lost to wartime diseases for every day lost by combat wounds, the Army ordered everyone to receive a series of shots from the medics before boarding the train for Boston—smallpox, typhoid, tetanus, cholera, and yellow fever. En route to Boston, the battalion received its final alert order to "prepare for LSV"—long sea voyage, destination unknown. Training was now over and the real world of war was about to unfold. Joe was finally on his way to "the seat of war in Heinie-land." In a letter dated April 12, 1944, from Camp Bowie, Texas, to Ken in Iceland, Joe wrote:

> *From: Private Joe Haan, 752 F.A. Bn, Btry. A.*
> *Camp Bowie, Texas*
> *Dear Ken—*
>
> *I received your very interesting letter today. It certainly was comprehensive in that it gave a very vivid description of Icelandic costumes and people. It certainly must be a beautiful country as the picture shows you sent. Is there any timber in Iceland? I had always pictured that country as a vast tundra where no life existed save penguins and scattered Eskimos living in isolated villages.*
>
> *Dan has not written to me in the past three months. The last time I heard from him he was 1st Sgt in Camp San Louis Obispo, California. He may be overseas for all I know. I would like to get some more pictures from you if you have any of the country. How do you get the film? It's almost impossible to purchase any here in the States. I had a fifteen-day furlough last spring when I was stationed in California. At that time, you could still buy film, so I took quite a few pictures out there. Did you take any pictures in England or were you not allowed to do so?*
>
> *I am now stationed at Camp Bowie, Texas, with the 752 Field Artillery Battalion. We have*

the big howitzer, 155 millimeter [shells weigh 100 pounds]. I just came into this outfit two days ago, transferred from the Tank Destroyer Battalion. What I would really like to get into is the infantry, that's what I'm trying for now but I don't think I'll get there because this outfit has received their alert orders. That sounds promising. In your opinion, how long do you think the war will last? It seems they have half the German Army over here in prison camps. It appears they are quite happy over the fact that they have been captured. It's surprising how many of them can talk English, most of them look very young, and not at all like the beasts they are pictured as. I must close for now, but hope to hear from you again soon.

—Brother Joe

Joe's battalion arrived at Camp Miles Standish in Boston on June 25, 1944, and departed the next day for the Boston Port of Embarkation (POE) where they boarded the USS *Wakefield* on July 1st. A Navy band played as the troops boarded the *Wakefield* and the Red Cross passed out doughnuts and orangeade. The latest news from Europe said that following the D-Day landing on June 6, 1944, the Yanks were now at St. Lo, France, and some were headed for Cherbourg. On D-Day, 175,000 troops landed on the Normandy beaches, and a steady stream of reinforcements was pouring into Normandy every day—exciting times for troops who had been training for so long.

The old ship creaked, strained, and rolled as it cut a zigzag course across the Atlantic to avoid being torpedoed by German submarines. Some of the boys got sick at sea, but Joe said he enjoyed his maiden sea voyage and spent his time reading, exercising, and on watch duty.

On July 9, 1944, the Wakefield pulled into Liverpool, England, where Joe's field artillery battalion boarded a troop train for Wales. Joe was enthralled with the way the Brits talked, saying that it "sounds like poetry." The battalion arrived at Court-y-Gellon in South Wales the next day and was met by an advance party that had arrived earlier. Four miles up the road, the troops received their first hot showers in more than a week. Hot food was provided from a temporary mess hall. Barracks were assigned, a permanent mess hall was set up, and vehicles, tractors, and artillery were procured.

On the radio, they heard "Axis Sally," an American expatriate living in Berlin broadcasting American music and Nazi propaganda from the German capital in her sexy voice. The GIs called her the "Berlin Bitch." After the war she was convicted of treason in Washington, DC, and sentenced to thirty years in prison.

A full schedule started the next day and continued for two weeks nonstop—physical hardening, map study, identification of enemy, defense from enemy aircraft, poison gas defense, blackout and camouflage, battlefield discipline, and small arms practice. Joe met several "Tommies" and local English civilians and remarked about the wonderful lilt to the Welsh brogue. Joe was fascinated by the funny accents he heard when he had his first pint of English bitters in a local pub, and he welcomed the strong British attitude against the Germans and their faith in Hitler's ultimate defeat. Joe said it made everyone feel good. An old British sergeant, a veteran of the World War I trenches in France, told Joe, "Nothing can prepare you for what you will face in combat." On July 10, 1944, Joe wrote to Ken in Iceland:

V-Mail to Sgt. Kenneth Haan, CIC Det. Hq IBC,
Iceland Base Command, APO 860.5
From Pfc Joe Haan 17047734, Btry A, 752 F.A.BN.
APO 403 C/O PM, NY, NY
Somewhere in England
Dear Ken—

I received your letter yesterday after it had travelled a good deal first to Texas then to England, where I am now stationed. I am not permitted to tell you what part because of the rigid censorship, as you know. I enjoyed the trip over here very much. I never got seasick, but there were a few of the boys who didn't fare so well. Did you travel all over the island when you were here? I think it is a very scenic little country with its quaint little villages and farms. We are not allowed to go very far from our station, but what I have seen of it I like very much. I wrote a letter to John Carmody. I am going to try to see him if I can, as you probably know I have never seen him. Did you get to see him when you were here? By the way, how many days' leave did you get [then]? I don't know how long I will be here but hope we get in on the big push before it winds up, which I don't think will be long. Must close. Here is Dan's address: APO 81, San Francisco.

—Brother Joe

The Allied D-Day landings on June 6 had succeeded dramatically, and hundreds of thousands of reinforcements from England streamed steadily into Eisenhower's massive invading armies. Though harder than expected and taking far longer than planned to break through the German defenses in Normandy, by early July over two million troops faced each other along a hundred-mile front in Normandy—800,000 Americans against 750,000 Germans, while 600,000 British and Canadians faced a nearby German force of 850,000. Following the hard-fought American breakout from Normandy on July 27, the outmaneuvered and outfought German Army was forced to begin its inevitable retreat into the heavily fortified Siegfried Line along the German border.

On August 15, Joe's battalion departed for the Southampton docks on the English Channel and arrived at Camp C-2 on the outskirts of Stockbridge shortly before midnight. Strict blackout discipline was enforced. Overhead, the troops heard the constant droning of thousands of friendly fighters and bombers on their way to and from France and Germany. Absentee ballots were issued for the US presidential election, and Joe voted for the first time in his life, noting that everyone in his unit seemed to vote for Roosevelt because he had done so much to save the country. The troops felt it was now up to them—"Adolph Schicklgruber, here we come!" They were assigned to General George S. Patton's Third Army, and their motto was, "We're all in this together."

The Southampton port was frequently bombed during World War II. Despite extensive damage, it was still the principal point of embarkation for troops heading for France, with over three million troops departing Southampton for the Normandy beaches in 1944 and 1945. Joe had read about the history of Southampton. He knew how the Vikings had defeated the English king and how generations of English soldiers had embarked for France from the docks of Southampton for their earlier wars, like Henry the Fifth at Agincourt. Joe was fascinated with how old everything seemed to be in England and that Southampton was such a well-defended fortress port. He knew that the Mayflower had originally set sail for America from Southampton with the Pilgrims in 1620 and that the Titanic began its fateful maiden voyage from Southampton in 1912. Now here he was, leaving Southampton like so many other soldiers centuries before him, this time to fight against German Nazis.

The next day, August 16, Joe's unit moved to Southampton Gate-10 where they remained overnight in readiness to board amphibious assault ships (LCTs) headed for France in the morning. Cots and blankets were distributed, and the troops had the opportunity to take their last hot shower for a long time. British barrage balloons prominently defended the area all around the docks, and searchlights glared deeply into the night sky, highlighting hundreds of planes coming and going overhead. Nervous energy and the constant droning of low-flying planes kept everyone awake until the approach of dawn, when the troops were aroused to prepare for immediate departure for Utah Beach on the coast of Normandy. Breakfast consisted of coffee, K-rations, and C-rations—canned meat and eggs, biscuits, dried fruit bars, cigarettes, and chewing gum. Red Cross workers distributed coffee and doughnuts as Joe's battalion boarded its assigned LCTs.

With his personal equipment and supplies, Joe said he carried well over seventy-five pounds of gear, or more—his M-1 rifle, ammo vest, double ammunition bandolier with 320 rounds, grenade bag, shovel, bayonet, combat knife, "sharp-as-a-razor" hunting knife, three days of combat rations, canteen, morphine, and cigarettes even though he didn't smoke. He also carried dozens of personal survival items in his canvas musette bag, including a camera, small books, pictures, letters, writing paper, and a .45 Colt officer's pistol he bought in Texas. What he really wanted was a German Luger.

The troops waited on board the LCT and were finally underway by 1:00 p.m., landing on Utah Beach in their landing craft at 3:00 p.m. near St. Mere Eglise. They marched four miles inland with their equipment and bivouacked for the night in tents, joining the other 800,000 American soldiers who had been relentlessly landing in Normandy since June 6. Everyone was in good spirits. The unit historian noted that crossing the channel and the subsequent amphibious landing were "a piece of cake."

Following the D-Day Normandy invasion in June 1944, General George S. Patton was placed in command of the US Third Army and positioned on the extreme right of the Allied forces spearheading eastward toward Germany. Patton's Third Army was part of the Allied forces that freed northern France, bypassing Paris. Patton used German "blitzkrieg" tactics with high mobility and aggressive shock maneuver. Rather than engage the German Army in a World War I-style frontal assault, Patton bypassed areas of German resistance and used the superior mobility of his units to defeat German defensive positions through rapid maneuver, rather than head-on fighting.

Joe was one of thousands of American troops sent to reinforce Eisenhower's victorious Allied Army. By the time Joe arrived in Normandy on August 17, the Allies had soundly defeated Hitler's centrally controlled German Army due to the resilience and ability of Eisenhower's Allied soldiers to adapt. The cost to the Allies was 210,000 casualties, including more than 50,000 Allied dead. But over the seventy-five-day period following D-Day, the German Army lost nearly 450,000 men—250,000 killed or wounded and 200,000 POWs—plus 1,500 tanks, 3,500 artillery pieces, and 20,000 vehicles that were abandoned or destroyed.

It had been the wettest July in forty years, and surviving remnants of the German Army retreated eastward through the mud toward the heavily reinforced Siegfried Line with their plodding, horse-drawn artillery. Patton implored his immediate boss, General Omar Bradley, and General Eisenhower to permit him to use his Third Army to encircle the retreating German Army and cut them off, forcing surrender, but the more cautious Bradley demurred. Instead, Patton was ordered to sweep rapidly around Paris to the south and then head directly east, unopposed, toward Nancy and Metz in Alsace-Lorraine along the German border. As the Germans evacuated Paris in August, Patton's orders to his Third Army were, "advance and keep on advancing . . . pursue the enemy relentlessly."

At noon on August 20, Joe's battalion headed south for Landivy, France, and arrived at 9:00 p.m., having travelled ninety-seven miles in nine hours. Wherever they went, the French people cheered, waved flags, clapped hands, and showered the American liberators with flowers, fruit, smiles, and blessings. Wine, cider, and cognac were served as French women tousled the hair of the American soldiers and kissed nearly everyone passing by. What a welcome.

Joe's artillery battalion continued south and southeast, covering 223 miles in a fifteen-hour trek taking them to the vicinity of Ormes, south of Paris, by August 23. The battalion's wheeled vehicles advanced another forty-four miles to Ladon. On August 25, the Allies liberated Paris, but Joe's battalion experienced its first delay due to a shortage of gasoline. The delay permitted tractors and guns to catch up with the remainder of the battalion and move twenty-one miles further east to Courtenay, where they formed a defensive position.

Rain had fallen all afternoon on the 25th and continued into the next morning as the sounds and sights of war became increasingly evident. Artillery firing could be heard in the distance all night. In the morning the battalion received twenty-four German prisoners to guard, their first. Joe volunteered for guard duty.

War soon became a reality—Private Ware struck a German mine on the road and was seriously injured when his truck was demolished, and Captain Collins was wounded in the chest, accidentally shot by a young battalion soldier cleaning his weapon. Everyone knew it was no longer make-believe war like stateside training.

On August 28, Joe's battalion moved fifty-five miles further east to a position half a mile west of Troyes. The next day they traveled another eight miles to a defensive position east of Troyes where gunners fired their first twenty-four rounds of field artillery at the retreating German Army. On August 30, the battalion moved eight miles east to Montrevil-sur-Barse and another six miles to Chauffour where the battalion's artillery batteries went into position and fired two missions at 7:00 p.m. A reconnaissance party led by Lt. Col. Webb went forward to scout the area at the front, and the main body of the battalion moved up under Major Albrecht. The next morning, the battalion moved another twenty-three miles east to a position near Epagne, but the advance came to an abrupt halt because it had now run totally out of gas, along with the rest of Patton's Army.

Following the Allied Normandy breakout in late July, Patton's Army swept through France in a lightning campaign, pushing the retreating and defeated German Army back toward its defenses along the German border. Patton's rapid advance was a cakewalk, but now the going was about to get really tough for Joe and his fellow soldiers. The battalion historian summarized the initial phase of General Patton's blitzkrieg march through France and the stubborn resilience of the retreating German Army:

General Patton's offensive came to a screeching halt on August 31, 1944, as the Third Army literally ran out of gas near the Moselle River, just outside of Metz, France. Patton expected fuel and supplies would be kept flowing to support his successful advance, but Eisenhower favored a broad front. Eisenhower gave Montgomery and his 21st Army Group on the Allied northern flank high priority for supplies for Operation Market Garden, resulting in Patton's Third Army running out of fuel in Alsace-Lorraine while aggressively exploiting German weakness on that front. Patton had proved that a major Allied advantage was in mobility with rapid blitzkrieg movements due to the greater number of US trucks, higher reliability of US tanks, and better radio communications. Patton believed that slow, deliberate, WWI-style frontal attacks were wasteful and resulted in high losses by permitting the Germans to carefully prepare defensive positions. Unfortunately, the time needed to resupply Patton with fuel was enough to allow the Germans to further fortify the fortress city of Metz, France. By October and November, Patton's Third Army was mired in a near-stalemate with the German Army in front of Metz, causing heavy casualties on both sides. By November 23rd, Metz fell to Patton.

It was now the first of September. Fall was in the air, with shorter, cooler days. After advancing 375 miles in two weeks, Patton's Third Army was stuck in place without fuel, allowing the Germans to establish a formidable defensive line along the Moselle River. The realities of war surrounded everyone. That morning the battalion captured its first enemy soldiers, and Joe now had an additional five POWs to guard. Joe noted in his journal the massive extent of destruction and that his experience in Alsace-Lorraine proved General Sherman's contention that "war is hell." He wrote, "Those that I fight I do not hate, those that I guard I do not love."

Devastation was evident everywhere, and each man in the battalion seemed to have a new, determined outlook. Carelessness had become extinct. Earnestness, coldness, and deadliness were expressed by all. Patrols and security guards were more cautious, making it difficult to move within the battalion perimeter due to increased security. Everyone was on alert, on the ball, ready to fight and kill with grim determination.

In the afternoon, word spread throughout the battalion that Lt. Wade and Lt. Munford, the assigned liaison pilot and observer, were reported missing from a reconnaissance flight over enemy lines. This was quite a shock, as both officers were held in high esteem by the troops.[8] It was soon learned that the two lieutenants were forced down and taken prisoner in the nearby town of Brethany. A failed rescue attempt suffered casualties with several American dead and wounded. That night, Joe wrote to Ken and summarized his recent movements as best he could to avoid censorship.

September 1, 1944

To: T/Sgt. Kenneth Haan, CIC Det. Hq. 1BC, APO-860 C/O Pm, NY, NY

From: PFC Joseph Haan 17047734, Btry A. 752. FA Bn. A.P.O. 403 C/O PM, NY, NY

Dear Ken—

Received your letter but did not have the time to answer it till today as we have been constantly on

8. Pilots and observers were assigned to artillery units to fly Piper Cub light aircraft. They worked as spotters and called in artillery fire to support infantry positions and direct attacks on enemy tanks and artillery.

the move. I am no longer in England but at one of the many fronts, which is France today. We have been here for quite some time. I am getting my share of souvenirs, so hope to have much to show and tell by the time this thing is over. I don't think the German Army will hold together much longer; they seem to be on the move back on all fronts. It has been raining here continuously, but today it is very clear and warm, so all the boys are writing letters. There are bombers flying over my head at this moment; I attempted to count them, but there are so many that it's like counting blackbirds. My unit has captured a few Germans and buried a few but haven't been involved in too much of the action way up front. I have passed through many towns that have been completely devastated, but some have been untouched. The French people treat us like royalty wherever we meet them. When we pass through the towns and villages, we are showered with fruit, vegetables, wine, and cider. Congratulations on the Bronze Star. I am quite anxious to know what your work is all about. I think I have a close idea as I met a soldier in England who was at one time stationed in Iceland and did counterintelligence work. I haven't received any mail in several weeks as we have been on the move, but hope to get some in a day or two. Will close for now, hope to hear from you soon.

—Brother Joe

During the night of September 23, the battalion received enough gas to move forty miles east to the vicinity of Guindercourt-aux-Ormes in pursuit of the retreating German Army, which had established a strong defensive line between

Metz and Nancy along the Moselle River. Eisenhower's "Redball Express" truck convoys started to bring gas and badly needed supplies such as food and ammo for units at the front that had outstripped their supply lines. The battalion was now under constant enemy bombardment and destroyed two German planes with machine gun fire. To get away from the steady roar of the big guns, Joe volunteered for machine gun outpost duty, guarding the battalion's outer perimeter along the front.

From September 9–12, Major Reese and an advance party were able to scrounge enough gas to move the battalion fifty-eight miles further east to a position near Colombey, then nine miles further into the front lines in the vicinity of Germiny, France. The next day the battalion moved forward another twenty-two miles near Ville-sur-Madon to a position one mile west of Lanueville-devant-Bayon. The battalion's artillery batteries fired all day and night at targets radioed into the unit command post by spotters on the ground, forcing the Germans to retreat across the river. The next day the battalion moved seven miles across the Moselle River at Bayon near Lorey. The effect of its previous firing was evident everywhere—the area was littered with enemy dead, an 88 mm German gun was destroyed, and enemy mortar and machine gun positions were obliterated.

During the night of September 16–17, the battalion moved seven miles further east to a position southeast of Dembasle and destroyed a battery of German 88s holding up advancing American infantry and tanks. The battalion's artillery also destroyed a horse-drawn German column. Up north, Field Marshall Montgomery launched the ill-fated Operation Market Garden, a bold British-American airborne assault into German-occupied Holland. The next day, Joe's unit moved another five miles east to a position southeast of Haracourt. General Lentz visited the unit command post.

On September 18, the battalion moved seven miles to a position west of Courbesseaux, and General Lentz made two more visits to the battalion command post.[9] On September 20, General Lentz changed the order of battle, directing the battalion to move forward and support the adjacent 35th Infantry Division.

Now the going got even more arduous. During the night of September 23–30, Lt. Col. Webb departed for a reconnaissance mission to the front. Within a few hours, the entire battalion moved into Gramercy. A new liaison pilot and observer were assigned and an anti-aircraft battery was attached to the battalion. Colonel Riley, commander of the 6th Armored Division Artillery, visited the battalion command post with further orders, and Lt. Col. Webb conducted another reconnaissance mission into the front lines. Late in the day, General Lentz arrived with orders for harassing and interdiction fire on all adjacent towns, villages, and woods throughout the night.

What Joe and his comrades did not know was that they were facing a fierce German counterattack and that the battalion would soon be surrounded and forced to retreat. For the next several days Joe's battalion was under constant bombardment and attack. On the third day at Gramercy, September 25, Joe was assigned to a reconnaissance party to conduct an observation mission into the front lines. While he was on patrol, Corporal Holloway, Joe's friend from "B" Battery, was killed by 88 mm shrapnel. Meanwhile, rain had fallen continuously and the battalion's vehicles were mired in thick, clinging mud. Returning from the reconnaissance patrol, Joe remained assigned to outpost guard duty which,

9. Major General John Max Lentz commanded field artillery in World War I and became assistant chief of staff for the Army Ground Forces in World War II, responsible for supervising and training Army ground troops. He joined XII Corps as an artillery officer in 1944 and became part of the US Third Army under General George C. Patton.

along with machine gun positions, were the most dangerous assignments in the battalion. Outposts were typically fifty yards in front of the main line of foxholes protecting the outer perimeter of the battalion. Joe said the Germans were so close that at times he could smell their sweaty uniforms and hear them talk.

Nights were always the worst on the front line, especially the constant pitch-black nights with cold rain falling. A sense of fatalism pervaded. It was difficult to dig in because of the rocky ground, so there was little protection in the forward positions. "Keep your head down or die" was the watchword. Heavy interdiction fire harassed the troops throughout the cold, wet nights at Gramercy, made especially lonely and bleak when one was assigned to a remote guard post along the far outer perimeter of the battalion.

On the fourth day at Gramercy, September 26, the situation became even more tense when enemy shelling concentrated on the battalion's artillery. Heavy bombardment continued unabated hour after hour, causing many American casualties and a perilous situation. Joe called the destruction around him "Dante's Inferno." When he saw Captain Miller receive severe wounds from white-hot exploding shell fragments, he deplored the utter insanity and futility of "this damned war." Attempts were made to obtain blood plasma, but to no avail.

A constant flow of "Redball Express" trucks driven by segregated black soldiers headed west to the rear lines with wounded and dead, while gasoline, ammunition, and C-rations moved in the opposite direction to Joe's position at the front. Late at night, Joe captured two German soldiers who approached his outpost along the battalion perimeter. Meanwhile, enemy artillery fire and American tanks constantly cut the battalion's wire communications so it was nearly impossible to talk to higher headquarters or the command posts. The battalion fired its guns continuously, day and night, and as enemy replacements appeared, the battalion shifted its guns back and forth, constantly firing at the steadily encroaching German Army.

The battalion's final day at Gramercy, September 27, started ominously. An early morning reconnaissance party under Major Reese left for Bey-sur-Seille west of Gramercy, but by 7:30 a.m., German forward units had penetrated the American perimeter and service area, forcing the battalion to retreat. The battalion march order was sent out for all units to move immediately to Bey-sur-Seille if possible. Three casualties were evacuated, an anti-aircraft vehicle was destroyed by enemy fire, and the service records of enlisted men in the S-4 logistics section were abandoned. During the American evacuation of Gramercy and subsequent retreat, two vehicles and three enlisted men were left in the area due to the deteriorating battle conditions—heavy fire from 88 mm German guns and surrounding enemy small arms fire.

By 9:30 a.m., enemy tanks advanced into Gramercy, and by noon, more enemy tanks and infantry approached from the rear of the town. Batteries "A" and "B" rotated ninety degrees to direct fire on the expected tank attack. Sitting in his outpost watching the German panzers advance, Joe said later that he "thought the jig was up," but an American anti-tank company engaged the German tank attack with indirect cannon fire. Several enemy tanks were destroyed and the remainder withdrew. Heavy enemy shelling continued through noon when two German ME-109 fighter-bombers attempted to strafe the area, causing one American casualty at the machine gun post and heavy shelling of vehicles. They were finally driven off by battalion anti-aircraft fire.

Joe's outpost detachment was the last to leave at 2:00 p.m. as German artillery shells rained down upon them. Two soldiers near Joe were killed instantly by flying shrapnel, and eight were seriously wounded. A truck driver was also killed while trying to get his truck out of the deep mud. Rain continued nonstop, and the battalion received harassing German fire all night as it plodded slowly westward, retreating through gummy mud and slime.

During the night of September 29–30, Joe's battalion safely reassembled at Bey-sur-Seille, but attacking enemy planes made it impossible for the battalion's air observers to get airborne and direct artillery fire. Colonel Webb held a group officers' meeting and staff meeting in the morning and said the battalion was ordered to hold the area at all costs and would remain in place for at least two to three weeks. Further defensive preparations were established around the perimeter of the battalion as enemy harassing fire rained down throughout the night. Battalion gunners—wet, cold, hungry, and very dirty—continued firing all night and throughout the next day and night, even though the battalion was no longer surrounded. There was just cold rain, mud, and menacing German landmines—Schu mines, "bouncing betties," and other booby traps.

Joe's battalion remained locked in place at the front lines throughout the months of October and November, when over ten inches of rain and sleet drenched the troops. Joe's battalion had advanced nearly four hundred miles from Normandy to the Moselle River in less than a month, but for the next hundred days they would move just fifty miles further east against a stubborn enemy.

And now the Germans weren't the only danger. When soldiers failed to keep their feet dry while sloshing day and night in deep mud and wet foxholes, the prolonged exposure to cold and wet conditions caused trench foot. It caused loss of sensation, tissue damage, and sometimes gangrene. In the fall and winter of 1944, trench foot put more men out of action than did German weapons. It soon became a court martial offense under Patton. The only remedy was to change socks frequently and have a buddy rub your feet. Meanwhile, locked in bitter combat in Alsace-Lorraine during the cold and wet fall of 1944, Patton's Third Army suffered 47,000 battle casualties, dead and wounded. To Joe it looked like the World War I stalemate repeating itself on the same French battlefields.

Digging a foxhole not far from the infamous French battlefields Verdun and St. Michel, still bombed out and mined from the First World War, Joe dug up an old German trench knife and belt buckle from 1916 with the inscription, Gott Mit Uns—god with us. German soldiers had Gott Mit Uns inscribed on their coins and belt buckles in the First World War. Twenty-six years later, Joe saw the same inscription on Nazi belt buckles and on the German coins in the pockets of POWs he guarded. Joe had also seen the inscription etched on a glass pitcher at the German farm back in Minnesota and had frequently asked about the meaning of the words, Gott Mit Uns. On the farm Joe would ask, "If Gott is mit uns, why am I treated like an animal?" Now he would ask, "Who is this god of death—this Gott of war, of carnage? Does Gott take sides in human affairs? Does Gott choose sides in war? Which Gott—the Kraut Gott, or the American god? Whose side are these gods on? Are we on god's side, or Gott's side?"

Gott Mit Uns

Under the roots of trees,
Dead ages lie down,
To cover this false promise
On rusting buckles:
"Gott Mit Uns."
So many Gods, so many creeds,
So many ways that wind and wind.

What the world needs is
More men that can be kind,
To cultivate more true creativeness,
And far less destructiveness.

Joe knew that at the nearby Verdun battlefield there were nearly one million casualties in 1916, and now hundreds of thousands more casualties on both sides littered the French countryside once again. He questioned the inherent contradiction in the inscription, Gott Mit Uns—a preposterous claim from both sides struggling to the death in futile war. He flaunted his questions to the warriors of old, and to all of humanity—"so many Gods, so many creeds, so many ways that wind and wind . . . to cover false promises on rusting buckles."

Late in October 1944, Joe's battalion remained in position on the front lines, blocked by the German Army and unable to move forward or back. This is when Joe spent three days in the same foxhole with a dead German soldier near the city of Metz in Alsace-Lorraine. He wrote of this experience in "Memories of Death," and in an essay, "Sharing a Foxhole with Friedrich Hofman," a memoir of the ravages of war, ignorance of blind faith, and ultimate bonds of common humanity.

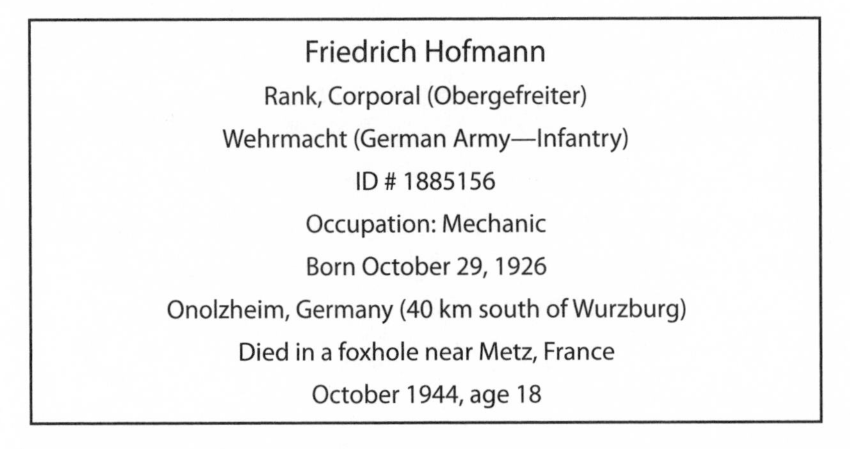
Friedrich Hofmann
Rank, Corporal (Obergefreiter)
Wehrmacht (German Army—Infantry)
ID # 1885156
Occupation: Mechanic
Born October 29, 1926
Onolzheim, Germany (40 km south of Wurzburg)
Died in a foxhole near Metz, France
October 1944, age 18

Memories of Death

"Resting on the Corpse of Friedrich Hofman"

Private First Class Joe Haan (Notebook II)

Alsace-Lorraine, France, November 1944

A dead man speaks,
For the violence that flares about me
Is shocking and sometimes stifling.
I am carried in a high wind,
Like the down of a flower,
Into a fray of which I have no interest,
For all of my energies, physical and mental,
Are concerned with other pursuits:
Distant galaxies, infinity and time,
Space and matter, the velocity of light,
The significance of a one-celled creature,
Does an amoeba think?
These thoughts transcend
All other events of the moment,
While I attempt to keep my poor body dry,
Sitting on the corpse of a dead man, the enemy.
Who a few days before, was the living,
With hope of a happy future,
Blue-eyed, blond-headed kinder
To love and fondle,
A frau to protect and respect, also die for —
"For which I have so young departed,
For I am the new dead who speaks,
Fired with nationalism and zeal
For der faterland, have I died in vain.
"But at this moment,
I serve a very practical purpose —
A footstool in the bottom of a muddy hole,
Whose excavations

I provided the energy hours before,
But now, I lie grotesque and undignified,
Discolored and unrecognized,
For my deeds of valor.
"Soon, putrification
Will blot out my memory forever,
For the worms will truly inherit the earth,
And organic Me, will be no more."

Sharing a Foxhole with Friedrich Hofman

An American Private's Memoir

Joe Haan (Notebook III)

Alsace-Lorraine, France, November 1944

I wish I had never met Friedrich Hofmann. Friedrich was a German infantry corporal of the regular Wehrmacht. I met him by chance somewhere in the province of Alsace-Lorraine, France in the month of October 1944.

It had been raining for several days in succession, which is nothing unusual in France come the autumn, as many a GI will testify. Our unit moved into a position, which up to a few short hours before had been the front line of the mighty Wehrmacht, all of which was very convenient for us as it saved us the monotonous and tedious task of digging foxholes. Friedrich beyond doubt had dug mine for me. In the short time I was to know him we struck up an intimate friendship, yet he kept me company for only three short days.

On his person he had a picture of his father and mother, also a picture of a very attractive woman who was either his sister, wife, or sweetheart. I was never able to learn which. He had been drafted into the Wehrmacht against his will to serve the Fatherland and pay the maximum penalty for being born a German. I have had occasion for meeting many Friedrichs under similar circumstances since that October day, but none of them have quite so impressed or haunted me as this Friedrich has; maybe it was his youthfulness, his blond hair that was exceptionally long, blowing in the fall breeze, or his glassy blue eyes staring lifelessly skyward.

Yes, Friedrich was a corpse, one I shall never forget; for many times I have met him since, usually in the wee hours of the morning, after which I awake—covered with cold perspiration, then the agony of despair, which stems from my sensitiveness to violence, and death holds me in its merciless clutch. Then I am shocked back to reality that I have survived a program of mass murder on a large legalized scale, and it isn't a bad dream after all, only this violent mental agitation, which runs in its cycle, have I left as a memory to remind me.

On the second day of sharing Friedrich's foxhole, and waiting for the General only knows what, in which I, an INFANTRY PRIVATE, am totally ignorant of, my curiosity overcame me so much I decided to become better acquainted with Friedrich. But how much, you ask, does one acquaint oneself with a corpse? The answer is quite simple—through the contents of his pockets. Rather gruesome, you might think, frisking the pockets of a dead man. When time is heavy on one's hands one is apt to do strange things to break the monotony, so let it be said an idle mind is mischief's workshop, though in this event my very idleness was to be the indirect cause for radical changes in regard to the philosophy of hate that I have for so long thrived on.

The combination testament and prayer book I took from Friedrich's pocket was old and brown from many rains that was in itself mute testimony of a long stay on the front lines; and a small trickle of his life's blood had found its way to a corner of the book. Within its soiled pages I found two four-leaf clovers. All this was fuel on the fires of agnosticism that long had been smoldering within me in regard to the matter of blind faith. Had he too prayed, as I had, in a vain effort to save himself, as our tanks, monsters of steel and energy, moved forward to crush or machine-gun anything in the line of an obstacle that might lie in their path?

INFANTRY hasn't a chance pitted against tanks, and tanks don't stop to take prisoners, at least they didn't in this situation. I had often imagined myself in a like position, caught in a German tank attack, like the man drowning, grasping for a straw, I would mutter a prayer. My faculty to reason would be stifled by fear, the invisible giant. I would not have the consolation that Friedrich must have had, knowing his prayers were born from faith. What, then, had I to turn to?

The dead enemy convinced me prayer was futile. If the prayer of the many men under arms could but be amplified, the clamorous din would out-roar the barrage from the cannon. This shocking reality had dawned on me like a bright light flashing in my face, after being confined in the dark recesses of the catacombs of suspicion and speculation, prayer would be like asking the omnipotence to grant me that three and three be not six.

The law of cause and effect must take its toll, these organic creatures called men. Their sole objective to kill or destroy must have their day of wanton butchery. It all seemed so unreal. Here I was thousands of miles from home on foreign soil, sharing this hole with a dead man, this creature I had been indoctrinated to hate. Somehow, I had never quite pictured the enemy as totally human. Gradually it became clear to me that here was a victim of circumstance like myself. I found I could no longer hate, but rather a confused feeling of pathos and sympathy came over me. The inoculation I had received with the virus of hate was torn between the positive and negative in mad frustration.

Without his gray-green uniform I would take him for an American, but in this maelstrom of turmoil I could have no regrets or offer no sympathy and retain my sanity. So I must let hate burn hot within me, hate the product of ignorance of things we do not know or understand. I found myself imprisoned with my conflicting emotions, without a god to turn to that I might seek salvation from this vexatious predicament into which I had unconsciously floundered.

It seemed all routes of escape were forever sealed and it would be merely a matter of time until I too would be lying dead in the mud, neglected and undignified, the inevitable fate of all soldiers who expose themselves to the hazards of war over a long-drawn period of time. Perpetual, merciful oblivion it would be at least, but I could not let my mind wander along this trail of thought, for hadn't several men of my acquaintance committed self-

maiming in their foxholes? I wondered if those at home whom we represented here in this mud would ever realize and appreciate what mental anguish and physical torture we, their infantry, were living through, with only one thought uppermost in our minds, to survive.

It all blends now into an incoherent nightmare, vague and inconsistent, except for the more gruesome experiences that leave their indelible impressions on one's memory. I shall not soon forget the severed limbs and shattered bodies of friends and enemy. The many dead who died with their eyes open because of the suddenness of death. The offensive in the Saar Basin where I lost my best friend, hit in the head by shrapnel, as I stood helplessly by and watched him die, his limbs thrashing violently in the mud till death stilled them forever. I soon learned when man's vital organs are pierced and torn by steel, his usual fate is sudden death. First aid is futile even if rendered by the hands of the most expert surgeon. All one can do is stand dumbfounded and be an unwilling witness to their departure.

This was Joe's "memory of death" as he was transferred to the newly arrived 26th Infantry Division (ID) in the fall of 1944. Known as the "Yankee Division" of World War I fame, the 26th ID was assigned to Patton in late September. The division entrenched into defensive positions near Joe's artillery battalion in October and launched limited attacks into the nearby Moncourt woods just east of the sector where it fought in 1918.[10] The following account is from the 26th Infantry Division record of events during October–November 1944:

10. Yankee Division, "26th Infantry Division–World War II," http://yd-info.net/page2/index.html#Bulge, accessed August 2010.

The newly arrived 26th Division was commanded by Major General Willard S. Paul, and in October 1944 the 26th relieved the 4th Armored Division in the front lines of Salonnes-Moncourt. The Yankee Division then participated in Patton's Third Army offensive of October and November, seizing Vic-sur-Seille, Marimont, Dieuze, and Sarre-Union, France, and in early December, the Yankee Division helped secure the fortified city of Metz that had fallen to Patton's Army in late November. Following the Metz assault, the 26th Division became part of Patton's famed Battle of the Bulge turning movement, where Patton's forces broke off from their east-to-west attack on the German front lines and rapidly advanced north more than 125 miles in driving snow and immediately assaulted the southern flank of the German "bulge" that extended far into the center of Eisenhower's long Allied north-south line. During the attack north, the Yankee Division was on the right flank of the 4th Armored Division, well known for its relief of Bastogne. Overcoming stiff German resistance, the Yankee Division crossed the Sûre River and seized Arsdorf on Christmas Day.

The historian from Joe's 752nd Field Artillery Battalion summarized the following events in the battalion's November 1944 records, leading up to the massive German Ardennes winter offensive that became known to history as the Battle of the Bulge:

By November 5th, the Germans were driven from Belgium; the Canadian First Army and British Second Army on the Allied left (northern) flank drove the Germans north into Holland; the US Ninth Army took its positions between the British and the US First Army, facing the Roer River, twenty-one miles west of Cologne and not far from Aachen, Germany, near the Belgium border; the US First Army was in front of Koblenz, Germany, when the US Third Army, US Seventh Army, and First French Army pushed into the Saar Basin and occupied Alsace-Lorraine; the Ninth and First Armies pushed on toward the Roer River; Patton's Third Army took the fortress city of Metz by direct assault [November] and continued to advance to the Moselle River along the German border with Luxembourg; the US Seventh and First French armies broke through at Saverne, France, seized Strasbourg, and pushed northeast to the German border, entering Germany on December 7, 1944; these setbacks for the Germans put a serious strain on German manpower; during October and November there were 300,000 German casualties and half were POWs; Hitler decided on one last desperate counterattack—the von Rundstedt Ardennes Offensive aimed at cutting off thirty-eight Allied divisions by extending the German line to the Meuse River in two days and to Antwerp, Belgium, in three weeks.

Shortly before the Battle of the Bulge, Joe was reassigned to the 1st Battalion, 101st Infantry Regiment, 26th Infantry Division, from the 752nd Field Artillery Battalion. The 101st, 104th, and 328th Infantry Regiments made up the 26th Infantry Yankee Division, recently arrived from Boston. At long last, Joe was in the infantry where he felt he belonged. He was finally out of the artillery that hurt his ear every time a big gun was fired—so horribly he would cry in pain. The only good thing about being in the artillery, he would note, was that it helped him learn the critical difference, amid the roar, between incoming and outgoing artillery.

Joe had been with the 752nd Field Artillery Battalion since he was demoted to private at Camp Bowie, Texas, shortly after the Louisiana maneuvers in early 1944. He was transferred to the Yankee Division after he got drunk and in a fight on his first European payday in Metz. He was demoted back again to one-stripe Pfc and was docked three days' combat duty for points and pay under Article 107 of the Army "Articles of War" for the time he was AWOL and in the stockade. Joe told the court martial board that he looked forward to getting out of the "chickenshit" artillery and into the infantry where he said he belonged.

Early in November, with Joe's artillery unit in support, the 26th Infantry was ordered to take the offensive and moved into Dieuze, France, which it did with few casualties. By November 20, the division advanced across the Saar River to Sarre-Union, capturing the town. This frightened many German civilians living there, ordinary people like Friedrich Hofmann. By early December, the division reached the French Maginot Line fortifications, opposite the German border. The soldiers were cold, wet, dead tired, and hungry from the exhausting house-to-house fighting.

Within the Maginot fortifications, the troops received hot meals, regrouped, reorganized, and received replacement troops and supplies. Dried off at last, replenished, and feeling better, Joe's battalion and the Yankee Division entered Sarreguemines, France, on December 8 and then moved back to Metz for R&R. But their badly needed rest was interrupted by the mammoth German Ardennes offensive as the Battle of the Bulge unfolded.

On Joe's second day in the infantry, December 16, German Field Marshal Gerd von Rundstedt launched a massive winter offensive at the weakest point in the Allied lines between Liege, Belgium, and Bastogne, Luxembourg. All hell broke loose. The 26th Infantry Division was ordered to disengage from the front lines to the east and move immediately north into Luxembourg to counter the German breakthrough in the Allied lines. The weather was exceptionally cold with blowing snow like a Minnesota winter. Some of the boys in Joe's squad had a hard time of it. Many were new replacements, just teenagers. They looked up to Joe, at the ripe old age of twenty-six, as an experienced veteran. Although never formally trained for the infantry, Joe looked tough and taught them tricks he had learned on outpost duty at the front, on the farm, on the road, and in training. He taught them how to survive, telling them, "Fear is inevitable. Just keep moving when you're fired at, and keep your head down."

Joe was selected as point man at the front of the battalion marching column as it entered the Ardennes Forest in Luxembourg. German 88 mm artillery fire started to impact on the side of a hill in the forest, about a half mile in front of Joe's position on the road. He spotted movement coming out of the woods in front and thought it was enemy soldiers. But what he saw was a half dozen European wild boars, frightened by the German artillery shelling and headed for the road a few yards in front of him. In an instant, the wild boars turned toward Joe, parallel to the road. They stopped, staring, no more than thirty yards away.

By now it was almost dark and Joe said to himself, "This will be the last chance you'll ever have to kill a European wild boar." He opened fire and killed the largest one, thinking of a wild boar feast when the regiment halted. But Joe's small arms fire alerted the advancing columns in front of his position and to the rear—they thought they were taking enemy fire. When Joe's commander discovered where the firing came from, and why, he was in deep trouble again. His young friends in the regiment admired him for his effort. A few days later, deep into the Battle of the Bulge, the wild boar incident was all but forgotten, except for the great pig roast Joe and his infantry buddies enjoyed deep in the Ardennes Forest that cold winter night.

On December 22, the Yankee Division attacked the German army at Rambrouch and Grosbous and beat off strong German counterattacks in the initial clashes of the Battle of the Bulge. The 101st Infantry Regiment captured Arsdorf on Christmas Day after heavy fighting along the Sûre River that forms the Luxembourg-Germany border below the confluence of the Our River. As punishment for the wild boar incident, Joe was "volunteered" for a Christmas night patrol behind enemy lines to scout a crossing over a nearby river. He selected one of the newly assigned young replacement troops to join him.

The Sûre River was the scene of severe fighting during the Battle of the Bulge. The Sûre runs through the Belgian province of Luxembourg and flows a hundred miles east and southeast into the Moselle River, seven miles southwest of Trier, Germany. Joe's regiment attacked toward the adjacent Wiltz River, but was forced to withdraw in face of determined enemy resistance. Action of the 101st Infantry Regiment on the Sûre River is where Joe received his Bronze Star Medal for "heroism for finding a suitable river crossing" for Patton's rapidly advancing forces. Joe silently killed a German sentry with his well-honed hunting knife he had carried since CCC days. The young troops he mentored longed to have such a deadly weapon.

Crossing the Sûre River on Christmas night, Joe and his patrol crept along a snow-encrusted ridge toward a German outpost. Joe overpowered a guard from behind, snapped his neck, and silently cut his throat. Joe and his patrol killed the other guard without raising any attention, captured the third, and called headquarters to let them know the regiment could safely start the river crossing. When he finally caught his breath, Joe said he could hear the singing of German Christmas carols, the same ones he remembered hearing on the farm in Minnesota. The following summary is from the Yankee Division history of the Battle of the Bulge and subsequent events:

> *In late 1944, the German Army launched a last-ditch offensive across Belgium, Luxembourg, and northeastern France, popularly known as the Ardennes Offensive and Battle of the Bulge, nominally led by German Field Marshal Gerd von Rundstedt. On December 16, 1944, the German Army massed twenty-nine divisions (250,000 men) at a weak point in the center of the Allied lines and made massive headway toward the Meuse River during one of the worst winters Europe had seen in years. Patton disengaged his forward attacking units in the South when he became aware of the scope of the German attack, and redirected a corps-sized element toward the North before setting out for a strategic meeting with Eisenhower, Bradley, and members of the allied high command. Thus, Patton was able to tell Eisenhower that his forces would be in position to counter-attack almost immediately. Needing twenty-four hours of good weather, Patton turned his Third Army abruptly north (a notable tactical and logistical achievement), disengaging from the front line to relieve the surrounded and besieged 101st Airborne Division pocketed in Bastogne, Luxembourg. By February, the Germans*

were in full retreat and Patton moved into the Saar Basin of Germany. Elements of the Third Army crossed the Rhine at Oppenheim, Germany, on March 22, 1945. Patton was planning to take Prague, Czechoslovakia, when Eisenhower, under extreme pressure from the Soviets, ordered American forces in Czechoslovakia to stop short of the city limits. Patton's troops liberated Pilsen on May 6, 1945, and most of western Bohemia.

For Patton's Army, July, August, and September resulted in rapid victory, but October, November, and the first half of December resembled the ravages of a World War I stalemate, which Patton wished to avoid. Then came Hitler's big gamble, the German Ardennes Offensive. During the first half of December, Hitler transferred nearly a million German soldiers facing the Russian Red Army on the Eastern Front to the Ardennes and positioned them in front of the weak center of Eisenhower's broad line of advance. The German Army broke through the Allied lines near Wilz, Luxembourg, and the Belgian border on December 17, two days after Joe joined the Yankee Division. Eisenhower quickly regrouped to squeeze the top and bottom of the "bulge" in the German lines, placing Field Marshall "Monty" Montgomery in charge of the northern flank and Patton's boss, General Omar Bradley, in charge of the southern flank.

The bulge was quickly dissolved, but three American divisions were badly chopped up in the process. Snow was more than ankle deep in the bulge, and temperatures were below zero Fahrenheit. The reinforcing 101st Airborne Division had been positioned in Bastogne, Belgium, since December 19 and was now surrounded by five German divisions. The American division commander refused to surrender, and Bastogne caught the attention of the world.

On Christmas Day, the skies cleared and the division was finally resupplied from the air. The 101st Airborne Division withstood the German siege until relieved by Patton's Army, which moved rapidly 125 miles from the south in a blinding snowstorm. Small, isolated American units fought desperately for survival, realizing that the only way to get back home was to destroy the German Army. Patton's center of gravity and the Yankee Division were now in the middle of the German bulge.

Two weeks after the German offensive opened, the German Army was forced to withdraw back into its Siegfried Line defenses on the German border. The Germans escaped disaster only because exceptionally bad December weather prevented the Allies from cutting off their retreat. The Battle of the Bulge resulted in nearly 81,000 American casualties, dead and wounded, but Hitler's big gamble had failed. The following summary is from the 26th Infantry Division history of the Battle of the Bulge and subsequent events:

> *R&R at Metz was interrupted by the Von Rundstedt Ardennes Offensive. The Division moved north to Luxembourg, 19–21 December, to take part in the battle of the Ardennes break-through. It attacked at Rambrouch and Grosbous, 22 December, beat off strong German counterattacks, captured Arsdorf on Christmas Day after heavy fighting, and attacked toward the Wiltz River, but was forced to withdraw in the face of determined enemy resistance. With the strategic villages of Arsdorf and Eschdorf cleared of the enemy, all units of the Division were facing the Sûre River, winding through its deep channel in the hills, and the lofty snow-covered ridges beyond. The attack was resumed by the 26th Division on the*

morning of December 26, with the 101st Infantry and the 104th Infantry prepared to cross the Sûre River. The enemy was very active on the opposite bank, and the efforts of the infantry and the 101st Engineers to secure crossing sites were met by heavy small arms and mortar fire, particularly in the vicinity of Bonnal and Esch Sur La Sûre. By the end of the day, using assault boats and footbridges initially, the greater part of the 101st Infantry and the 104th Infantry had crossed the Sûre. Enemy aircraft were active over the bridging sites, and the 390th AAA Battalion destroyed fifteen enemy planes and damaged three. After regrouping, 5–8 January 1945, it attacked again, reached the Wiltz River, and finally crossed it, 20 January. The Division continued its advance, took Grumelscheid, 21 January, and crossed the Clerf River, 24 January. The 26th then shifted to the east bank of the Saar, and maintained defensive positions in the Saarlautern area, 29 January–6 March 1945. The Division's drive to the Rhine jumped off on 13 March 1945, and carried the Division through Merzig, 17 March, to the Rhine, 21 March, and across the Rhine at Oppenheim, 25–26 March. It took part in the house-to-house reduction of Hanau, 28 March, broke out of the Main River bridgehead, drove through Fulda, 1 April, and helped reduce Meiningen, 5 April. Moving southeast into Austria, the Division assisted in the capture of Linz, 4 May. It had changed the direction of its advance, and was moving northeast into Czechoslovakia, across the Vlatava River, when the cease-fire order was received.

Joe received the Bronze Star for Valor for action about ten miles southeast of Bastogne near the town of Arsdorf, Luxembourg, on 25–26 December 1944. The commander of Joe's regiment, Colonel Walter T. Scott, received the Silver Star for heroic action during his regiment's Sûre River crossing. On January 20, 1945, General Patton wrote a letter of commendation to the officers and men of III Corps, including the men of 26th Infantry Division and Joe's 101st Infantry Regiment:

> *The speed with which the III Corps assembled, and the energy, skill, and persistency with which it pressed its attack for the relief of Bastogne constitute a very noteworthy feat of arms.*

General Paul added the following commendation to the 26th Infantry Division:

> *When you initially attacked for seven days and nights without halting for rest, you met and defeated more than twice your own number. Your advance required the enemy to turn fresh divisions against you, and you, in turn, hacked them to pieces as you ruthlessly cut your way deep into the flank of the Bulge.*
>
> *Your feats of daring and endurance in the sub-freezing weather and snow-clad mountains and gorges of Luxembourg are legion; your contribution to the relief of Bastogne was immeasurable. It was particularly fitting that the elimination of the Bulge should find the Yankee Division seizing and holding firmly on the same line held by our own forces prior to the breakthrough.*

I am proud of this feat by you as well as those you performed earlier. We shall advance on Berlin together.

Feb. 1, 1945
Headquarters 26th Infantry Division
W.S. Paul, Major General, Commanding

Citation for Award of the Bronze Star Medal

To Private First Class Joseph B. Haan, 17047734, 101st Infantry Regiment

HEADQUARTERS 26TH INFANTRY DIVISION
28 April 1945

Private First Class Joseph B. Haan, 17047734, Infantry, Headquarters Company, First Battalion, 101st Infantry Regiment, 26th Infantry Division, United States Army. For heroic achievement in connection with military operations against an armed enemy near Arsdorf, Luxembourg, on 25–26 December 1944.

On the night of 25–26 December 1944, Private Haan, a Headquarters Company patrolman, went forward with a reconnaissance patrol along the south bank of the Sûre River in the vicinity of Arsdorf on the mission of locating a suitable location for an assault crossing and bridge site for the Battalion's planned river crossing.

Moving through bright moonlight and along the precipitous, ice-covered bank, they encountered an enemy combat patrol and after a fierce fire fight forced the foe to disperse. After locating a suitable crossing point and bridge site, Private Haan and

his comrades crossed the river in rubber boats and cautiously worked their way up a steep hill on the north bank.

The patrol surprised a three-man enemy outpost, killed two, and took the remaining foe prisoner. Infiltrating fifteen hundred yards over the high ground and into enemy territory, the patrol discovered and reconnoitered an unmapped road and found it passable for all vehicles of the Battalion up to its junction with the main road leading into Bavigne.

Private First Class Haan and his companions skillfully worked their way back to the reverse slope of the hill just opposite the proposed bridgehead and sent back their vital information to the Battalion Commander. The Battalion made immediate use of the patrol's information, proceeding to construct two footbridges and one infantry assault bridge across the Sûre River while Private First Class Haan and his comrades protected the bridgehead on the hostile side of the river.

Despite intermittent enemy artillery fire and several strafing attacks by hostile aircraft, the patrol members clung to their position until the bridges had been completed and the river crossing affected without a casualty by the assault infantry elements. As a result of this outstanding patrol action, the Battalion was enabled to cross the Sûre River and establish a bridgehead 1,000 yards wide and 1,000 yards deep before being discovered by the enemy. Private First Class Haan's heroic action contributed materially to the success of a major operation in the Battalion's drive into the flank of the enemy's Luxembourg salient. His courage under fire and aggressiveness in action against the enemy reflect the highest credit upon Private First Class Haan and the armed forces of the United States.

By Command of Major General PAUL:

/s/ C. A. HILEMAN, Lt. Col., AGD
Adjutant General

With the Germans in retreat after the siege of Bastogne was broken, the week after Christmas was relatively quiet. When the bulge was fully neutralized in early January, Eisenhower had seventy-three Allied divisions massed along a broad front ready to launch directly into the German heartland in the final Allied offensive against seventy-six defending German divisions.

The wintry days were short, with constant sleet and snow, and it was now dark by 4:30 p.m. The fanatical zeal of young German soldiers, indoctrinated in the Nazi youth program, became increasingly evident. The task at hand for the Allies was to break through the German Siegfried Line, cross the Rhine River, and destroy what remained of the German Army as the Russians advanced rapidly on Berlin from the east.

By mid January 1945, the 101st Infantry Regiment had regrouped and the troops had rested. They received new boots and clothes, and had hot showers for the first time since they were in Metz. Later in the month, the 101st attacked the German lines successfully and reached the Wiltz River, which was immediately crossed. The weather was cold with snow, sleet, and rain, and Patton attacked relentlessly, regardless of conditions, "to the limit of the troops."

The Yankee Division continued to advance to the east and took Grumelscheid on January 29, crossing the Clerf River on January 24. The constant themes of bitter cold and steady artillery shelling caused some units to reach their breaking points. Joe said he wondered why he was still alive. Mud and constant movement were made worse by a diarrhea epidemic causing cramps and fever, but everyone was reminded, "We're all in this together." On February 1, the division reached the Saar Valley between France and Germany and moved to the east bank of the Saar where it maintained defensive positions in the Saarlautern area until early March 1945. Worn out and exhausted with battle fatigue after months of continuous combat, rest was a welcome relief for Joe and his Yankee Division comrades.

The division started its final "Drive to the Rhine" on March 1 and crossed into Germany March 9, the day Joe received the Purple Heart when he killed two fanatical German soldiers and was wounded in action "fighting hand-to-hand against an armed enemy." It turned out to be a flesh wound on his ankle, but no broken bones. Joe was treated by regimental medics at the 101st aid station and returned to duty in a few days. While recuperating, Joe wrote to Ken in Iceland on March 11, 1945.

From: PFC Joe Haan, 17047734, Hq., Co., 1st Bn.
101 INF, APO 26 NY, NY
Somewhere in Germany
Dear Ken—

I received a letter from Bub. She gave me your address, so will drop you a line. I certainly was surprised that you were back in the States again. I bet it was good to get back there after being away so long. How do you like the city of San Antonio? I have been in and out of that city for the last eight years, so I am quite well acquainted there. I used to know a few people there but don't remember their addresses. Have you been out to Breckenridge Park and the Trail Driver's Museum yet? They also used to have a rattlesnake farm out there where you could buy rattlesnake sandwiches. I tried one myself, not bad stuff. I was slightly wounded since I come to the Infantry, just enough to receive the Purple Heart. It looks like we'll soon be in Berlin, now that we have our armies across the Rhine River. I guess the Japs will be our real headache. Write soon, must close for now.

As ever, —Joe

By early March, thousands of American troops were pouring through the once impregnable Siegfried Line. Since launching its final offensive into Germany following the Battle of the Bulge, the Allies had taken 250,000 prisoners and an equal number of German soldiers had been killed or wounded. Joe's company reached Brotdorf, Germany, on March 17. The town surrendered without a shot, but Joe's unit kept moving without stopping to taste the German beer or wine. The Yankee Division reached the banks of the Rhine River on March 21 and crossed at Wiesbaden and Oppenheim south of Mainz four days later. When Patton crossed the Rhine on the 22nd, he stopped halfway and dramatically urinated into "Father Rhine"—a long, high, and steady stream in full view of the troops and combat reporters surrounding him.

I drove to the Rhine River and went across on the pontoon bridge. I stopped in the middle to take a piss and then picked up some dirt on the far side in emulation of William the Conqueror.

—General George S. Patton, March 1945

On March 27 the 101st Infantry Regiment reached the Main River near Frankfurt and secured a bridgehead across the river the next day. Joe's 1st Battalion continued east through Frankfurt, but slow and tedious house-to-house fighting was needed to clean out remnants of the German Army in the towns and villages. Joe's unit reached Hanau on the 28th where they faced vicious hand-to-hand fighting in the rubble. Joe said the days at Hanau were a blur. What was disturbing was the fierce fanaticism of the young German soldiers, many just teenagers willing to fight to the death.

The Yankee Division broke out of the Main River bridgehead on Easter Sunday, April 1. The division drove rapidly northeast through the German countryside to Fulda, on a direct beeline toward Berlin, forcing thousands of Germans who were trapped behind the rapidly advancing American lines to surrender. The fighting at Fulda was tough and determined, but resistance was finally overcome by the evening of the second day. On April 5, Joe helped capture Meiningen, Germany, but the 26th Infantry Division was then ordered to head off a possible German counterattack from the southeast and move into Bavaria, Austria, and Czechoslovakia.

Though saddened to learn of President Roosevelt's death on April 12, the troops knew they had won the war. By mid-April, 325,000 German soldiers had surrendered and the Russian Red Army was at the outskirts of Berlin. Slave labor camps and poison gas dumps were overrun by Patton's Army, and German civilians were awestruck at the power of the advancing Allied Armies. It was now just a mopping up operation.

In a formal ceremony on April 28, Joe was awarded the Bronze Star Medal for heroism in combat during the Battle of the Bulge, December 25–26, and the Purple Heart. His friends said he should have had the colonel's Silver Star. Joe still had one stripe as a Pfc and wore all of his combat decorations and medals at the ceremony. He said he looked like a general.

The troops learned that Hitler had killed himself on April 30, and on May 4 the Yankee Division assisted in the capture of Linz, Austria. Patton now prepared to move immediately northeast into Czechoslovakia across the Vltava River, but the next day Joe and members of his unit overran the sprawling Gusen concentration camp in Austria. The atrocious scenes shocked even war-hardened combat veterans like Joe, who brought back dozens of horrific pictures. Memories of Gusen and man's intolerable inhumanity to fellow living creatures were etched forever in Joe's mind. Having felt so much emotional and physical pain in his life, Joe had great empathy for the poor creatures who suffered so terribly in the German concentration camps. That night he wrote in his journal, "If there be a god, may he forever damn the Nazis and their master race."

On May 7, 1945, the 101st Infantry Regiment moved into Stuben, Czechoslovakia, freeing the people in the homeland of his mother's family. That day, the regiment received the following message from Third Army Headquarters, relayed to the 26th Infantry Division Headquarters from General Eisenhower, terminating the European war. It stated in part:

> *A Representative of the German High Command signed the unconditional surrender of all German Land, Sea, and Air forces in Europe to the Allied Expeditionary Forces and simultaneously to the Soviet High Command at 0141 hours Central European Time, 7 May under which all forces will cease active operations at 0001 hours 9 May. Effective immediately all offensive operations by Allied Expeditionary Forces will cease and troops will remain in present positions.*

For Joe, the war was over and everyone celebrated, but there were rumors that the 101st would soon head for the

Pacific to fight the Japanese. Waiting for orders, the regiment had it easy for the next three months, and all the troops could talk about was how they had survived and whether they would go to Japan or head for home. Joe had the chance to hunt deer and explore the area in southern Germany, not far from where Neanderthal man was discovered. He did some souvenir hunting, sending three boxes of German artifacts to his nephews in Minnesota. He knew they would like them. On May 28, Joe wrote to Ken in Iceland from Stuben, Czechoslovakia:

> *Dear Ken—*
>
> *I have been intending to write this letter for some time but have been busy with guard duty inc. It is hard to believe the war is over. I'm still booby trap conscious and am ready to hit the ditch whenever I hear any kind of swishing sound, such as a truck coming down the highway. They sound just like mortar shells.*
>
> *I am in the same town we took the day the peace was signed, that is one day of my life I will never forget. I have a German camera which I took some pictures of the Germans turning in their weapons, but it will take some time before I get them developed. Czechoslovakia is the seventh country I have been in. I landed in Liverpool, England, then went to Newport in South Wales to be processed. I stayed five weeks there, then shipped to France from Southampton, England. I landed on the Utah Beach on D+60, we saw our first action at Troyes, France [seventy miles east-southeast of Paris]. I was in at the first battle of the Moselle River, also the siege of Metz. The first and only tank battle I ever saw was at Nancy, France, when I was still in*

the Field Artillery and twelve German tanks broke through our infantry, and got within 800 yards of our Battery. I thought the jig was up that time, but our Tank Destroyer came up just in time to intercept them before they did too much damage. Seven of them were knocked out and the other five took off.

I transferred to the Infantry on the 15th day of December at the time of the German counteroffensive in Belgium and Luxembourg. That's when the going really got tough. We contacted the Germans in northern Luxembourg on the 20th of December. I had never received any training in the Infantry, but the Tank Destroyer training was similar. The 26th Division also helped in the direct relief of the 101st Airborne at Bastogne, Belgium. We were hitting the left flank of the German spearhead. We took our toll of Heinies but paid plenty ourselves. I lost plenty of friends up there who came with me from the Field Artillery. There were twenty of my old outfit who left there together, and there were only a few left.

How many points have you got? I counted my points over again after the new battle stars came out and found I had eighty points. I am expecting an oak leaf cluster which will give me the minimum to get out of the Army. I received a letter from Dan a few days ago. He sent me a bill of Japanese currency and said his outfit was somewhere in the Palau archipelago, just as you predicted. How did you know? In all the months over here, I had one pass and that was the 1st of April. I had a three-day pass to Paris, France, plus travel time, which took six days. Paris is certainly a wonderful place. There is no sign of the war there, past or present, as far as the condition of the city, except for the many uniformed soldiers of many countries.

I have been in many of Germany's cities. One was Frankfurt. They are completely destroyed; we drove for miles through Frankfurt and there was nothing but rubble to look at. There were not more than a handful of curtains left there. So, Paris with all its caves, street buses, lights, and people, really looked good to me, as I had been at the front for many months. I visited all the historical sights such as Napoleon's Tomb, Arc De Triomphe, Eiffel Tower. The main street of Paris, as you probably know, is the Champs Elysees (pronounced shons-il-e-say). I never could catch the pronunciation until I broke it down that way. Every day is a Mardis Gras on this avenue. There are hundreds of sidewalk cafes full of idle women, but beautiful. They all seemed to be well dressed, but a little hungry. Inflation has taken quite a hold in France, so everything is sky high. I paid 500 Francs for a bottle of perfume, which is equal to $10. Later I found the Army PX, and with a special ration ticket for combat men on pass, got the same thing for 100 Francs. I sent Bub and Sis a bottle each and hope they get them OK. Have you ever heard of Place De Concorde? It is supposed to be the largest public square in the world. That is the place where Louis the 18th was executed with Marie Antoinette during the Revolution. It is near the Seine River in Paris. Their palace is still standing there also; if its rooms were placed end to end, it is said they would extend for five miles. I enclosed a German bill and a French invasion Franc; also, the insignia of the German Army. If you would like to have any souvenirs, I would be *glad to send you some. I have some German pistols, but we are not allowed to send automatic weapons; however, I did send a German rifle and bayonet to Bub. I hope it goes through all right. I sent Wayne a German helmet and a few other things, as he has been asking me for souvenirs. At the time, we are stationed in southern Czechoslovakia in the foothills of the Austrian Alps. We can see the snow-covered peaks in the distance. I'd like to take a trip up into them before leaving here. Will close for now, hoping to hear from you soon.*

As ever—Joe

On August 14, a formal ceasefire order was received from General Eisenhower while Joe and his unit were in Passau, Germany. World War II was officially over. With nearly 17,000 casualties and numerous awards, the 26th Infantry Division was deactivated in Germany and there was no more worry about going to the Pacific to fight the Japs. That night there was another big celebration, but still no word on when they would head for home.

After four months exploring the German countryside, Joe finally departed the European Theater of Operation (ETO) on October 15, 1945. He received his Honorable Discharge from the Army on November 6, 1945, and separated as Private First Class (Pfc) at Camp McCoy, Wisconsin, with $647.55 in mustering out pay. Joe was proud he had survived another test of the survival of the fittest. He was free at last—wiser, tougher, more experienced, with a little jingle in his jeans, and no attachments to anyone or anything.

War Poems

Joe wrote several poems during the war, but many did not survive. Like his poem, "War," they reflect a tormented state of mind suffered by a sensitive young man exposed to danger, cold, hunger, and deadly combat for weeks on end. Beginning with his experiences on the hated Minnesota farm, Joe wrote poetry and songs to ease his inner tension, talk with himself, and make sense of what was going on around him. Writing about the insanity and futility of war and his life at the orphanage and on the farm was Joe's attempt to figure it all out.

Soldier's Lament

Joe Haan (Book II, #9)

A violent thing I do today,
In futile battle, men I slay,
Who have been short years, and a day,
In time that here, they had to stay.

In all our young, infernal ways,
We were drawn to ruthless frays,
Violence, high and glorious,
No man now is envious.

Warriors, we, are in the strife,
To sad, sad music of this life,
As muffled drums are slowly played,
Our total death remains unswayed.

Unexplained forevermore,
A useless passage through the door,
A door that opened premature,
Like many others, gone before.

Grieve not for those who no longer be,
Lost now, in vast eternity,
Return again, oh wretched soul,
To pain and sorrow, and useless toil.

Those That I Fight

Joe Haan (Book III)

Those that I fight, I do not hate,
Those that I guard, I do not love.
No likely end could bring me less,
Or leave me happier than before.

No law or duty, bade me fight,
No public men or cheering crowds,
A lonely impulse of delight,
Drove to battle without vows.

I balanced all, brought to mind,
A waste of breath, the years behind,
Does not balance, not this life,
Nor this death, this human strife.

The Open Mouth of Hell

To Joe Haan from EML, Book III

Like a speeding locomotive
That comes rushing down the track,
You hear Eighty-Eight's a whistling
Just before you hear 'em crack.

And you swear each pack's your number,
That it's heading for your hole,
There to rip you all to pieces
As its own special goal.

Comes another, then another,
Whipping by, or landing near,
Till your mitts are wet from sweating
And your heart is cold with fear.

Then your non-com starts a yelling,
Signals up to the attack,
For, while Eighty-Eights can kill you,
They must never hold you back.

So you rise and get to rolling,
Through a hurricane of shell,
With your face toward his cannon,
And the open mouth of hell.

Joe's journey across Europe, 1944–1945

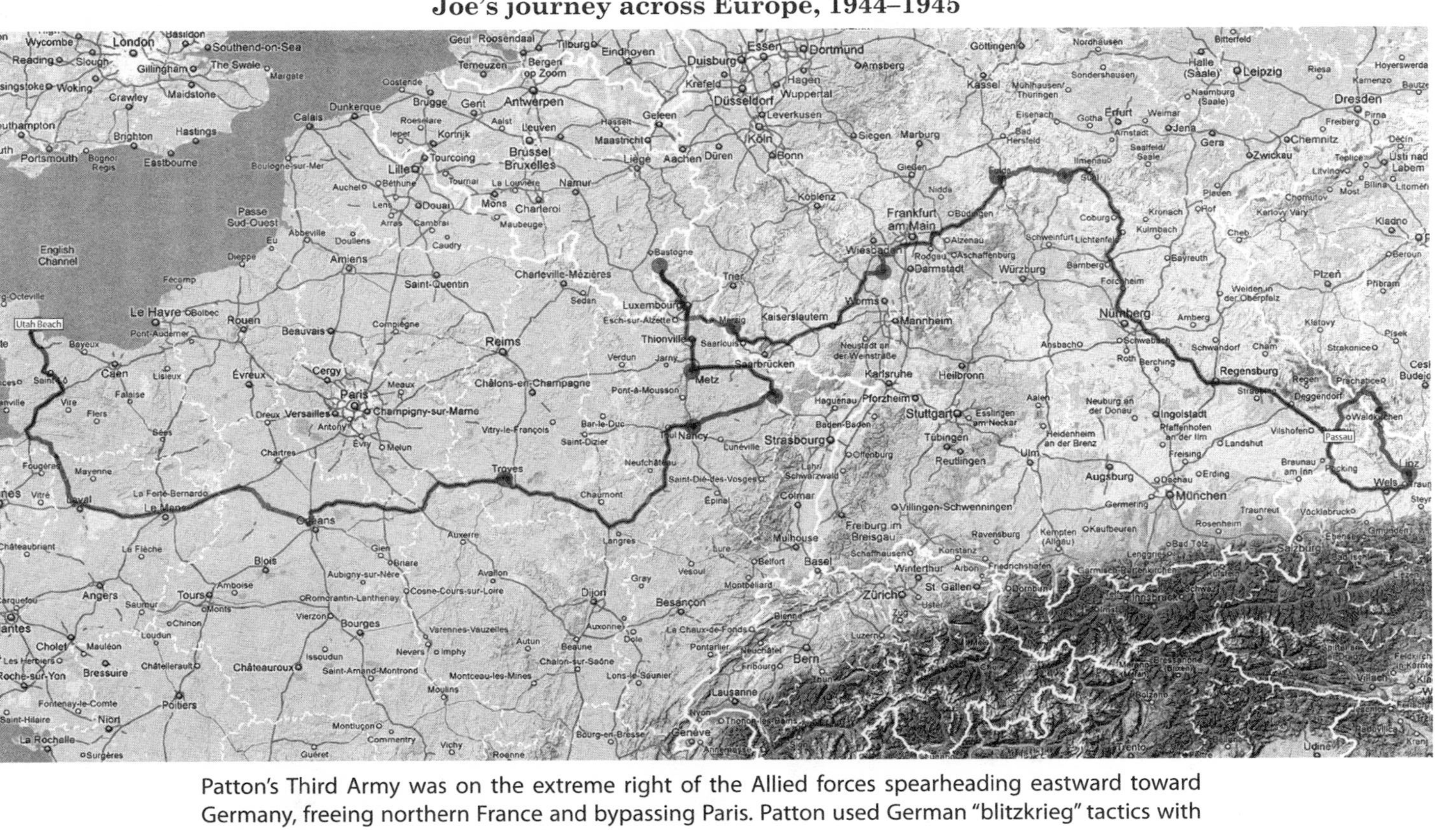

Patton's Third Army was on the extreme right of the Allied forces spearheading eastward toward Germany, freeing northern France and bypassing Paris. Patton used German "blitzkrieg" tactics with high mobility and aggressive shock maneuver.

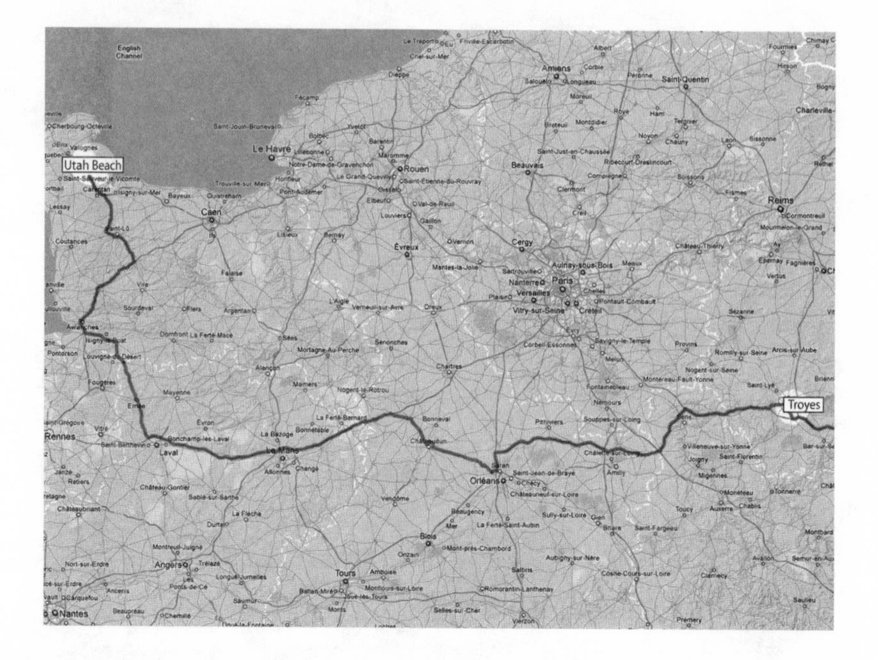

Map 1—Utah Beach to Troyes

Utah Beach, Normandy France, August 17, 1944—Joe left Southampton, England, on an LCT at 1:00 p.m. August 17, 1944, and landed on Utah Beach on the coast of Normandy, France, at 3:00 p.m. Spent the night in Saint Mere Eglise four miles inland—"piece of cake."

Landivy, France, August 20, 1944—Joe arrived in Landivy, France, as a conquering hero—bombarded with kisses, flowers, cider, and wine from the adoring, liberated French people.

Ormes, France, August 23, 1944—Joe arrived in Ormes (near Orleans, south of Paris) August 23, 1944. Found pictures of German massacres of French civilians. Wheeled vehicles advanced forty miles further to Ladon.

Troyes, France, August 28, 1944—Joe arrived at Troyes, France, south of Paris August 28, 1944, where he saw his first action against the retreating German army.

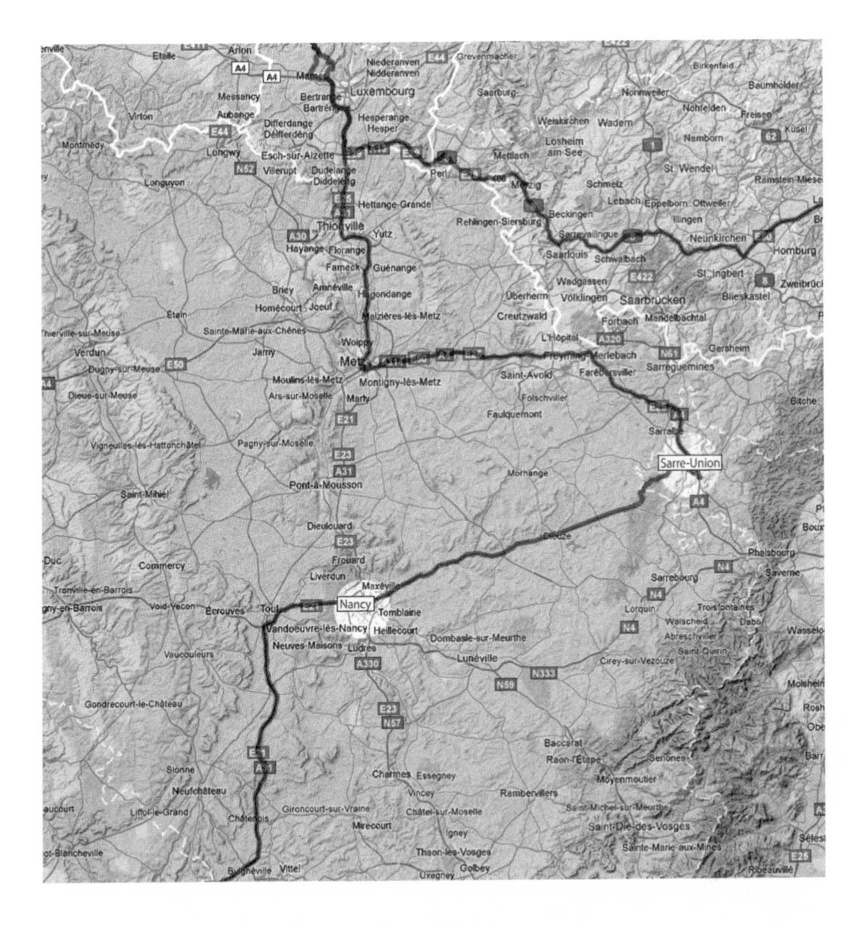

Map 2—Nancy to Sarre-Union

Nancy, France, Sep–Oct–Nov 1944—Joe spent September, October, and most of November 1944 in the vicinity of Nancy, France, on the same ground as the old World War I battlefields twenty-six years earlier. During the first battle of the Moselle River, Joe found a rusting WW I German belt buckle with the inscription "Gott Mit Uns" and he pondered its meaning . . . "under the roots of trees, dead ages lie down, to cover this false promise on rusting buckles: 'Gott Mit Uns.'" In late October, just east of Nancy, Joe spent three days trapped in the same foxhole with the corpse of German Corporal Friedrich Hofmann.

Sarre-Union, France, November 20, 1944—As the German Army retreated further east toward the German border, Joe's unit captured Sarre-Union, France, on November 20, 1944, and then immediately turned back west to help tighten Patton's noose at the Siege of Metz.

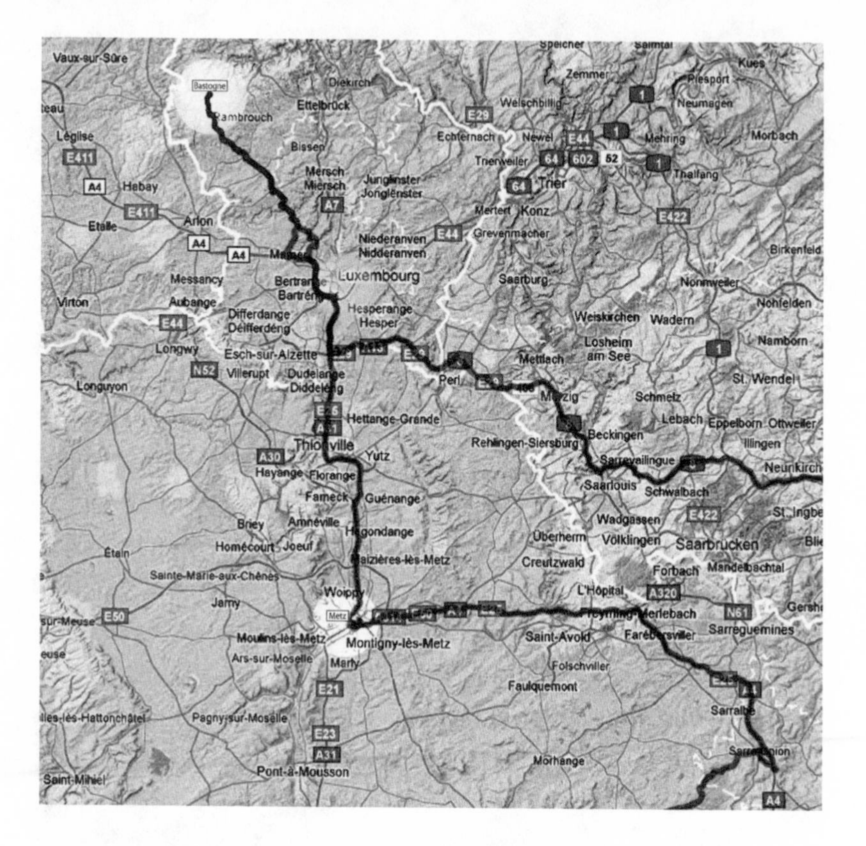

Map 3—Metz to Bastogne

Metz, France, December 1, 1944—When the city fell to Patton's Army following the Siege of Metz, Joe's division was placed on R&R in the city where they had hot meals, showers, and their first payday since arriving in France. That night Joe got drunk on French Sauterne wine, got into a fight, was placed in the stockade, and busted back to Pfc for the last time. Like an answer to a prayer, on December 15, 1944, Joe was transferred from the relatively safe field artillery to the 101st Infantry Regiment. The Battle of the Bulge started the next day, and Joe's unit immediately headed north into cold, blowing snow, not knowing that Field Marshal Gerd von Rundstedt had massed an attacking force of 280,000 men for Hitler's final offensive in the Ardennes. Leading his unit as point man out of Metz, Joe soon came into contact with the left flank of the attacking German army at Rambrouch and Grossbous.

Arsdorf/Bastogne, Luxembourg, December 25, 1944—After shooting a wild boar in the Ardennes Forest, Joe was assigned to a dangerous Christmas Day patrol behind enemy lines in an effort to secure a crossing for Patton's Army over the Sûre River. For his heroic action about eight miles south of Bastogne, Belgium, on Christmas night, Joe was decorated with the Bronze Star Medal for Valor.

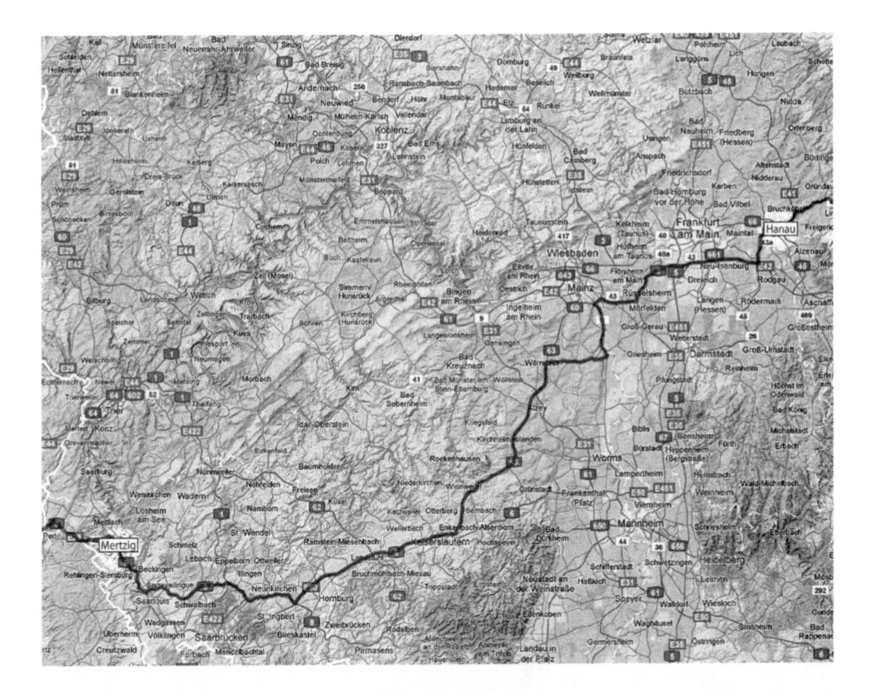

Map 4—Mertzig to Hanau

Merzig, Germany, March 15, 1945—The Battle of the Bulge resulted in 80,000 American casualties, killed and wounded. Joe's 101st Infantry Regiment saw some of the toughest fighting, especially in the vicinity of the Sûre River in late December and in January as the assaulting German Army was pushed back to the Siegfried Line. Joe's unit spent the month of February in defensive positions along the German border and crossed into Germany in early March, where Joe was wounded in fierce hand-to-hand fighting as they cleared towns and villages door-to-door.

Oppenheim, Germany, March 25, 1945—Joe crossed the Rhine River at Oppenheim southwest of Frankfurt on March 25, 1945, and started clearing towns and villages in house-to-house fighting.

Hanau, Germany, March 28, 1945—Hanau was finally taken on March 28, 1945, after fierce house-to-house fighting.

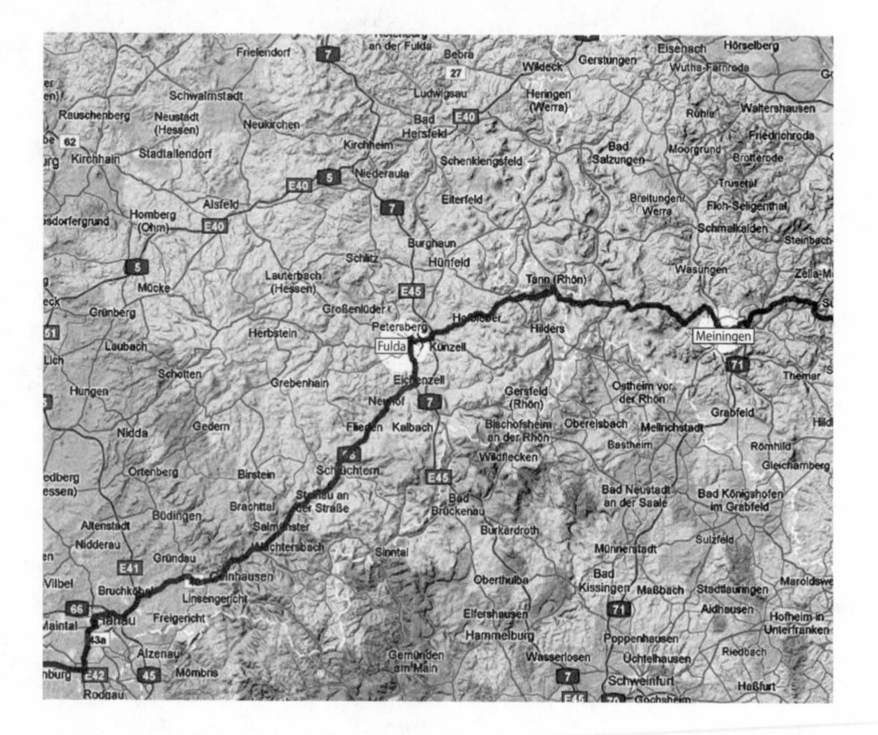

Map 5—Fulda to Meiningen

Fulda, Germany, April 1, 1945—Patton's Army broke out of the Main River bridgehead and moved rapidly northeast to Fulda, in the direction of Berlin, trapping tens of thousands of Germans soldiers who were forced to surrender.

Meiningen, Germany, April 5, 1945—After capturing Meiningen on April 5, 1945, Patton's Army was ordered to turn sharply southeast and move into Bavaria and Austria.

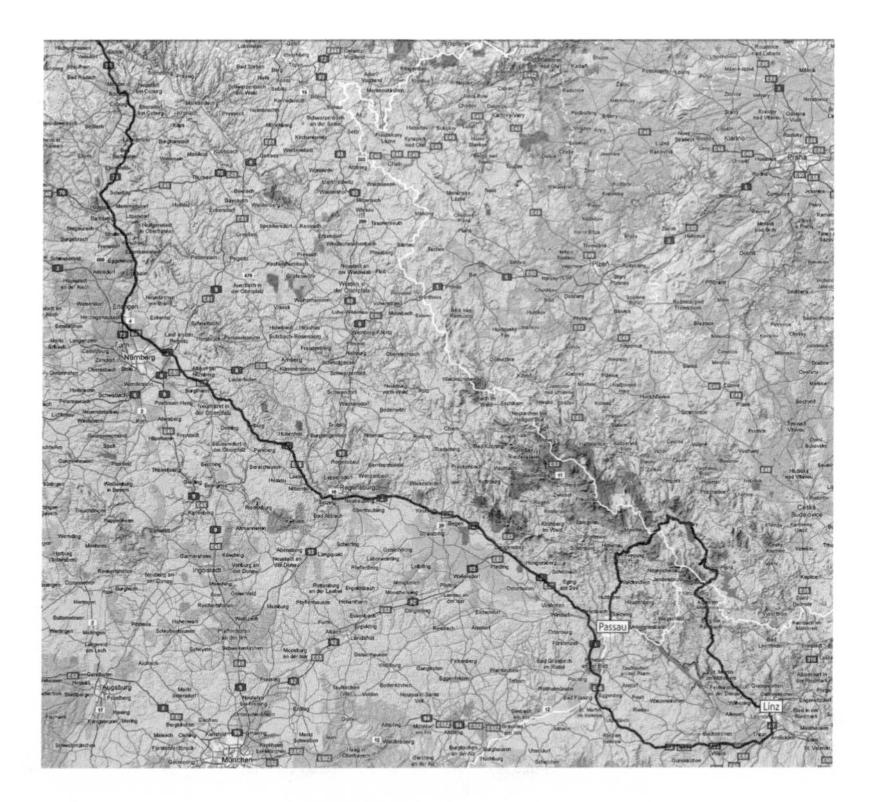

Map 6—Linz to Passau

Linz, Austria, May 4, 1945 and Gusen Concentration Camp May 5, 1945—Joe's regiment assisted in the capture of Linz, Austria, on May 4, 1945, and on the next day participated in the liberation the Gusen Concentration Camp a few miles northwest of the city. The horrors of the concentration camp were documented by Joe with pictures of German atrocities—" . . . if there be a god, may he forever damn the Nazis and their master race."

Stuben, Czechoslovakia, May 28, 1945—Joe's unit moved into Stuben, Czechoslovakia, on May 7, 1945, where they received a message from General Eisenhower announcing that the German Army had surrendered.

Passau, Germany, June 1–August 14,1945—Joe moved back into Germany during the summer of 1945, waiting word on being reassigned to the Pacific to fight the Japanese. Joe was still in Passau, Germany, on August 14, 1945, when General Eisenhower announced that World War II had officially ended.

X

After the War

1946–1992

Joe was discharged from the Army at Camp McCoy, Wisconsin, on November 6, 1945, and had nearly $650 in cash when he hitched his way to St. Paul—older, wiser, far more mature, but still angry. The Army had no "decompression plan" for returning combat veterans—they were simply paid off, mustered out, and sent home by the millions to decompress on their own.

Joe had recurring nightmares when he got back to St. Paul about life on the farm and the night he and his patrol killed the German sentries along the Sûre River in Luxembourg during the Battle of the Bulge. His dreams were about that Christmas night when he snapped the neck and slit the throat of a German soldier. A third sentry bawled and dirtied his pants because he thought Joe would kill him too. Joe's patrol took him prisoner even though he got in their way, The captured German soldier was so scared of Joe's violent broken German that he followed Joe's orders like a robot. But the bad dreams kept coming back, and Joe would wake up in a sweat just as the sharp knife pierced the German sentry's throat, cutting the carotid.

But Joe never complained or said "poor me." Joe felt he was lucky to be alive and picked up his life without complaint, as a survivor. After getting drunk several times with Army buddies, Joe stayed with Cecilia and Rose in Minnesota for several weeks. Then he decided to go to Oklahoma, where he had met Helen Jessie four years earlier. Helen was a member of the Choctaw Nation in Oklahoma and had the natural beauty and sense of spiritual calm Joe associated with primeval people of the ancient past.

Joe seemed to understand Helen and her family better than anyone in his life so far, and they accepted Joe and seemed to understand him because Joe was so much like them. Joe felt that he was born to be an Indian or a primitive creature who had to teach everything to himself, and that's how he felt when he was with Helen. It's quite possible no other person in the world could have married Joe or put up with him—and vice versa. Joe needed someone who could calmly and stoically accept his sense of pain, massive exuberance, liveliness, energy, and high spirits. For over forty-five years Helen lived up to that call of duty and beyond. In Oklahoma City on April 20, 1946, Joe wrote to his older brother, Kenny, who was a law student at Harvard University at the time:

Dear Ken—

I have been intending to write you for some time, but I have a bad habit of procrastinating when it comes to letter writing. How do you like married life? I can't say I ever expected you to take the plunge. How many years are you going to law school in the East and where do you expect to practice? Helen is taking a course in cosmetology; she only has three more months to go. As for myself, I still feel as unsettled as the sands of the sea. I can't make a decision as to what I should do in life. I don't know what's the matter with me. If I could make up my mind I would be halfway there. Say, Ken, if you still have that fellow's address that lives in Alaska, if you have, please send it to me soon, as I may take a trip up there this spring. I wouldn't mind making my home up in that country. I am sending you a picture of Helen; hope you get it OK. By the way, she is half Choctaw Indian but has none of their wild ways. Bub sent me a letter from Dan's first wife. I am sending it on to you. Drop me a line when you get time, and don't study too hard in them law books.

—Joe

Joe and Helen returned to St. Paul after their wedding in Oklahoma and stayed with Bub and her family in Birchwood on White Bear Lake near St. Paul. They also visited Rose and her family near Northfield in the spring and summer of 1946. This is when Joe filed a lawsuit against the German farmer and State of Minnesota for putting him into indentured slavery, but the lawsuit fizzled because more than ten years had passed since the expiration of the Indenture Contract on his eighteenth birthday in February 1936.

During his postwar "decompression," Joe would often drink too much. It never took a lot of alcohol to do the trick, and it would frequently cause problems. Later in 1946, Joe heard about the ironworking construction boom in Texas, so he and Helen packed up and moved to Houston. They went on to have two sons, Jack and James, in 1948 and 1949. Joe's nephew David Mahmood, Bub's son, had several memories of Joe after the war:

My first recollection of Joe, or "Little Joe" as he was called by my parents, was when he came back from World War II and lived with us in our little house in the St. Paul suburb of Birchwood, Minnesota. That would have been 1946 or so, making me about eight years old at the time. Joe Haan was certainly a fascinating character—especially to a little kid. He was slim, wiry, not bad looking, and smarter than hell. Joe was somewhat deaf in those days, but nowhere near as bad as he became later in life.

Joe was married to Helen, a Native American from Oklahoma. As a young woman, she was very good looking. I remember in the evenings watching Joe comb her hair. She would sit on a hassock and Joe would comb her long black hair that went down to her waist. Joe was obviously very much in love with her.

I remember Joe playing his guitar and harmonica at the same time. Everyone thought he was a very talented musician. He played what I consider Woody Guthrie-type songs or the Pete Seeger music that first came out of the 1930s.

Joe had a huge trunk full of World War II memorabilia that he shipped from Germany and had sent to our house. It was a very large steamer trunk and had all sorts of German flags, bayonets, officer's swords, a German helmet, Luger pistol, German medals, and other things he took off dead German soldiers. He had a German helmet with a bullet hole in it. I remember the helmet being very well constructed with a full soft-cushioned leather liner in it, made very well. He had a huge German battle flag in like-new condition.

Joe told a story of how he and a buddy, blasting their way through a building in Germany, ended up with German jewelry and diamonds and that before they embarked for the United States they had to give it up. They were told that looted goods could cause them to go to prison.

In 1946, my father, Ferris Mahmood, was a superintendent on a construction job and he put Joe to work on the job as a laborer. One of the foremen had a German accent. When Joe was on a scaffolding twenty feet up in the air, the German foreman yelled something at Joe that must have sounded like the German farmer. Joe jumped off the scaffold and landed on top of the foreman, ripping him to pieces. Ferris thought Joe had killed the guy. Joe's temper scared the hell out of everyone on the job.

I can remember Joe having bad dreams and waking up in the middle of the night from the dreams. My parents thought the war had a serious effect on him psychologically, aside from what happened to him on the farm and in the orphanage. When Joe drank alcohol, he was like a wild Indian, capable of damn near anything. I know at the time, Cecilia, my mother, was relieved when Joe and Helen left our home. I can remember Joe meeting someone at the Jackson Buffet bar in St. Paul and drinking too much. I think it was his father, Dan McCann, and Ferris bringing Joe back to the house in really bad shape.

Joe was more than an outdoorsman—he was a survivalist. He was someone who could really live off the land. He set traps around the lake near our house and in the swamps. He caught beaver, skinned them, and stretched the pelts out on a board. I still remember the pungent odor of animal hides drying in the basement. One time we were out in the woods and Joe found a den of skunks. He killed the skunks with some large rocks, and Joe and I came home stinking of skunk. Joe skinned the skunks and stretched their pelts on boards. The odor filled the house with the smell of skunk for weeks to come. He did it in the basement of our house and it drove Cecilia nuts. I thought it was great.

I remember Joe pointing out to me as a kid the stars at night and the different constellations. He really understood the stars and was comfortable being guided by them in the outdoors. To me, it seemed that he was born a hundred years too late.

Joe would build "trot lines" out of ordinary white wrapping string. He would put dozens of hooks on lines attached to the main centerline, with lead sinkers on the main line. He explained to me that the line would lie on the bed of the lake and the short strings with the hooks on them would float up and catch the fish. It was really ingenious. We went down to the lake in the late afternoon when no one was around. It was fascinating to watch him take the trotline, swing it over his head like a lariat, and get the line out into the lake as far as possible from the shore. In the morning we went down and retrieved the trotline that had caught a string of sunfish, crappie, and bass. That evening we had a big fish dinner. Of course, it was illegal, but that's how Joe learned to do it on the farm.

I remember Joe telling a story of when he was in the service at an Army fort out West and he and a buddy decided to walk across the desert to the mountains. The distance was far greater than what they anticipated, and Joe said he almost didn't make it back because they ran out of water.

How he got to Houston and became an ironworker, I don't know. But, he was there when the City of Houston was growing rapidly and there was a tremendous amount of work. He apparently became a successful and well-paid ironworker.

Sometime in the 1980s at Christmas, there was a story written in the Houston papers about Joe passing out wine to people on skid row. When asked by a reporter why he was giving wine to alcoholics at Christmas, he said, "That's what they want."

I can remember Joe claiming to be an atheist and arguing with my mother, Cecilia, who was a devout Catholic. Joe admitted, however, that when he was in a foxhole and bullets were flying overhead, he did pray to God—just in case.

At death, he saw himself as fertilizer going back into the ground. Given a proper home life and education, it would have been interesting to see what he might have become. There is no question he led a fascinating life, but a tough one. Obviously, he was a very talented individual.

—David Mahmood, August 2010

Joe went on to make his living in Houston as a taxidermist and fully vested, card-carrying union ironworker for the rest of his working life. Joe's knowledge of diverse, yet connected subjects, his talents with his mind and his hands, and his many odd and interesting eccentricities made him well known in Houston. He wrote a tribute, "High Steel," to his co-workers on his last day on the job in 1980 and he would often recite poetry. He spoke to college students in Houston on taxidermy, paleontology, geology, and his fossil collections because he was so widely read on many subjects. In addition to evolution and paleontology, he had a life-long passion for history and philosophy that tended to support his stoic agnosticism.

When Joe and Helen were settled in Houston, he joined the Ironworker's Local 84 apprenticeship program in June of 1947. Joe became a journeyman in August 1949, an honorary member in October 1981, and a lifetime retired member in January 1983. The requirements for an ironworker were as rough and tumble as Patton's infantry, and Joe wouldn't have had any other type of job—fearlessness and courage on the inside, and on the outside good physical conditioning, agility, and strength. Tom Dilberger, a fellow ironworker, wrote in *The Ironworker* magazine about the trade:

> *At that time, the apprentice tests were hard. There were three parts—physical, mental, and psychological—and failure on any part meant disqualification. The test was given every three years, and if a man failed, he was out of luck. He had to wait for the next test. There was also an age limit of twenty-nine. Anyone older than that had to find another line of work. Although there were no blacks in the union, it was not segregated. It was about 60 percent white, and the rest were American Indians. Indians had to take the test and measure up just like everyone else.*

Like Joe's relationship with Helen, a job as an ironworker was unique and probably the only job he could have accepted and handled because of his fierce independence, drive, and constant demands. Joe was at his best when he worked alone on the hardest and most dangerous jobs. The smart foremen soon got to know Joe and understand him, because he was the best and fastest at what he did and they knew it. But he worked strictly on his own terms. The number of times union foremen would tell him to slow down on the job, Joe couldn't say. He could tie steel several times faster than the average worker, and Joe would tell them to get out of his way. That's how he always worked and that's why he was known as "el Tigre Chiquito."

Joe was successful and thrived because he showed up on time at the right place, had the fortitude to do what was required regardless of weather, heights, or danger, and he held the standard higher for the next man coming up behind him. *Ironworkers Local 84* in Houston published "Requirements for Iron Workers" that described Joe to a tee:

> *Good physical condition. The materials used for ironworking are heavy and bulky, so above-average physical strength is necessary. Agility and a good sense of balance are also required. It is important to mention that an ironworker must be willing to work in high places, have a good sense of balance, and be alert to potential danger to themselves and others. (See http://www.ironworkers.org/becoming/)*

When Joe moved to Houston, the Texas Local 84 Ironworkers Union was already well established in South Texas, having received its charter with the International Ironworkers Union in 1904. The charter also covered Mexico and extended into Central America by the 1970s when Joe took a job for a time in the Dominican Republic. After the war, Houston's economy boomed due to the expanding Texas oil industry and Local 84 ironworkers worked on seemingly unlimited numbers of jobs on high office buildings, bridges, warehouses, and roads throughout the area. Joe preferred high steel. Local 84 was known for having the best apprentice facilities in the country and had over 1,100 apprentices attending classes by the 1970s. The apprentice facilities are still in use today with state-of-the-art updates to ensure that apprentices are the best in the field. When Ironworkers Local 84 celebrated its anniversary, the University of Houston history department identified the bold and daring in its research of Local 84 folk heroes, and Joe was one.

There are those who might say—
'They don't deserve that big iron pay.'
So come all you, who speak as such,
Let's see if you dare to do as much.

—Joe Haan, 1980

The Golden Gate Bridge, St. Louis Golden Arch, and Chicago's massive 110-story Sears Tower were all built by ironworkers. Joe became proud of his craft as the most daring man to walk Houston's death-defying high steel tightrope. Nearly every structure built during Joe's post-war career—office towers, high-rise apartments, schools, sports stadiums, shopping malls, hospitals, bridges, industrial buildings—required the daring and rough-and-tumble skills of well-trained ironworkers, making them the most highly respected and best paid tradesmen in the construction industry.

Joe was proud he had helped build Houston's landmarks and shape the skylines of one of America's most rapidly growing cities. It was gratifying for him to be able to stand back, admire his work, and say, "I helped build that!" On many days—cold and warm, windy and calm—Joe worked high in the clouds erecting the skeletons of tall Houston skyscrapers. He set steel rebar in concrete to reinforce the framework and built complex steel ornamental structures, the taller and windier the better, as far as he was concerned.

Building the world's greatest steel structures became an amazing feat that fascinated Joe, especially the engineering. Most ironwork in Houston was done outdoors and could be carried on year-round except in very severe weather, but in many cases indoor work was coordinated with bad weather to keep people on the payroll. Safety devices such as nets, safety belts, and safety scaffolding were developed to reduce the risk of injury caused by the dangerous amount of climbing, balancing, and reaching overhead that was required.

Joe scoffed at weather delays and safety requirements even though he saw many steel workers fall to their deaths due to foolishness or a misstep. El Tigre Chiquito was known as the most fearless of them all, and he worked hard to live up to his nickname. Writing in *The Ironworker* magazine, ironworker Tom Dilberger discussed the specialties and difficulties of a good ironworker:

> *A raising gang has a foreman or pusher, and men with four different specialties. The hooker-on physically puts the steel wire slings, or chokers, around the beams, girders, columns, etc., that are going to be raised by the crane for the connectors to set. He must know all the different capacities of the chokers he's using, so as not to put a choker on a piece if it is not rated for that weight. He also unofficially runs the gang, because he sets the sequence for the pieces of steel that go up to the connecters.*
>
> *A tagline man then uses ropes with hooks spliced into their ends to guide the beams up to the connectors. If one of the beams he's guiding snags on a beam that's already set, he must signal the crane operator (who is not an ironworker) to slack off the load so the tagline man can clear the piece. Then he directs the crane to continue raising the*

piece. The tagline man is usually the youngest man in the gang and is being groomed to be a connecter. He must be in excellent shape, since he may be asked to go connecting at any time.

The signalman communicates with the crane operator. Sometimes he will use hand signals, and at other times there is a "phone system" hooked up to the cab of the crane. The signalman must be alert all the time because the unexpected can happen. A good signalman can save a man's life, and a bad one who doesn't pay attention can cause trouble. He is usually the oldest man in the gang, and is considered something of a sage . . . It was the dead of winter and the temperatures were very cold but this had little effect on the plank carriers. The job at hand was such that with the constant trips, plank after plank, it was always enough to keep us warm even on the coldest of days with just the lightest of clothing possible. They always had a saying: "the heat's in the tools."

Joe set the standard for the daring Houston workers who walked the steel framework of tall buildings under construction—daredevils called structural ironworkers and known in the Texas press as "cowboys of the skies." Joe's usual job was to unload, erect, and connect fabricated iron structures and pieces to form the skeleton of a larger structure, and to do this hundreds of feet off the ground in all types of weather. Structural ironworkers would typically work on the construction of office towers and other tall industrial, commercial, and residential buildings, which became Joe's specialty. They would also work on bridges, stadiums, and prefabricated metal buildings from time to time. Joe always said he preferred "High Steel" and not the easy stuff like pre-cast beams, columns, and panels that could be easily assembled on the ground. Rigging was an integral part of the ironworking trade. Joe became an expert rigger, with a strong technical knowledge of fiber line, wire rope, hooks, skids, rollers, proper hand signals, and hoisting equipment. He tended to ignore training on government safety issues.

Joe and his fellow ironworker riggers would load, unload, move, and set machinery, structural steel, curtain walls, and other materials. They used power hoists, cranes, derricks, and forklifts and aerial lifts. Sometimes they lifted loads by hand with a series of block and tackle systems Joe first learned to use on the German farm. Welding and burning equipment were tools of the trade. Joe became an expert arc welder in the process, even artistic when he had the chance, which was frequent. Many of Joe's pieces of steel artwork survive, like birds he artistically cut freehand from tempered steel, with layers of carefully hammered feathers textured into the metal surface.

Over the years, high steel became part of Joe's life, granting him the same opportunities, problems, and issues he experienced during the war. Though offered promotions many times, Joe refused higher-paying supervisory positions where he could use his knowledge but would have to be the boss. Joe always preferred to be a "common soldier," like a "Pfc grunt" in the Army. And he was immediately ready to attack any type of prejudice or injustice and was steadfastly intolerant of intolerance, especially when it came to fairness, equality, and fundamental human rights. Joe's poem "High Steel" has appeared in *The Ironworker* magazine and is a classic in the ironworking trade. It was written when he retired from Ironworker's Local 84 on October 17, 1980, and was dedicated to his fellow devil-may-care ironworkers:

High Steel

Joe Haan, Ironworkers Union Book # 386783
October 17, 1980 (Book II, misc.)

In all the world of adventurous men,
The high steel boy is one of them.
On gird or truss or bridging high,
Many a hand has had to die.

Grab spinning hook, walk narrow beam,
This job's not what it might just seem.
Through sleet and wind, rain so cold,
This work's for men—few men so bold.

An unsung song of toil and pain,
In exchange for our small dollar gain.
Take a trip from the Golden Gate,
View high steel in the Empire State.

Wherever you may cast your eye,
You see their work up in the sky.
The many bridges that span the land,
Assembled by the ironworker's hand.

And now, before all things are said,
Let us pay tribute to brothers dead.
For theirs was not to reason why,
They chose a task to death defy.

So they get the iron in their veins,
Risk life and limb for some few gains.
Up in the morn before break of day,
What fate decrees, no man can say.

Always walk iron with a little dread,
In exchange for this, our daily bread.
Where winds blow strong, men grow pale,
When caught up there in a raging gale.

There are those who might some day say—
"They don't deserve that big iron pay."
So come all you, who might speak as such,
Let's see if you dare to do as much.

Joe enjoyed his home on Landor Lane and his immaculate tropical garden and overflowing taxidermy lab. He liked to keep things neat and was fascinated with all types of plants, especially tropical varieties that thrived in Houston's warm, humid climate. He raised his own vegetables and proudly boasted exotic flowers and the hottest jalapeno peppers. A large crock of homegrown hot peppers was always available in the kitchen, and Joe enjoyed showing his tenacity in eating the very hottest. Julia Quist remembered her first trip to Houston in 1973 when she and her husband Paul rode their BMW motorcycle from Fairbanks, Alaska, to Houston on their way to see Paul's brother who was assigned to the Pentagon in Washington, DC.

> *Staying with Joe and Helen for one week in 1973 was one of the most fascinating times in my life. It was like being on the set of an independent movie directed by the Cohen Brothers with a character that would display the madness of John Malkovich and the gentleness of Gregory Peck (more of the first).*
>
> *I remember how excited Joe was when he saw Paul's motorcycle pull up in his driveway, the little dance that he did before he was lost in Paul's big*

bear hug. Then he paused to acknowledge me by asking, "And who are you? You look like an Indian, but I hear you are a Greek." And he went on for the longest time talking about Ulysses and the Odyssey in detail and it was good—it felt like I had never heard the story before.

Then we went in the house—there was a gigantic clay dinosaur in the living room—and we met Helen. Helen had a sewing room in the house, and it was packed. But the rest of the house was all Joe's, full of stuffed birds, animals, and many mountings. We drank beer and whiskey and Helen taught me how to fry chicken. Joe loved her fried chicken and he said it more than once. It seems that we had two things to eat during our weeklong stay, venison chili and fried chicken.

When we woke up in the morning, Joe was already gone—he went to work early in the morning and came back in the early afternoon. He worked during the first couple of days that we were there and he took the rest of the week off. The first day that he was at home, he made all kinds of commotion to get us up and going. I was up before Paul and had tea with Helen while she was preparing a hearty breakfast for Joe. He totally covered his breakfast with jalapeno peppers, his special "hot pepper jam" as he called it. There was nothing sweet about that jam; it had just enough heat to peel off barnacles from a battleship. Joe tried to convince me to eat some and he tried every day while we were there. The last day he said, "You are stubborn like a Greek mule; I may have to scalp you after all."

The few mornings that Joe was at the house, he worked in his botanical garden. He had hundreds of non-indigenous herbs and plants, mainly herbs that he imported from Japan and Ceylon. He knew their common and botanical names and spoke about them as if they were exotic visitors. Scalping me was an offer he also made on the morning of his first day off while he and I were getting to know each other. My hair was black and long then, and the wind during the motorcycle travel, as well as the cheap soaps on the Motel 6 overnighters, had taken a toll on it. Helen had given me a wooden, wide-toothed comb and I was fighting the tangles. Then Joe came up with some oily taxidermy stuff, and rubbed it through my tangled dry hair. The next thing I knew, the comb glided through my hair like a hot knife through butter. He combed it for a couple of minutes and said, "That's good. Otherwise, I'd have to scalp you."

The walls of the bedroom where Paul and I slept were covered with trophies of wild birds and animals (some domestic). Joe had altered the natural looks of some, like the "jackelope," Joe's Great Carnivorous Texas Hare—what looked to be a large domestic rabbit with a nasty grimace, exposing ferocious fangs. There was also a bat and a full-bodied wild cat and many, many more stuffed animals that appeared ready to invade your sweet dreams and turn them into nightmares. However, there was a "Joe" story behind every animal. As Joe said, he did not stuff them, but brought them back to life.

On Sunday, the last day of our visit, we all piled in Joe's car and he took us to the boat show at the Houston Astrodome. I was not sure why he took us there. Joe seemed to despise everything about the show and was very relieved to hear that Paul was not too impressed either, so he decided we must leave immediately. As we were leaving the building, I realized that Joe hated the pomposity of the show but was very proud of the structure and he wanted to show us that he had been part of its construction. He wanted to share this with us, but without too much fanfare. We said goodbye to Joe on Monday morning. He stayed home until we left. I remember turning back to wave just before Paul turned at the end of Landor Lane, only to see him running toward the racing BMW. This is my lasting image of Joe.

—Julia Quist

Joe always enjoyed Paul's visits. Over the years, going back to the 1960s, Paul often came down to Houston with his college friend, Tim Carlson. They enjoyed Joe's stories and had a lot of fun together. Paul had learned to recite "The Cremation of Sam McGee" and "The Shooting of Dan McGrew" in high school, and he and Joe would put on quite a show in Joe's backyard. Then Joe would take them around his Houston haunts—the hobo jungle with cardboard huts near the railroad tracks not far from Landor Lane, and all-black honky-tonks in the neighborhood.

Joe would explain to Paul and Tim what it was like being the only "white man in a sea of black." He had to put bars on all the windows of his house after drug dealers took over the Landor Lane neighborhood and broke in one day and stole his guns.

Joe told them about the night he crawled through backyards on his stomach, like a commando on patrol behind enemy lines, to cut the rope of a dog that had been tied up all day and was barking incessantly, only to be attacked by the dog and forced to kill it with his bare hands and knife. Joe told them stories about the proper burial for a drug dealer's brain; the pursuit of the great Lanny LaRue, king of the rattlesnake hunters; how to decapitate a human or animal with the sharpest knife in the world; how to do the "Korean Deathlock"; and what it was like to fight a water moccasin while seining in Buffalo Bayou. Tim recalled:

> *Joe bought a few acres of land out on Buffalo Bayou. He planned to build out there, but Hurricane Camille flooded the property, and Helen was afraid of snakes and wouldn't go there. Joe liked to go out and walk through the brush.*
>
> *He took me over to the neighbor's house one day and said, "Look at what he's wearing around his neck." The guy was sort of a treasure hunter and wore a Spanish doubloon in a string around his neck.*
>
> *"Show him what's in your garage," Joe said. We walked to his garage and slid open the door. In the garage was a steel cage with a full grown Bengal Tiger pacing around! "Show my friend some of his tricks," Joe said.*
>
> *The crazy guy got in the cage, picked up a beach ball and tossed it to the tiger. The tiger batted it back at him. This went on a few times until the tiger quit. The guy walked over to pick up the ball, but the tiger picked him up, grabbed him by the thigh, lifted him up, and gently shook him. The guy was yelling at the tiger to let him go, but we could see four holes in his jeans with red stains spreading outward. He decided to exit the cage. Joe and I agreed . . . he was nuts!*
>
> *This was also the only time I ever saw Joe shoot a weapon. He had an old .22 rifle that he kept for*

burglars and occasional squirrels. Joe had told us about the time in Germany when an Army truck drove into his camp filled with ammunition. The Captain said anyone who wanted to practice could help themselves. Joe and a buddy consumed four rifles using up the ammo and melted the barrel of a .50 caliber machine gun in the process. Joe walked over to the bayou, reached down and picked up three small stones. He threw them up in the air with his left hand, then hit all three of them before they hit the ground.

Paul and Tim were fascinated to hear Joe tell about hopping a freight train, what it was like riding the rails in the 1930s, and what the Depression-era CCC camps were like. They marveled at his many experiences during World War II—the Battle of the Bulge, house-to-house fighting in Germany, the Gusen Concentration Camp, and the wild boar incident in the Ardennes Forest. Joe would take them to see his friend's Rhodesian Razorback dogs that performed incredible tricks, like taking the keys out of various cars at the command of the owner. Tim recalled a number of these stories:

One day Joe took me to meet the Dog Man. This was a young black guy who lived about a mile from Joe. We drove up to the house, parked and walked over to where several men were standing. Joe asked Dog Man to show me what his dog could do. Dog Man turned to one of his Rhodesian Razorbacks and said in a calm manner, "Go get his keys." The dog ran over to Joe's car, jumped in the window, pulled the keys out of the ignition, and ran back to put them in Dog Man's hand. Next, it was, "Go get him a beer." The dog ran into the house and came back with a bottle of beer in his mouth. I was impressed.

Joe used to go to Joe Barr's house for an occasional visit. Joe Barr had a very old parrot that sat on his front porch, and Joe would sometimes bring his boys with him when he went to visit. On one occasion, Joe was watching his boys who went over to play with the neighbor's kids. They were playing hide-and-seek and Jimmy ran into the garage to hide. When the kid who was "it" looked around, the parrot blurted out, "Look in the garage... look in the garage . . . " The first time I met Joe, he had a cage full of white rats in his back yard. He said it kept the burglars out. They were really tame, but they still made Helen very squeamish. Hector the Great, a miniature Chihuahua, was Joe's pride and joy. Joe had him trained to stand on his back legs in the palm of his hand while he raised his hand as high as his head.

Joe always had a great time when Wayne, Paul, and Tim were around. He enjoyed the times the boys spent with him over the years, talking philosophy, telling stories, and singing songs over a little Lone Star, Budweiser, and Sauterne. Joe told them he was like Diogenes seeking an honest man. He would show them his homemade Ouija board with mysterious numbers and strange letters for forecasting everything imaginable, and his divining rod for finding water and valuable minerals, and everyone would have a good laugh.

In addition to his scientific and artistic interests, Joe had developed a solid knowledge and understanding of the American Civil War based on in-depth reading and many trips to Civil War battlefields over the course of fifty years or more.

Through friends in Houston who shared his interests, Joe found the original unpublished Civil War letters of Corporal William Cunningham, a Wisconsin volunteer member of the Iron Brigade that was decimated on the morning of the first day at Gettysburg, July 1, 1863. Joe knew the story of the Iron Brigade, having first walked the battlefield of Gettysburg in the summer of 1938 on the very ground and woods where the Iron Brigade made its last stand against Lee's advancing Confederate Army.

William Cunningham's Civil War letters were written to his girlfriend Mary Parrish back home in Avoca, Wisconsin. They recount the pain, suffering, defeat, and tragedy he endured during the Civil War as a member of one of the few western regiments to serve "back east" with the Army of the Potomac. The letters moved Joe because they told a universal story of a patriotic and idealistic young soldier caught up in events far beyond his control. He wrote to his girlfriend back home and expressed eternal hope and optimism, following defeat after successive defeat. Joe believed he had known William Cunningham as a fellow comrade-in-arms, and he copied the letters in 1973 with his nephew Wayne. The William Cunningham letters reminded Joe of his wartime experience in France, Belgium, Luxembourg, and Germany, but Joe had survived his war and William Cunningham had not.

Joe seemed to understand what happened to William Cunningham and his best friend, Sergeant Spencer Train, that first day at Gettysburg. Joe may have lived with a burden of guilt for having been spared in combat during the violence he experienced in late 1944 and early 1945. Joe had heard other World War II vets talk about a feeling of "survivor guilt" for having lived while their comrades had died. These ambivalent feelings are expressed throughout Joe's poetry, and especially in "Ode to William Cunningham," where he describes William Cunningham in McPherson's Woods at the time of his final, fatal martial clash, as though Joe were present there with him.

Ode to Corporal William Cunningham

2nd Wisconsin Infantry, Iron Brigade, Army of the Potomac 1861–1863
Joe Haan (Notebook II)

He seemed to have an ancient sense of justice,
Reincarnated from some distant past,
A total abhorrence to subjugation, the binding of men,
In spite of the fact that he had made
But twenty short trips about the sun.
To all free-loving men, he knew,
No nation could exist, half slave, half free.

The sounds of far-off war trumpets
Amplified this message to William Cunningham,
So the angry guns would speak,
And many noble men
Would walk into the maw of death,
And endless bitter tears would flow
In half a million simple homes,
For so many young Wills would be no more,
Only known as the vast "Unknown,"
Lying in a desolate field, undignified in death.
Truly did they inherit the earth.

Private William Cunningham
Was unique in more ways than one:
In an age when the greater percentage
Of young men his age were ill-educated,

His power of expression stood out
With a rather limited vocabulary,
A certainty his intellectual achievement
Was recognized by his comrades in arms.

As war banners unfurled in the winds,
Martial tunes were struck in 1861,
Simple young farm boys
Congregated from near and far
Upon the parade ground
At Madison, Wisconsin.

And oh, how their spines did tingle
In the limelight of history and public acclaim,
And would not history proclaim
They exemplified the very best in courage,
With a sense of justice that could not be equalled.
All willing martyrs, no conscripts these.

Red hot cannister and grape shot
Cut great swaths in their ranks
That first day at Gettysburg,
And after overwhelming pain, oblivion.
The Iron Brigade would be no more,
Only many vacant chairs,
And years of gnawing agony for loved ones.

Over this enigma of life
And sudden violent death,
For how does one reason out,
This wasting of human intellect,
The squandering of one
Who showed so much potential
For further achievement in any field?

Some men are priceless,
Others of little value whatsoever.
This contrast is self-evident on every hand;
Sometimes a gem occurs in a field of dirt—
For justice is an artificial thing,
Created by homosapien man
Out of the primordial past, from which he evolved,
Where no such thing as mercy or justice existed.

Even now, some men lay down their lives
On the altar of sacrifice,
For principles they feel
Are the only correct ones,
Though they may realize
They shall never pass this way again,
Manly unsung heroes, these,
No man yet, shall they displease,
With malice toward none, charity for all.

Over the years, Tim and Joe went on Civil War trips to Pea Ridge and into Mississippi and Georgia. In 1974, just before going to the Dominican Republic, Joe had a great time in Washington, DC, with his nephew Wayne and his son Pete, tramping Civil War battlefields in Pennsylvania, Maryland, and Virginia. Joe was still very agile at the age of fifty-six. Joe's audience couldn't believe his dance on stage with a belly dancer at a Greek restaurant in downtown Washington, DC, which he did one-footed while biting his big toe. Joe was always quick and agile like a cat and very strong—he said it was a Haan trait. He said that it had helped him survive over the years, along with his well-developed intuition. Joe said his intuition saved him several times during the war—subliminal warnings of impending danger he had learned to heed, causing him more than once to hit the deck just in time or refuse to volunteer for a dangerous patrol assignment. In the spring of 1997, the spirit of Joe led Wayne and two of his Fubar friends from St. Olaf, Rawhide, and Gunder, on a Civil War trip down the Mississippi River to Vicksburg. Joe would have loved the journey and the memories it evoked.

Remembering Joe at Vicksburg

—B. Wayne Quist, 1997

Early in the month of April, they journeyed
Through the length and breadth of the State of Mississippi,
Down the Great River to Hannibal, St. Louis,
Fort Donnelson, Shiloh and Memphis,

And further south in search of "Sam" Grant,
Along the Mighty Old Man River,
Banks overflowing with Minnesota waters,
Muddy, sprawling, meandering—a giant spill of melted snow,

Working its way to the Gulf of Mexico, and beyond,
To evaporate and rise in wet and humid clouds,
With rain and snow yet once again, the process starts anew.

They saw the River, working and plodding its way
Past Vicksburg, Port Gibson, down the Natchez Trace,
An ancient footpath linking Nashville to Natchez on the River.

Moving ever southward over Emerald Mound,
Testament to early Mississippians who once
Resided and prospered along the fertile banks
Of the black-earthed Mississippi Delta,

Fertile northern soils washed by eons of erosion.
Moving again along the ancient Trace,
Through Jefferson to Natchez on the River,
Clouds of fragrant flowers, antebellum-style,
Colored azalea, dogwood, flowering April spruce.
Sleeping, resting with the dead.

Beginning to work slowly northward,
Along the Trace, footsteps of a past long gone,
To Sam Grant's landing at Bruinsburg on the River,
Below the Vicksburg ramparts,
After running the gauntlet
With 23,000 Yankee troopers,
The largest amphibious operation
In the history of the world,
Before D-Day 1944.

Wending the way from Bruinsburg, back to Port Gibson,
Lunching at an unpainted country store,
Lazing in a napping noonday sun,
They followed Sam Grant and 45,000 Midwest Yankees
To the Battlefield of Raymond, northeastward,

In the direction of Jackson, away from Vicksburg, Grant style.
Always victorious, through counties black and poor,
Black folk with unstained bloodlines, no mulattos these,
Turning west upon the foe, Confederate General Pemberton,
Wrapping him up at Champion Hill,

The greatest battle of the American Civil War, some say,
Yet today—no marker, no memory, no nothing to remind
That something more than scrubby pine had ever ventured forth
In an area known as Champion Hill,
Fifty-four thousand engaged in battle,
The greatest perhaps, and yet today forgotten.

Then to the Big Black, a railroad trestle,
A battle and a river crossing,
The line of Confederate retreat into the City of Vicksburg,
Backed up against Old Man River,

A Siege—long, hot and dusty days—
Bombardments everlasting, scant food and rancid,
Rats as morsels, cooked with pea ground bread,
And finally, ignominious surrender to U. S. Grant
On the Fourth of July, 1863.

The same day as victory back east at Gettysburg,
Breaking the back of the Confederacy—forever—
The Union saved, Old Man River free again
To move its cargo up and down the Father of Waters,
Northern farmers, no longer hostage to move wheat to market,
"Free at last, free at last, thank God Almighty we're free, at last."

And they moved ever northward, in further tribute
To an Oxford Man of Letters.
"Faulkner drank," the neighbors said, "his father too."
Moonshine bottles, 182 empties,
In the Rowan Oak woodshed,
Old Turkey and Jack Daniels when times were good,
Moonshine good enough for sippin' on other, leaner days.

Approaching Rowan Oak, a pleasant country breakfast
In the Coffeeville Café, a time warp—
Billy Joe, the log cabin, a gentle April rain—
A misty Saturday morning, bookstore on the Square,
Coffee, the Veranda, a football player, the Colts,
Supreme Court Justice, Rebels, Ole Miss,
Faces, names, and Holly Springs.

A trip South, along the Mississippi,
In the month of April 1997, thinking of Joe,
Great fun, many laughs, and many sights
Mortal eyes shouldn't have seen.

Since his days on Cobb Creek at the German farm, Joe had wondered how cavemen, thousands of years ago, would have communicated and he composed a language he called "XOTÄNEF" that attempted to transcribe the sounds of cave men, as he imagined them, into the Roman alphabet. The language Joe developed over many years consisted of a thirty-two-letter alphabet and working vocabulary, along with a two-part description of the grammar, twenty-five-page pronunciation guide, and accentuation rules. Joe had come to believe that Neanderthal man used sophisticated language to communicate, and XOTÄNEF was his attempt to show how early primitive people spoke tens of thousands of years ago. Though Joe never found anything similar to his XOTÄNEF language, recent DNA evidence published in 2007 supports Joe's theory:[11]

> *Scientists who have been trawling through the DNA found in Neanderthal bones have discovered that the now extinct species had a "language gene" that is only found in modern humans. Their controversial findings create the tantalising possibility that Neanderthals were in fact capable of speech much like humans and communicated with each other through their own language. As language is seen as one of the key cornerstones that has set humans apart from other animals and*

11. Richard Gray, "Cavemen may have used language," Daily Telegraph, London, 20 Oct 2007. http://www.telegraph.co.uk/news/uknews/1566748/Cavemen-may-have-used-language.html (accessed August 2010, printed under license with permission).

allowed sophisticated cultures to develop, many anthropologists now believe it may have allowed Neanderthals to have their own culture. It is a stark contrast to the traditional image of Neanderthals as simple-minded cavemen, and the latest research has shed new light on how Neanderthals evolved from our common ancestor more than 400,000 years ago. Professor Svante Paabo, who has been leading the Neanderthal genome project at the Max Planck Institute for Evolutionary Anthropology in Leipzig, Germany, said the presence of the language gene would change the way people view Neanderthals. He said: "It is not a compliment to be called a Neanderthal, but we are finding that the Neanderthal DNA looks much more like contemporary humans than chimps. The human variations of this gene involved in the use of language are not found in apes, and for a long time there has been speculation Neanderthals would have a different gene and so a different linguistic ability. By looking at their DNA, we have found that from the point of view of this gene, there is no reason they would not have spoken like we do. It is a very contentious area with a lot of different views."

His team's findings support previous work that has attempted to model the Neanderthals throat and larynx from their remains. While some scientists have insisted they would have spoken, others have dismissed the idea. Until recently common scientific opinion has painted a picture of Neanderthals as a slow and dim-witted species that was outwitted by its smarter cousins who went on to become modern humans while the Neanderthals died out.

But there is now a growing consensus that Neanderthals were perhaps far more sophisticated than they have been given credit for. They were capable of making stone tools, and even cleaned their teeth. The discovery of the gene, called FOXP2, has provided the strongest evidence yet that this heavily built species was capable of speech, although the researchers are unable to say what extent their linguistic ability would have been. FOXP2 is thought to be crucial to the development of language as it governs the fine control of muscles that is needed to form words with the larynx, lips, and tongue.

Professor Paabo has been leading research to create the first-ever profile of the Neanderthal genome from the remains of nine Neanderthals, thought to have been killed and eaten by cannibals 42,000 years ago, that were found in a cave in Northern Spain. The bones are carefully collected and frozen in the cave to avoid contamination before the DNA is extracted in the lab and profiled.

But some scientists have warned that it is not possible draw any conclusions about the Neanderthals' ability to speak from the research, which is published in the journal Current Biology . . . Dr. Simon Underdown, an anthro-pologist at Oxford Brookes University, insists, however, that the new research will revolutionise the way people look at Neanderthals. He said: "This research should finally blow away the last vestiges of the Neanderthal as a dull-witted cave man."

Dominican Republic Notes

Joe Haan (Notebook III)

In 1974, Joe traveled to the Dominican Republic on an ironworking job with the Houston Ironworkers Union. Joe's letter to Helen and his subsequent notes included many observations of the local community.

August 3, 1974

To: Mrs. Joe B. Haan

Greetings to all at home. And so I find myself now in a rather small town of San Pedro, which means Saint Peter, approximately forty miles from the capitol of Santa Domingo. "Domingo" translated is "Sunday of Saints."

A message to those who assumed that poverty was rampant in the USA—the contrast between here and there is definitely incomparable, for here it is apparent on every hand. The many new sights, sounds, and odors that have greeted my senses all have been stimulating as well as depressing, for poverty is always pathetic. When one walks upon the street to practice charity, then you fall into the role of the Pied Piper of Hamelin. If you give a centavo, the receiver of such a gift will follow you about in the street like a faithful dog, ever ready to be presented with one more tasty bone.

At times, I find myself completely isolated in my thoughts and without communication, as if I were an alien being in an alien world somewhere out in infinity. The general populace is extremely friendly and amiable. A small wave of the hand to any group of people rewards you with innumerable smiles and a very great amount of handshaking. This, all again, in contrast to the hostility and enmity that we find at home between the races.

Here the ethnic blend is Negro and Spanish with perhaps ten percent Caucasian. The language is Spanish but on rare occasion you meet with an anomaly, a very black man who speaks with a perfect English accent: "I say, chap, where are you from, now? As for me, I am English, as my father has come from Antigua long years ago, and I am a British subject." Thus they speak.

I would like all racist and bigoted-minded men to spend some time here and they would become much more tolerant, for it could not but leave indelible impressions etched upon their memory, and it could not but have less than positive results.

There is a grand and colorful growth of flowers in great profusion, such as a very exotic tree like our common mimosa. The tree is called "Flambojohn." It is very large in girth, several feet, and no doubt very old. The seedpods are twenty inches long with a large brilliant flower of the darkest shade of red. Mango, papaya, and coconut trees are to be seen on every hand, forming a perfect tropical setting.

We are on the coast. Our house is two blocks from the water, which is blue and green to the shoreline. There are outdoor cantinas there, where one may gaze out on placid water after it breaks over a coral reef five hundred yards off shore. The beer is quite expensive here, eighty centavos per quart, but of a very good quality. It has absolutely no hangover effect such as our home product. The hedges about the better homes are hibiscus, a solid mass of blooms, or crotons five feet tall pruned square, both very delicate plants without any tolerance for frost. This morning we took our servant home. She has eight children. In front of her home stood a giant ficus rubber plant thirty feet high.

A huge black moth just flew in. I tried to catch it but to no avail. Our house is new made of blocks, no screens on the windows or doors, only glass shutters, so all forms of insect life have ready access to our rather dignified abode. Peddlers without number beat a path to our door, dispensing a great variety of fruits and vegetables. A huge avocado seven inches long sells for five centavos. There are large crabs that come out of the water and walk about; one came in our door. They sell for a dollar a dozen, and they have much larger claws than our Blue Gulf variety.

Today is Saturday. I went to the outdoor market where one may purchase many homegrown products. There is a mob of humanity milling in the street, which reminds me of a large anthill recently disturbed. There are several merchants who display meat of unknown identity on dilapidated wooden tables in the open air. The proprietor is having a very difficult time, for a swarm of flies is making a suicidal attempt to lay their eggs upon his stock in trade. Under the table lie three dogs, mangy and to all appearance on the threshold of starvation. They cannot see the meat but the scent is there, and so they look upward with a look of supplication in their eyes.

Overhead hangs a rather large picture of the Virgin Mary where she might view much human suffering. She, too, appears to be hungry, or as if abandoned by her divine son and father. After three hours I returned to this same stall and the meat remained unsold; it has now become discolored and shrunken. The Virgin looks sadly down as if she had failed some mission for humanity, for here meat is somewhat of a luxury for the average citizen, and so the dogs may yet receive a tasty morsel.

The national pastime seems to be the government-sponsored lottery. A ticket sells for 25–60 centavos, and everyone participates. Hundreds of people display and sell these tickets seven days a week, the winning numbers being posted on a huge billboard every Sunday at 11:00 a.m. At that time masses of people congregate in the central plaza. As the time approaches for the winning numbers to be announced, everyone becomes quite emotional, for the remote possibility exists whereby you might be removed from an environment of dire poverty to one of extreme wealth. And so monies are spent by the very poor in desperation, while actually the odds of winning are a million to one. I have observed a very common display of a crucifix about the neck of the average player. At times they grasp it tightly in their hands, and they only wish that the gods will smile favorably upon them in this game of futile chance.

And so, this narrator having summarized some of the scenes here, has yet to form any concrete conclusion about the Republica Dominicana. I remain aloof in my thoughts and be not too sentimental about the human race in its struggle for existence and identity. There are many things yet to be said of the sights, sounds, and odors here, and the very unusual nature of the people who exist in a vacuum or a form of perdition, which is not of their making.

—Joe Haan

San Pedro, Dominican Republic

Joe Haan, Dominican Republic, 1974

Man on lonely beach with walking stick, lost,
Rental system for rich man's cemetery vault,
Burning bodies, goats and pigs in cemetery,
People chopping grass with machete,
Bicycles and burros for transportation.

Police with ancient Lee Enfield rifles,
Color of water, fish to be seen,
Filthy market, starving dogs,
Tame pigs roam streets like dogs,
Garbage in street, no disposal, dump in every block,

Horse-drawn carriage, 1900 vintage,
Man leading two pigs on leash like dogs,
Guards armed only with machetes,
Old, narrow-gauge railroad,
Aluminum dish called canteen, in three parts.

Spear fisherman on reef, lobster for 5 pesos,
Slaughterhouse on beach,
Thousands of flies in cab of truck,
Headache, nurse shot, soldiers everywhere.

Exotic fruits and vegetables, unidentified,
Pre-Columbian burial site, jade hatchet paint,
Ricardo the Great who makes coffins,
Funeral procession quarter mile long,
Visited two churches, asked why they killed their god.

Woman weeping bitter tears six years after father's death,
Licensed prostitution a way of life,

Man at fire station rings bell at 12 noon,
Large bowl of soup, mostly macaroni, 40 centavos,
Chicken cooked with feet and head attached,
Remove only eyes and toes.

When it rains, streets are mud like chocolate pudding,
Oxen pulling train, sugar cane supervisor on horseback,
Sugar cane towns, police friendly to people,
Soup house on Sunday, beggars demand soup,
Many flies, blind man eating soup by me.

People walk in streets, old Dodge cars,
Two motor bikes collide, crowd around victims,
Most rugged coral beach with spout holes,
Man on mule in hills, shotgun on lap,
Many small pushcarts, wheels lean 10 degrees.

Policeman with fighting cock,
Café business on every sidewalk,
Horse-drawn surreys, 1900 vintage or older,
Violent frenzy of cockfight,
I bet and win, return winnings to loser.

Chickens sold on street, alive, by peddlers,
Weigh them on merchant's scale,
Hundreds of small shops,
Dicker on price, goods beyond reach,
Family with 12 children, all attractive.

Tree with roots growing out of top
Hanging back to the ground,
Police embrace people openly on street,
Man drunk or crazy directs traffic at main plaza,
Police applaud, so does large crowd from sidewalk.

Police hitchhike to work, soldiers carry guns home,
Dogs and cats roam streets unmolested, open cantina door,
See first mongoose run across the road,
Buy giant shrimp, fresh water, one foot long,
Natives eat innards of crab, eggs.

Foreman on job lends money, exorbitant rate of interest,
Sept 24th, people calibrate birth of virgin sister,
Very young girls want to come to America,
Where streets are paved with gold, they think,
Old man, clothes patched in 150 places,
Quite unbelievable unless seen.

Children of all ages clothed in rags,
Wander about street like stray dogs,
Small boys steal rich man's avocadoes,
Medium size dog on street, mongrel strain,
With crucifix about his neck.

Combination store and bar in very poor residential area,
Observe sale of one egg, two eggs, half pound of flour,
One and a half pounds of rice, one pound of beans,
One stick of mesquite.

Small child enters, wishes to purchase milk,
Tall merchant behind rough board counter
Waves her violently away,
Till we rescue her from her economic dilemma
With 25 centavos and an added 10 centavos,
Owner's face beams with broad smile.

Horse with broken leg, very crooked, but healed,
Abandoned, very lame in street,
Horse harness made completely of manila rope,

Stone obelisk in highway intersection,
Prevent cars from colliding.

White herons, very numerous, land in street,
Policeman killed by own gun in public plaza,
Much goat meat for sale,
Half a goat for 12 pesos, eaten in one meal.

Man with seven children, no job,
Beautiful voice of opera quality,
Male children up to the age of seven
Run completely nude about the street.

When president leaves capitol,
Army moves ahead to protect him,
Two boys beg, do flips and walk on their hands to impress me.

Tobacco plantation, American-owned, all acres,
Pay scale 25 centavos per hour,
Very best land, black and fertile,
Drying corn and beans on asphalt highway.

All roads in bad condition,
Washed completely out in places,
Power truck runs off cliff, kills four hombres,
Four-year-old child goes about
Begging for pan, her daily bread.

XI

Joe's Poems and Songs

What follows, beginning with "Salute to the Stars" and finishing with "The Round Game," are a series of Joe's poems, written over the years. They explore themes that were typically "Joe" throughout his life—the nature of the universe, space, time, quantum physics, particles, distant galaxies, comets, asteroids, cosmic dust, violence of nature, evolution, geology, volcanoes, ancient man, dinosaurs, fossils, cockroaches, vanity, futility, heresy, free thought, deaths of gods, equality, prejudice, ignorance, chance, pestilence, and the pollution of the planet by "Spoiler Man," a statement ahead of its time.

The poems are personal and reveal Joe's innermost thoughts—thoughts that constantly occupied his mind. The theme of survival—creative evolution—was always present in Joe's thought. He would often speak of the constant lessons of survival that human beings accumulated in their DNA over thousands and thousands of years. Joe would often say as a prelude to a lecture on space and time:

Our earth has made four and a half billion trips around its sun—forever long, has it evolved—oozing life some three billion years ago—surviving extinctions, cooling, warming, asteroids, comets, volcanic eruptions, ever-changing climates. Time and time again, adversity altered life's earth-forms—from single-celled organisms, to viruses, algae, and to grasses, fishes, amphibians, great dinosaurs, mammals, apes, and other primates. 'Spawned of the Tree of Life,' heroic homo sapiens man first stepped forth a mere 130,000 years ago, spreading out from Africa some 80,000 years later, taking another 40,000 years to learn to farm as it moved into Asia, Europe, then the Americas just 12,000 years past—all the while surviving earthquakes, floods, hurricanes, ice ages, drought, starvation, lethal viruses, and ever-warring tribes of fellow man even yet today, befogged by myths of priests and holy wise men. The lessons of life on Earth are these—to live, mankind must adapt, freed of shackles and convention; all species must evolve to thus survive, for written in the code of mankind's genes, immutable imprints of survival there reside.

—Joe Haan to Paul Quist

Joe's Poems

Salute to the Stars

—Joe Haan (Book II, #1)

Far more galaxies there be,
Than fishes in the deep, dark sea.
In the vastness of the sea of space,
Time is lost in an endless race.

Yet, no man knows what lies without,
Beyond the realm of truth and doubt.
Suns without number greet our eye,
Beckon to us in a twilight sky.

Far beyond the reach of man,
Scattered by an unknown hand,
Insignificant, anonymous man,
Exists on earth, like grain of sand.

Oh, starlight caught in guided path,
Enslaved by some gravitational wrath,
Give thy heat and wonder light,
To us, poor victims of endless night.

Know you're not—you're not alone,
In the darkness and the gloom,
For the light shall never fail
Through dimensions' time we sail.

The Question

—Joe Haan (Book II, #2)

The vanity of man's quest,
Even though he does his best
To find and answer—"how and why?"
Not be born—and never die.

Gods of creation will always be,
Just beyond the next galaxy,
Man the fool—fooled be he,
By prophets of illegitimacy.

Of all the things that we can see,
In endless search for identity,
We look, we learn, and we ask:
"What then, is our earthly task?"

Profound thoughts of few men,
Specks of grain in a dusty bin,
Who are they who think so fine,
Are they the ones who are divine?

Oblivion

—Joe Haan (Book II, #3)

Time had no womb to enter in,
For eternal time has always been,
Count the tides and count the suns,
Count lives of men whose course has run.

Organic things within the sea,
Do they dream of things to be?
Ferocious sharks go gliding by,
Little fishes then will die.

Men rush madly to their chore,
To a job that they abhor.
The sands of time erode away,
The value of their task today.

Like little fishes in the pond,
They too, dream of things beyond.
When all your atoms have finally fled,
Then you have found an eternal bed.

Thinker

—Joe Haan (Book II, #4)

Few men think, but think they do,
Have you asked, "Who are you?"
Walk upon a higher plane—
Is profound thought too much pain?

If the mind is finely wrought,
Logic is the only thought.
Search yourself, and you will find,
The grand prerogative of mind.

Some little men will assert,
Their noble right to desert.
The myth of those gone thus berserk,
Humble man, now out of work.

For pseudo-sachems do abound,
Ignorant man, they always hound.

Sachem is a title given to the head of some Native American tribes.

Fido's Fate

—Joe Haan (Book II, #5)

My polytheism dictates to me,
A God, in every galaxy.
For man must have his Gods and Dogs,
As down life's road he slowly plods.

Both are words made by man,
In a lifetime, they too soon will span.
Oh, will my Fido be with me,
In my waited trip through eternity?

Will the carrier of rabid bite,
Too, find heaven in its flight?
But backward spell the word of Dog—
You also have the word called God!

Death of a Galaxy

—Joe Haan (Book II, #6)

As the galaxies shift in an endless drift,
To be lost forevermore,
What we see, is never to be,
For there is no finite shore.

All are voyageurs on an endless track,
From the womb of time begun—
Who are they, oh, so brilliant light,
From humble atoms spun?

Trapped in the vortex of dynamic spins,
This final nova, thus begins.

The Particle

—Joe Haan (Book II, #7)

Oh, little, small, molecular man,
Existing in thin spectrum band,
Bound within atomic cocoon,
Like an insect, or flower that bloom.

Energy in an organized state,
Is animate matter's lonely fate.
Phenomenon of nature's scheme,
Monkey man will ever dream.

What purpose life, enigma still,
The human mind will always fill.
Chemical-molecular, a changing mix,
That's the law of nature's tricks.

So remember, man, as you pass me,
We all will meet eternity.

Futility I

—Joe Haan (Book II, #8)

Thinking men pay a bitter price,
Who think of things that are not nice.
Of perilous trip that you've been through,
Oh, thinking man, who are you?

Let now your consciousness freely wheel,
That your latent psyche may reveal
Who we are, and why are we
Never free from strife that be.

Nature's laws dictate to us
A vital message that we must
Resolutely march, with head held high,
For alas—so doomed are we to die.

Think on, my friend, it's not too late,
Determine now—what is your fate?

Free Thought

—Joe Haan (Book II, #10)

So many lies, of man's fate when he dies,
Here is a word from a few who are wise:

Whether flora or fauna, cellular bound,
All shall return to atoms, unwound.

Anonymously come, anonymously go,
All goals forgotten, as lives cease to flow.

Futility II

—Joe Haan (Book II, #11)

Birth to death is a lonely struggle,
Life is such a fragile bubble.

What little knowledge we do attain,
In our short span, is all in vain.

But leave a track on the road of life,
Be a champion of intellectual strife.

Logic and reason stand alone,
Against mass minds, where myths are born.

Carry your burden to that distant goal,
Through obstacles, much grief, and toil.

Bigotry, intolerance, arrested minds—
Martyrs must struggle, till their truth they find.

So man's senses will resound,
Where nature's beauty does abound.

A Star's Terminus

—Joe Haan (Book II, #12)

Oh, let me reach, to touch a nearby star,
Tho they be, so distant, so very far.
For what you see, no longer be,
In the space of this great fantasy.

Time exists not for only thee,
Nova, soon, will all you see.
With scorching heat, perdition's hell,
From your deep bowels, magma swell.

All the fire, lost in vain,
To orbit forever in empty plane.
So winds, cast out, no longer blow,
The seeds of life no longer grow.

Drift, now dead, great inanimate thing,
For no longer will you, such bright light bring.

M-G-3E

The 4th Dimension

—Joe Haan (Book II, #13)

Place a cube, in a sphere,
DODECAHEDRON—lying near.
Twelve pentagons upon your side,
The smaller cube, you hide.

What is that, containing all,
Bigger cone to outer wall?
Oscillate cube at speed of light,
Orbit within outer cone's sight.

DODECAHEDRON—so all, too,
Will be passing, always through,
From the cube to outer cone,
Back again, is constant blown.

All are caught in static trap,
Make their trip—out and back,
No one, then, is master there,
When all live within one sphere.

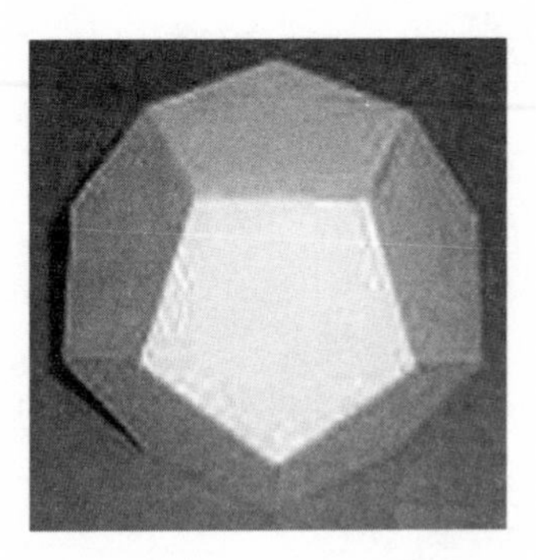

Each dimension's orbit, there,
Forever will be unaware
That they mutually ever share
Space within the lonely sphere.

A dodecahedron is a twelve-sided polygon with each of the twelve faces a pentagon. Scientists recently suggested the universe might be shaped like an expanding dodecahedron, explaining NASA's measurements of cosmic microwave background radiation left over from the Big Bang. Ancient Greeks said the dodecahedron corresponded to "quintessence," the element of the heavens. Plato wrote, "God used this solid for the whole universe, embroidering figures in it."

Birth of a Sun

—Joe Haan (Book II, #14)

(By The Who, "Flung Dung, from Sun," is sung. JBH)

Spiral nebula spinning in time,
Will compress and not unwind.
What will be your cosmic fate
As our velocities never abate?

Gather your atoms close to you,
To heat atomic cauldron stew.
But cataclysmic cycles wane,
So endless spirals, not in vain.

At last, conceive, gigantic sun,
No—your task is just begun.
Trap all matter drifting near,
They shall be your self-own sphere.

Catalysis will play its role,
As nucleic acids cease to boil.
Molecular things there, now will be,
So even monsters, you may see.

Then the beast will take its toll,
That emerge from planet soil.
Oh, survival now, survival then,
Eternal law—you cannot bend.

A spiral nebula is a galaxy having a spiral structure, such as the constellation Andromeda, visible to the naked eye. Arms containing younger stars spiral out from old stars at the center.

Volcano

—Joe Haan (Book II, #15)

Oh, Mother Earth, can't you see
That volcanic ash is strangling me?
Held within the laccolith throat,
For heated magma burns and roasts.

Lay to waste a beauty land,
By a monster, mountain-mad.
So flee, my children, filled with fear,
I will burn, and also sear.

Martyrs now, is all you be,
That fiery gods can only see.
Mother Nature, kind and cruel,
A cryptic message, which is dual.

How to escape her wicked hand,
As it rains that blistering sand.
"Oh, where is succor?" cry we in pain,
For none escape, caught in this scene.

So, all you little things that be,
Caught up in this fiery sea,
All shall die, return to me,
For all of your eternity.

Laccolith—an igneous intrusion injected between two layers of sedimentary rock forcing the overlying strata upward, giving the laccolith a dome-like form with a generally planar base.

Pestilence

—Joe Haan (Book II, #16)

Oh, the gods that cannot see,
Horrible disease that should not be.
Never can I see azure skies,
For I was born without eyes.

So to a man, I lend a hand,
With the wound that will not mend.
And I vainly speak to my god,
As endless victims are laid to sod.

Where are you, oh mighty power,
As pestilence will soon devour
All your children, hour-by-hour,
Until they are no more.

Human morons—the world abounds,
Monkey minds, so unsound.
Where then seek, and try to see,
What represents equality.

Life, then, is just a game of chance,
So practice now, your deadly dance.
The veil of tears that we call life,
Battle lines of continued strife.

And new dimensions always grow
The ranks of men, to reap and sow.
This we know, for we are sure
That pestilence is never pure.

Dinosaur Feast

—Joe Haan (Book II, #17)

Behold, beware, for I am king,
Of all that I survey.
For this voracious appetite,
Eats a ton of meat today.

The ground will tremble underfoot,
As prey be hunted down,
Turf and stone, and tender frond,
Will all be trampled on.

The bellows sound within my throat,
Conveys a message, still,
That I shall gorge upon your flesh,
Ground in a mighty mill.

Many centuries, I do prevail,
For the weak go to the wall,
The banquet laid for him that's strong,
To devour all that's small.

Meat is meat, and very sweet,
So nutritious is it all,
We devour kith, eat our kin,
Before the starving fall.

Equality Dead

—Joe Haan (Book II, #18)

Of gods and kings, and noble men,
Who dwell in castles, grand,
At sumptuous feast, you gorge yourself,
Produced by slavery's hand.

The wine you crave is from the grave,
Of those who've gone before,
From grapes of wrath, you take your bath,
And forever close the door.

On frozen ground, lie derelict men,
Whose time has finally run,
They grow the grape, fill the vine,
From which the wine was spun.

Blood is wine—wine is blood,
Shed by serfdom's kind,
For haughty, wealthy, selfish men,
To opiate the troubled mind.

The Carnivore

—Joe Haan (Book II, #19)

Out of the depths of dark and cold,
Come scaled invaders, cruel and bold,
Scan with reptilian evil eye,
All be devoured, what we spy.

Encroaching, now, on every plain,
For all defense has been in vain,
Master race that we shall be,
Our shadow cast is five-by-three.

Fifteen feet of monstrous stride,
Giant girth some eight feet wide,
We are fishers of little men,
Driven to our traps and pen.

Like little herring, they will be,
Flesh for champions, such as we,
All man's technical things he knew,
Discovered in times, passing through.

No sentry guards the city wall
For in the gathering, they all did fall
Into carnivorous hungry maw,
Ground by sinewy crushing jaw.

In this harvest of all mankind,
Nowhere on earth will you find
Surviving human, soul or mind.

Burned and broken, rusted down,
We've now reversed the hallowed ground.

The Nucleus

—Joe Haan (Book II, #20)

Microscopic things we know,
Give off at times, a purple glow.
Fragment of a miniature sun,
Light years, here, before earth begun.

Oh, how small can matter be—
Is an electron all we see?
No finite border in this world,
Where quadrillion atoms, all unfurled.

Alpha ray, who are you?
Protons, neutrons, two-by-two.
Helium atom, now you will be
With two electrons that were free.

Beta ray, glow and die,
Positron has gone by.
From within, electron fled,
One more positron, not shed.

Tamper not, with this sphere,
If radioactive death you fear.
Gamma rays, you'll feel, not see,
A poisoned land, forever be.

Deception

—Joe Haan (Book II, #21)

Down a jungle trail I trek,
Through a verdant paradise.
Beauty here, has no compare,
When seen by human eyes.

Varied orchids are in bloom,
Wherever footsteps trod,
I reach and pluck of but just one,
That emerged from near the sod.

But before I pick, I take a stick,
To rustle leaf and stem,
For fer-de-lance be lying near,
The death of many men.

So, how is it, in beauty's glow,
Where spectral hues abide,
Tragedy may be lurking near,
And danger on all sides?

What justice, this, you may now ask?
Where reptile venoms flow,
It is but coincidence?
No man shall ever know.

But if the reptile bite you miss,
While in this deadly zone,
A curare dart may strike you yet,
And from this world, you're blown.

The fer-de-lance is the most dangerous snake of Central and South America. Curare dart is a South American poison arrow.

Over Population

—Joe Haan (Book II, #22)

In the year, one trillion and 903,
Men accumulate to high degree,
Look across all broad land,
Billions of starving bodies stand.

A solid mass, a human wall,
No room to lie, or breathe at all.
With whimpering voice, and shaking hands,
Threaten all with fierce demands.

From demon gods, whose seed did sow,
That more failed, not to grow.
So now we suffer and, alas,
No food about, only grass.

And soon, the grass will all be gone,
A devastated, blackened lawn.
Hark—godly herald in the midst,
Evolving from this murky mist.

Stands three hands above our plane,
The very one that is our bane.
Beseech us now to never sin—
Brother, bring more babies in.

So, soon, the oceans we will fill,
Again, evolve the fishy gill,
There, too, we will more crowd the sea,
And nothing else, can ever be.

But, if the oceans ever dry,
For all the reasons, you know why,
Then dead men stacked, you will see,
Ten miles high, alongside me.

Quantum Jump to Within

—Joe Haan (Book II, #23)

A massive electron, that am I,
And I'm not all—so here is why:
My mass is made of many things,
When divided, so it brings

A million quarks in nucleic eye,
Minute things that never die,
For the mesons made by me,
They, too, shall always be.

But, what this quark, I say,
That makes electrons tick away?
Quarks are made of little erks,
That bring about atomic jerks.

Ten septillion tiny erks,
Make but one eighth of a jerk.
The jerks are made of murks,
And murks, then too, are made of zerks.

Honorable Professor Tum Quan Thump-Confuse-O-All, from Outer Crymonia Antimatter Man.

Mesons consist of a quark and an anti-quark, and have a spin ratio that is zero or an integer.

The Spoiler Man

—Joe Haan (Book II, #24)

Upon a planet, in time there grew,
A parasite-like, most hungry shrew.
It had two arms, two legs, a head,
Mother Earth will take them dead.

They covered her from head to girth,
With concrete substance, little worth.
Drove huge drills right through her skin,
To see just what might lie within.

There they found the gold called oil,
To cover fertile land and soil.
Spoil and ruin, all that would grow,
No more grain, to reap and sow.

Burned her hide with many fires,
Defiled her streams, pollution sired.
Changed the atomic nature of things,
So total destruction—that, it brings.

Mountains high of plastic dung,
On once verdant land, is flung.
Good ground covered with fancy stone,
To mark the place of dirty bone.

Once the air, so fine and sweet,
Corrupts now, what we daily eat.
Oh, Mother Earth, you must revolt,
Condemn this spoiler as we molt.

Keep that black and slimy ooze
Within the ground, or we shall lose.
Eradicate from your broad land,
This destructive holy band.

The Slaves

—Joe Haan (Book II, #25)

The world is full of holy men,
Who know all gods' secrets, then.
No question asked shall remain,
Go unanswered in their domain.

All untrained and fearful slaves,
Will pay their dues, for they are knaves.
Earn your bread with blood and sweat,
Or you will certainly fail to get
Sacred blessings from this priestly set.

But do not fail to share that bread,
With godly men whose scripture said:
"Give your total half to me,
For I am the One, the Holy See.
I am too good to labor, slave,

For that's the task of common knave.
If you fail me, my just share,
Even if it's on a friendly dare,
I'll bar your path to eternity,
Wherever you might, so'ever be.

And if you fail, on second chance,
Then forever do a painful dance.
In Hades fired—forever, fervent,
The fate of each unfaithful servant."

Leopard's Feast

—Joe Haan (Book II, #26)

Graceful oryx (gemsbok), and impala too,
Nibble tender grasses, wet with dew,
Across the leagues of comely veld,
Is antelope land in which they're held.

As twilight descends upon the plain,
And a closing day begins to wane,
Fauna, from all points around,
Gather at the watering ground.

Lithe and speedy, racers here,
Come to drink, without fear,
But, what lies in thornbush grass,
Waiting for impala to pass?

Swift and sure, with powerful leap,
Leopard springs from muscled feet,
Landing then, on impala there—
Tearing bone and flesh, even hair.

Oh, all of us herbivorous things,
Pray we might have heavenly wings,
Or make us all eaters of meat,
And give us fangs, not grinding teeth.

Oryx (gemsbok)—large African antelope of striking appearance with long, spear-like horns.

Paradise Disorganized

By Father fa-nang-ler, Ex Soul Trapper
—Joe Haan (Book II, #27)

I just returned from paradise,
What I observed shocked my eyes.
No method or manner have they there,
And no one really seems to care.

I asked the keeper of the gate,
"What's the population rate?"
"My good man, god only knows,
We have them stacked, unnumbered rows."

I then inquired whether a quota be,
He raised his staff for me to see,
"You see there, high up in the sky,
Room enough for all to die."

"Sir, may I enter the glittering room,
And see the precious golden throne?"
"Oh, no! And never, earthly friend,
That's reserved for haloed men."

So, what fools we mortals be,
To be thus snared in a heavenly sea.
Do not take that scripture bait,
Avoid a boring, endless fate.

Prejudice

—Joe Haan (Book II, #28)

In one life, by jury tried,
Twelve men saw that I had died.
I must confess, to all reveal,
Their narrow minds, my death did seal.

They were of an aristocracy,
And I, but a lowly commoner be.
At the bar I stood, with fear so pale,
A sentence that would soon prevail.

The second life, they laid to rest,
Because I had not done my best.
What I failed, or tried to do,
Was to accept their religious view.

The third life that came around,
Was brutally returned to ground.
For Bruno's ashes, asking why,
Giordano had so soon to die.

Once I dwelt in limestone cave,
Could not stand the Sachem rave.
Struck huge club upon his head,
For that now too, convicted dead.

Dedicated to Giordano Bruno, 1548–1600, burned at the stake as a heretic by the Roman Catholic Inquisition; Italian philosopher, proponent of the infinity of the universe, an early martyr for modern scientific ideas.

Escape Smilodon

—Joe Haan (Book II, #29)

In prehistoric time gone by,
Primates had to question, "Why?"
As they trod, hill and dale,
Seeking food, to no avail.

For the game had fled,
All grasses, trees, all were dead.
From the rain gods, water not,
To parched lands, death it brought.

Across this dry and dusty plain,
The hunt—the search—was all in vain.
Ravenous smilodon, so hungry too,
For fresh red meat, that's new.

Tiger's scent of hunting man,
"I will eat him, if I can."
Tired and worn, this hominid thing,
Who runs as only panic brings.

"The will! The will! I must survive,
Therefore, must I run and hide.
I'm no match for this deadly beast,
I must escape his bloody feast."

So he moves at panic pace,
In a final desperate race,
A granite crevice is lying near,
One steep approach is almost sheer.

That's succor sought to comfort find,
For smilodon is close behind.
Within this split of igneous rock,
I now escape from the tiger's knock.

To that crevice, tiger rushing came,
Sensing tasty, sub-human game.
But, alas, the crack is thin,
And hungry tiger cannot enter in.

"So at last, I have escaped
A painful, brutal, bloody fate."
Crouched within this granite vein,
Cramped and torn, with muscle strain.

"Oh yes, tomorrow I'll live again,
I'll trample mountain, plain and fen."
But now, the shift—tectonic plates!
In this tigered-tomb, my death now waits.

Smilodon was a saber-toothed cat with exceptionally long canine teeth. Hominids include chimpanzees, gorillas, orangutans, and humans.

The Mermaid

—Joe Haan (Book II, #30)

At ebb tide noon in a small lagoon,
A mermaid frolics under tropical moon.
Her head is covered with silver hair,
An iridescent body, scaled so fair.

Shoreline sands, laid down in time,
Organically fertile from ancient slime.
A perfect, rustic, verdant scene,
Varied flowers bloom, for mermaid queen.

Beyond the lagoon, a reef does rise,
A natural groin of nature's disguise.
No shallow water, or peace is there,
For great white shark, has there his lair.

Venture not, beyond the lagoon,
Unwary swimmers meet their doom.
For hungry shark must constantly eat,
So caudal flippers not cease to beat.

The trusting mermaid, swimming then,
Approached the watery killer's den,
The sea came red with bubbled froth,
A beautiful mermaid, forever lost.

Evolution, or Geological Time

—Joe Haan, 1966 (Notebook II, #31)

Let us go back, on the primordial-track,
To ancient archeozoic ooze.
When the jellyfish swam, with his intellect dumb,
In the twilight zone of life.

Through the endless depths of eternal time,
They evolved at a lowly pace,
Never aware, this protein mass,
That it would father a vertebrate.

As the Trilobite made his entry bow
Upon the stage of life,
The Proterozoic was soon to pass,
Like a shadow in the night.

The Cambrian Seas that enfolded lands
Were lush with organic life,
While the barren grounds lay meaningless
In the long Paleozoic night.

The Brachiopod and Trilobites
Were soon to have their day,
In the Ordovician and Silurian,
In whose time they held their sway.

The Devonian scene saw little change,
In the relentless march of time,
But the warming Carboniferous
Brought a very modern clime.

The mighty age of reptiles,
Which now lie in Permian Sands,
Were terrible to look upon,
In this Prehistoric Land.

The Mesozoic dinosaurs,
For all their strength and bulk,
Disappeared from earth forever,
Leaving behind an empty hulk.

The Jurassic and Triassic
Were the stage on which they played,
Till the Cretaceous curtain descended,
To write "finis" on their days.

Then dawned the Cenozoic Age,
With the early Paleocene,
Which preceded Eohippus
Of the early Eocene.

Now wild-eyed little lemurs,
Swinging fast from tree-to-tree,
Knew not, in the distant future,
True humanoids, they would be.

Heresy's Crime

—Joe Haan (Book II, #32)

In the year fifteen hundred forty-three,
A great mind must no longer be.
For Copernicus did depart this world,
Around the sun, his planets twirled.

Glad tidings at religion's throne,
For heresy's crime, he stood alone.
So come the year fifteen and sixty-four,
A great new mind came through the door.

For what Galileo was soon to do,
Was prove Copernican theory true.
But all the world abounded, then,
With ignorant, stupid, bigoted men.

Papal kings would then agree:
"No one shall think—just think like me.
So recant, now, you heretic giver,
Or at the stake you soon will quiver."

Fired faggots, fueled hot on feet,
Evils rage, you soon will meet.
Recant! Confess the crimes you live,
Gods—our holymen—will then forgive.

Death of the Gods

—Joe Haan (Book II, #33)

Our pagan gods—they all are dead,
Allah, too, has also fled,
Buddha, Shinto—where are you,
And Shiva, god I never knew.

Oh, Brahmin's search has been in vain,
A soul like me, the gods might gain.
Vishnu, now, I worship thee,
The gift of life, she gives to me.

Where be divine Christus, the holy loss,
The one last god, sent to the cross,
So cruel—man kills with fear, his gods,
Who lie beneath our earthly sods.

So, resurrect the thinking mind,
From shackled fear, chains that bind,
Liberate, oh gods—forevermore,
Humble men, from torture's gore.

From sixteen-eighteen till forty-eight,
Witches, burned at man's black stake.
Pitiful, painful, mournful cry,
Everlasting woes that never die.

Conflict of the Gods

—Joe Haan (Book II, #34)

Trouble not the mind with fearsome fantasy,
Create not more dissembling mystery,
So reason may drive all fear away,
And destroy man's ignorance in this, our day.

Superstitions flourish where ignorance thrives,
We see cruel demons in the skies.
Shinto, Buddha, Mohammed and Christ,
Divine leaders, all, who swear they are right.

Vishnu, cruel Shiva, Brahma brother,
Children of god destroy one another.
Martyrs bleed, and die like swine,
While gods feast holy with red wine.

Capricious Mother Nature, too:
"Has the lord now told you what to do?"
Mountains quake and crush the babe,
A future fool of religion's rape.

Many questions thus remain,
Unanswered by gods so vain.
Father Zeus, on Olympus high,
Pagan lords will never die.

Stars' Atomic Divinity

—Joe Haan (Book II, #35)

Oh, brilliant, burning, atomic sun,
When was your fire first begun?
What lit your smoldering, hydrogen hell,
So deep within your magma well?

Quite an eternal living thing,
Warmth and light in space, you bring.
So worship you—man always will,
For life in space you do fill.

Gigantic mass of electrons, free,
Ionized, for a time to be.
One proton always will escape,
And then it's helium, it will make.

For every atom in your veins,
A sun does burn in endless lanes.
All particles, then, forever will,
Be caught in this great gravity mill.

The Axis Tilts

—Joe Haan (Book II, #36)

The axis tilts, the oceans rise,
To drown the young—dumb and wise,
Monkeys perched on the highest limb,
Not taught to flout, or even swim.

Tidal waves, sure soon to be,
Will claim fearful monkey's tree.
If only un-lunged we were, and gilled,
And webs between the toes, so filled.

The muddy waters will claim us all,
Except the ones on mountains, tall.
But voracious oceans must be fed,
Children returned to Permian bed.

Yes, from the sea, all have come,
And in her waters we have swum.
For water's water is most of thee,
Our true mother is the sea.

Where magnetic pole we once did see,
There, its place no longer be,
And fragrant flowers cannot bloom,
Tropical forests, face also doom.

Permian: the period of geologic time, 250 to 290 million years ago, when many marine invertebrates disappeared and reptiles flourished.

Cockroach: Blattaria Supremus

—Joe Haan (Book II, #37)

Behold! At last, we stand supreme,
For us an end, a horrible dream.
In a billion years, we had begot,
Our fossilized brothers in the rocks.

Long before the imposter man,
Left their tracks in earthly sands,
We were mummified in carbon tombs—
Vast coal beds were once our homes.

Our prime enemy now has fled,
Radiated, burned—the biped dead,
What gamma rays have done, you see,
Did mutate us, to larger be.

Now we stand some five feet tall,
With long antennae one another call,
No molecule of air do we need,
A message sent, for all to heed.

Our ecclesiastic leaders plainly see,
That even god must look just like we,
Visualize no other image, then,
God could not look like biped men.

Blattaria (cockroaches) arose at least 280 million years ago and have not changed much since. There are about 4000 species worldwide, ranging from six-inch tropical cockroaches in South America to smaller North American varieties.

Allosaurus

—Joe Haan (Book II)

In prehistoric Jurassic time,
One dinosaur was so sublime.
Twenty ton of sinuous bulk,
Carnivorous allosaurus was that hulk.

Follow in his thunderous wake,
Underfoot, the ground will shake.
A million years old, that am I,
All living things, I do defy.

Ornithopoda, so lithe but frail,
In my shadow, they all quail.
Feast you now, on plant legume,
Meat for me, you will be soon.

Of all the beasts you would find,
Huge of body, small of mind,
Seek no answer to why I be,
I devour all, is plain to see.

The whole earth is now my wide domain,
Hunt the mountain, glen, and on the plain.
No gladiator to challenge me,
My eggs to others, food they be.

Allosaurus ("different lizard") were large carnivorous theropod dinosaurs (tyrannosaur) that lived about 150 million years ago in the late Jurassic period. Ornithopods ("bird feet") were bird-hipped dinosaurs that started as small, bipedal running grazers and became one of the most successful groups of herbivores in North America during the Cretaceous period.

The Coconut Cartel

—Joe Haan (Book II, #40)

All this land belongs to me,
Far beyond what you can see.
A million acres of coconut grove,
And on its fringe, trespassers rove.

Woe to them, who trample there,
For we have poison, trap, and snare.
Not one morsel shall they get,
Till our conditions, all are met.

This sacred land, that I behold,
Was father's-father's, never sold.
All to us, was given free,
Allah's hand, signed this decree.

So now I command, you starving bands,
Walk not upon my holy lands.
Only those who are my slaves,
Will have coconut in their cave.

Ask us to comprehend,
How ancient laws you will bend.
Mounds of coconuts shall go to waste,
They shall not receive, even a taste.

The Round Game

—Joe Haan (Book II, #44)

Oh, humble man, snared on a sphere,
The moon is close, the sun not near,
So, little primitive-minded man,
In a time they soon will span,
Do lay to waste the time allowed,
As all the players stand so proud.

What a mystery this round thing be,
It seems to defy our gravity.
Soccer, football, the basket game,
Have left so many players lame,
Pursue the round thing, gladi-man,
Join the teams of those who ran.

In the ranks of players be,
Few intellectual stars you see,
A little pigskin, inflated air,
A million spectators, it will snare.

So now play on, your futile games,
Stupid man, a mind inflamed,
Squander all, your little gain,
View the games, they're all the same.

My only hope, that I hold dear—
No round games played on other spheres.

Joe's Songs

Why Soldier Why

—Joe Haan (Book II, #40)

I'm a young man that's gone away,
I've took a trip today,
To fight a war, and die, I may,
For what, I cannot say.

I know not what I'm fighting for,
It may be to open freedom's door,
So from our wounds, blood does pour,
While deafening cannon roar.

I loved the world, the world loves me,
Yes, just to live, to love and be,
Help me now to strive and see,
Make all mankind free.

We are taught to take another life,
In painful, senseless insane strife,
We plead to you, who sent us here,
Our crimes committed you shall bear.

(Capo 3 Fret Chord G+Ab)

Love Lost

—Joe Haan (Book II #41)

A paining heart is mine
For I will always pine,
To revive again those happy memories.
Memories are pain, and it is vain,
To trap again a heart that I set free.

In all your youthful life,
You will find painful strife,
Competing for love, not meant to be;
So you're shackled down by painful throngs,
A burden of love you could not see.

Life's now a lonesome road,
Where all love's grown cold,
You're driftwood on the river of regret,
Floating with the tide, one cannot hide,
For tragedy will catch you in her net.

(Capo 2nd Fret Chord C+D-key)

Infidelity

—Joe Haan (Book II #42)

I am trying to forget
A girl I left behind,
But in spite of all I do,
She is always on my mind.

For I love her so,
The world must know,
And you will always find,
Where love's long dead,
The soul has fled,
And you will always pine.

(Refrain)

The postman brought the word today,
And I've an aching heart,
Every time I read those words
The bitter teardrops start.

I'm sorry that you went away
So the path of love does bend,
For I must let you know tonight,
I married your best friend.

(Capo 3 Fret Chord C+Eb)

The Latin Lament

—Joe Haan (Book II #43)

Oh, this is a story, a tale of woe,
Of sad love unfinished, down in old Mexico.
I met an angel with coal black hair,
Who vowed she did love me, and always would care.

(Refrain)

I mourn forever, wherever I go,
Why fate has deceived me, I shall never know.
One thing is certain, I'll never forget,
A dark-haired senorita in a life of regret.

The night winds were blowing, across desert sands,
When I asked this fair maiden for her little hand.
But fate had decided, this could not be,
Death, did take this darling from me.

(Refrain)

I mourn forever, wherever I go,
Why fate has deceived me, I shall never know.
One thing is certain, I'll never forget,
A dark-haired senorita in a life of regret.

(Capo 1st Fret Chord in C)

Suzanna

—Joe Haan (Notebook II)

My darling dear is no longer here,
For she has gone and left me all alone.
So I sing this song, for I belong,
Wherever that little girl may be.

(Refrain)

Oh, I love her so, no one will ever know,
Just how much she really meant to me.

I travel here and I travel there,
But I'm always, so always, all alone.
So come back to me, wherever you may be,
For you're a queen upon my throne.

(Refrain)

Oh, I love her so, no one will ever know,
Just how much she really meant to me.

They say that your love will live forever,
That there is no way it could ever die,
So I worship thee, as you can see,
For no one else can ever be, that I can see,
So I say a very sad goodbye.

(Refrain)

Oh, I love her so, no one will ever know,
Just how much she really meant to me.

My darling dear no longer loves me,
So there is nothing I can do, but lay me down and die.
Oh, come back to me, wherever you may be,
For my heart is breaking, and I am so all alone.

(Refrain)

Oh, I love her so, no one will ever know,
Just how much she really meant to me.

(from every stage)

XII

Joe's Epilogue

Joe died in Houston on January 7, 1992, from heart failure. He was almost totally deaf at the time. Helen sold the house on Landor Lane and eventually returned to her native Oklahoma to live with relatives. Joe's oldest son, Jack, lives in San Antonio where he has worked as a carpenter. He has one daughter, Nave, Joe's only grandchild. Joe's youngest son, James, lives near Sacramento where he has worked as a building contractor, champion fish carver, and spiritual fishing guide into the remote Sierras.

Joe's epilogue is a short statement that summarizes the fate of the characters in this drama of life—namely Joe—and this brings us back to memories of the many times Joe toasted "the bird" as he recited the old poem he loved, "Mr. Flood's Party." Joe met many Eben Flood characters on the road when he was riding the rails in the 1930s and later in Houston's skid row district. Many of them, like Joe, never had a birthday party or even attended a party of any type in their lives.

Every Christmas in his later years, Joe would go downtown Houston where vagrants congregated to stay warm, and he became known as "The Iron Man" who handed out money to the homeless. "Throw a nickle on the drum, save another drunken bum," was his cry. When asked by a Houston news reporter why he also handed out free wine at Christmas, Joe's honest response was, "Because that's what they want."

Joe often saw many Eben Floods on Houston's skid row and he kept going back, especially in his retirement years. Joe ran across Edwin Arlington Robinson's poetry in one of America's libraries when he was on the road in the 1930s—homeless, alone, always broke—and every time he had a chance to take a drink of something potent, he would inevitably toast old Mr. Eben Flood. In his bones, Joe felt he knew Eben as a kindred soul, a brother.

Joe knew Mr. Flood from the feeling he got from Robinson's austere style and bleak subject matter. Mr. Flood appealed to Joe's sensitivity to human pain and suffering because he had endured so much of it—psychological, emotional, and physical pain, as well as anguish and suffering.

Joe always struggled with the dichotomy between the bleakness of "survival of the fittest" on the one hand, and the unlimited scope and depth of the human heart on the other. He knew both extremes. People who understand the feeling of a Sauterne sedative know how it could ease the pain and provide the very few amusing parts to Joe's life. Laughter was infrequent in Joe's presence, except for his wry and twisted smile and bawdy laugh of "Drink to the dead already, boys . . . and Hurrah for the next man who dies." This was because pain was the overriding emotion that dominated Joe's entire being.

Visiting old slave quarters in Savannah or Charleston during his Civil War expeditions reminded Joe of his time at the Owatonna Orphanage and on Cobb Creek back in Minnesota amid the loneliness of the German farm. He shared their slave experience. He knew how they felt, beaten and worn from the ravages of pain and not being free. Even though a nonbeliever, Joe would have said:

> *"Thank god for the solitude and beauty of nature,*
> *Thank god for the bountiful stars in the skies,*
> *Thank god for people like Mr. Eben Flood—*
> *May he rest in peace—and may he party on,*
> *In his 'valiant armor of scarred hopes outworn.'"*

Mr. Flood's Party

Edwin Arlington Robinson (1869–1935)

Old Eben Flood, climbing alone one night
Over the hill between the town below
And the forsaken upland hermitage
That held as much as he should ever know
On earth again of home, paused warily.
The road was his with not a native near;
And Eben, having leisure, said aloud,
For no man else in Tilbury Town to hear:

"Well, Mr. Flood, we have the harvest moon
Again, and we may not have many more;
The bird is on the wing, the poet says,
And you and I have said it here before.
'Drink to the bird.' He raised up to the light
The jug that he had gone so far to fill,
And answered huskily: 'Well, Mr. Flood,
Since you propose it, I believe I will.'"

Alone, as if enduring to the end
A valiant armor of scarred hopes outworn,

He stood there in the middle of the road
Like Roland's ghost winding a silent horn.
Below him, in the town among the trees,
Where friends of other days had honored him,
A phantom salutation of the dead
Rang thinly, till old Eben's eyes were dim.

Then, as a mother lays her sleeping child
Down tenderly, fearing it may awake,
He set the jug down slowly at his feet
With trembling care, knowing that most things break;
And only when assured that on firm earth
It stood, as the uncertain lives of men
Assuredly did not, he paced away,
And with his hand extended, paused again:

"Well, Mr. Flood, we have not met like this
In a long time; and many a change has come
To both of us, I fear, since last it was
We had a drop together. Welcome home!"
Convivially returning with himself,
Again he raised the jug up to the light;
And with an acquiescent quaver said:
"Well, Mr. Flood, if you insist, I might."

"Only a very little, Mr. Flood—
For auld lang syne. No more, sir; that will do."
So, for the time, apparently it did,
And Eben evidently thought so too;
For soon amid the silver loneliness
Of night he lifted up his voice and sang,
Secure, with only two moons listening,
Until the whole harmonious landscape rang—

"For auld lang syne." The weary throat gave out,
The last word wavered; and the song being done,
He raised again the jug, regretfully,
And shook his head, and was again alone.
There was not much that was ahead of him,
And there was nothing in the town below—
Where strangers would have shut the many doors
That many friends had opened long ago.

XIII

"The Greatest Generation"

An Afterword

Journalist Tom Brokaw wrote about the steadfast bravery and distinctiveness of the World War II veterans in his book *The Greatest Generation.* As members of that distinctive cohort, Joe and his comrades fought and died to save the world from the twentieth century's deadly totalitarian movements, only to hand off their victories to another generation—sated, spoiled, and fatted Americans who squandered their birthright in hedonistic excess, rarely appreciating the values their fathers fought to preserve.

Now another life cycle following the Greatest Generation is mopping up the excesses of a gluttonous "me too" generation, seeking to bring the world back into equilibrium, as Joe and his generation did in their time. As "god's angry man," Joe would have written of the excesses of the early twenty-first century in words he would have shouted loudly to the world as the last iconoclast.

Blasphemy

The voice of Joe Haan, god's angry man

On this, a once and mighty native land,
We come together, in helping hand,
To friends and ever-warring tribes:
Protect us now, from foes, besides,
Give us your oil of fatted fate,
But never hate the Apostate.

Bring forth we then, a book of truth—
From a son of Europe's daughter—
A message to the world, to all who believe,
Or disbelieve great Zeus and the many Prophets—
Abraham, Moses, Jesus, Mohammed, JBH—and others:

[Peace and blessings be upon them all].
And upon each and everyone,
The innocent and the free—
Believers fought against, and wronged—
To them does Life bring victory.

Goodness and righteousness is called to them,
Fight not, for peace is the commanded task,
For all whom Life guides, is rightly-guided,
And all whom Life leads astray
Are first made mad before destroyed.

So yet is there a right way, to behold the truth—
Choose governments of free will,
Free to choose a god—or none,
Free to choose an exalted god, or no one.

Submit to Man's laws, accept opinions of others,
Enjoin good, forbid evil, honor universal truth.
With hands, tongues, hearts, minds,
Seek unity, agreement,
Reject oppression, lies, immorality, debauchery,
Bounded with manners, principles, honor, purity—

All true believers, not weak or powerless,
Superior—victorious in all ways—
Under Man's laws,
With freedom and liberty for all,
Regardless of consequence.

For the wise seek to acquire the best possible knowledge,
As war and carnage come again to ancient lands;
Reaction, revenge, retribution—
Long lines of extremism invoking religious myth
Justify mass murder, suicide, death—
Religious wars between peoples of the World,
Cultures reinforced by hostility, distrust, hatred.

Impious expansion, conquest, invaders,
Tensions for hundreds of years,
Some still hating and cannot love—
Over time—disillusionment, hostility, rejection—
Millennial defeat by "enemies of god,"
Successive loss of dominion,
Authority over family, house, and home.

For that, and more—
Hating an upstart daughter of Europe,
Devil incarnate, myth-makers say:

"You, creator of unbridled freedom,
Satanic temptress, soulless culture, materially advanced,
Lacking spiritual meaning, existential validity,
Assembled artificially—unnatural, unorganic—
Dominated by theft of people's souls, and natural resource,
Lacking dignity and courtesy,
Dangerous embodiment of ruthless capitalism,
Imperious incarnation of evil, you daughter of Europe."

A people hated for who they are, and what they do,
Rendering unto Caesar what is Caesar's,
Unto God all else, a people sovereign,
Church and state apart.

A great and noble experiment—
Unrestrained freedom to choose, make money,
Use god's earth of rightful things,
Commanding humankind to be free,
Conscience liberated from restraint,
Living harmoniously under god,
Constantly improving,
Laws made by Man.

For if the mind of Man be shackled,
Tied and bonded as to a hated German farm,
Angels of death do then descend,
Energy and faculty perish,
Lightness of the air grows heavy,
Dull and filled with gloom,
Bleak and cheerless—a veil of bitter tears.

Having "Sworn upon the altar of god,
Eternal hostility against

Every form of tyranny
Over the mind of man—"

We must remain, forever free,
Without profanity, false piety,
Or baited blasphemy.

—B. Wayne Quist, August 2010

From Joe, a word of caution to the world—

"As man marches down
The endless corridor of time,
To an unpredictable future,
He shall either walk in the sun,
Or return to the primitive darkness
That was his past."

And from Alaska, a closing reminiscence

—Paul Quist, Fairbanks, Alaska, August 2010

Here's what a typical evening might have been as Tim Carlson and I, two college kids, gathered with Joe around the kitchen table with a jug or two of Joe's Sauterne and a case of Lone Star beer. The scene was the early 1960s on a hot sultry night in north Houston, with loud male cicadas clapping in the background. These nights were often a cross between a Socratic symposium and a professional wrestling clinic.

You see, Joe couldn't talk to you without touching you, manhandling you, his hand on your shoulder, on your head, or holding both your arms. There was no escape. He had your total attention and he dominated. Joe always spoke loudly because his hearing had been impaired by World War II artillery. And as he grasped your limbs, you could feel his intensity, see his furrowed brow, deep-sunburned creases along his cheeks, and riveting blue eyes. Joe was mesmerizing. Everything about Joe commanded your total attention, and he got it. The dialogue and conversations developed a rhythm of their own, and the subjects would run the gamut from survival to the metaphysical.

The evening might start with a depiction or reenactment of one of the great battles of history—Alexander the Great in Persia, Julius Caesar in Gaul, or General Patton and Joe at the Battle of the Bulge along the Sûre River a few miles south of Bastogne. He might follow with a lengthy dissertation on Joe's *Origin of Species*: "In the beginning, Man created god . . . you'll never look at an ape in the same way again."

Before long, the guitar and harmonica have come out and Joe would sing "This Land Is Your Land"—he loved Woody Guthrie. Then a Jack London story, where he built a fire in the Arctic winter of our minds, which might lead to Robert Service and "The Cremation of Sam McGee." He would follow this with a lecture on igneous, sedimentary, and metamorphic rocks, and never-ending questions and his answers:

"Want to know how to skin a lynx without cutting its eyelids?" He told us. "Want to hone the sharpest knife in the world?" He showed us. "Want to know the best way to hop a moving freight train? Well, let me tell you," and he would, as more answers to his questions continued:

"This is how you make a Clovis spear point like Helen's forefathers did 12,000 years ago. You have to watch the size of your flakes as you chip away the flint. And this is how to stay alive in a freezing foxhole with your dead enemy as your only companion." Then, as we would step outside, the inevitable toast would ring loudly into the hot and sweaty Houston night:

Hold your glasses steady boys,
For this life, it's a pack of lies—
Drink to the dead already, boys,
And Hurrah for the next man who dies!

Now, here's the wrestling part. At some point in the evening, you were sure to find yourself by Joe's lush garden in the backyard. Suddenly you're flat on your back in an instant, looking up at the stars. It's Joe, practicing his karate hold on you. Just as suddenly, he throws the Korean Deathlock on you, and there's absolutely no escape until you cry, "Uncle."

The curriculum at Joe's symposium was both mental and physical, and as the night wore on, the Sauterne and Lone Star lubricated the sense that we were at the center of the universe participating in an ancient ritual, a symposium with the grand master, an unforgettable human being, a remarkable teacher. We were his fortunate students.

As you entered the front room of Joe's house, you were immediately greeted by a six-foot-high Tyrannosaurus Rex dinosaur Joe had molded from clay. Throughout the house, the walls were covered with more than a hundred stuffed animals and fish, every kind of deer, javelinas, many varieties of snakes, shark jaws, antelope, hawks, eagles, and rats. Joe had turned his house into a natural history museum with stuffed animals and reptiles of all sizes and shapes; beautiful butterflies and poisonous insects; lifetime collections of minerals varying from meteorites to semi-precious stones found or mined by Joe over the years; Civil War Minié balls, hundreds of arrowheads, strange metals, and flags; coin, stamp, and currency collections; German bayonets, helmets, flags, and Lugers he brought home as war souvenirs. If Joe identified with it, the rare item was in one of his many collections displayed throughout the house.

Driving by Joe's house in north Houston, no one would ever suspect that its occupant was so much different from the neighbors. Joe bought the one-story rambler in the 1950s for $7,500, and it's probably worth that today. By the 1970s, the white middle class neighborhood had evolved into an all-black, desperately poor enclave with an economy based on drugs. Every night, a procession of vehicles would line up on Landor Lane, stopping two houses down from Joe. An eight-to-ten-year-old kid would run out to the car and collect the money. The car would pull forward to the house next door to Joe's, and another young kid would run out to deliver the drugs to the waiting car, which immediately sped away. It was a business, a well-greased system, and it went on all night, every night. After a break-in when someone stole his guns, Joe installed steel bars on every window and heavy steel doors and locks.

After that, the neighborhood left the strange old taxidermist/ironworker alone. Joe was friendly with his black neighbors, but he was white. They wondered to themselves why any sane white man would choose to live in a place where all the neighbors dreamed of escaping, but couldn't, as they were trapped in poverty. But behind those barred windows was a man who empathized with their plight more than they would ever know. He was a man trying to make sense of a chaotic universe, a man who wrestled daily with man's inhumanity to his fellow man. Joe knew we are all children of our history and he knew he belonged there at his first home on black Landor Lane. He chose not to leave because it was home and he felt his neighbors' poverty and felt their crying needs.

The latest of many drug murders in Joe's neighborhood had occurred the night before we arrived in Houston on one of our many visits. The ambulance had come and awakened Joe late at night. The next morning, Joe walked across the street to the park where the murder had taken place. There on the grass was a mass of blood and a clump of human brains, the dead man's brains that had been literally blown out of his head, but too messy for the busy ambulance crew to pick up and remove with the dead body.

Joe went home and came back with a shovel and bucket. With care, he put the man's brains in the bucket and carried them to a quiet corner of the park. He buried them in an unmarked grave, pondering all the while the senseless loss of human life. Joe had been there before, on grave duty in France, after the Battle of the Bulge, and later in Germany. Another senseless death, another night in the Houston ghetto.

By the 1970s, north Houston resembled the third world, as we witnessed when Joe showed us around his neighborhood. He took us into an all-black convenience store with very few goods for sale—just pop, candy, cigarettes, and a large screened-in beer and liquor area. The clerk was stationed like a sentry at the front door, sitting on a stool. Directly behind her was a large tattooed man who didn't smile, with a sawed off shotgun chained to his left arm.

Then we walked across the street to Joe's all-black local bar. He went there frequently enough that the patrons all knew him by name. They knew that he was a little different, but not much else. Few white men would dare venture into this all-black bar. Except for occasional guests Joe would show around, no other white person ever entered the neighborhood, much less the local bar. But it was okay that we were there with Joe; that was the subliminal message in one of the most interesting bars I've ever seen.

There were no signs anywhere advertising its name or type of business. You had to know it was a bar. The walls were made of recycled plywood. The ceiling was a blue tarp that served as the roof. The bar itself was made of three fifty-five-gallon steel barrels with two-by-twelve planks serving as the bar top. Patrons sat on metal folding chairs around cheap card tables. The entire nature of the bar gave the impression that it could pack up and move out in a few minutes. The floor never had to be swept and never was because it was dirt. Lou Rawls albums played on the 78 RPM record player, "Breaking My Back Instead of Using My Mind" and "I'd Rather Drink Muddy Water." We ordered three Lone Stars from the obliging bartender who walked over to a ten-year-old kid behind the bar and handed him some money. The kid returned a few minutes later with three beers he had purchased at the convenience store we had just left across the street.

This was Joe's world, his own sociology laboratory. He openly shared it with us, in sorrow at the human condition but also proud that he was able to live and survive there.

Joe had worked with steel all his working life. Through an ironworker companion, he came by some exceptionally high quality steel with just the properties he needed to make the sharpest blade in the world. He took it from there, heating the steel to cherry red and carefully cooling it in gentle oil baths. Then he would pound it time and again to perfectly align the atoms. Through time, trial, and self-taught metallurgy, Joe developed what he called "the sharpest knife in the world." His favorite demonstration was to take a silk scarf and throw it in the air. As it passed gently over the stationary knife, drifting silently, the scarf was cut in half.

I pondered the sharpest knife in the world late one evening when the knife was at my throat. Joe was wound up about some injustice that needed correcting when he grabbed the knife, put it up to my throat, and said the bastards should be decapitated. At the time, I didn't know this was simply Joe's way of making his point. Putting down the knife, he kissed me on the cheek. He reassured me that he meant no harm to his nephew, but all evildoers should beware. I've often thought of the sharpest knife in the world over the years and am reminded of Somerset Maugham's *The Razor's Edge:*

> *The sharp edge of the razor is difficult to pass over, thus the wise say the path to Salvation is hard.*

The neighbor, two houses down the street from Joe, had a terrier dog. For several nights in a row, the dog took to barking all night long. Joe would get up at 5:00 a.m. every day and put in a hard day's work bending steel. He needed his sleep, especially on hot summer nights without air conditioning. Joe had several conversations with the dog's owner, but to no avail. Exasperated with the ceaseless barking, Joe slipped silently out of bed one night and crawled stealthily like a commando through two backyards with the sharpest knife in the world between his teeth. He said the dog didn't know what happened. It just lay down and stopped barking.

Often, when I'm lying in bed at night before sleep falls, I recall the first time Joe took me on a trip through the universe. It was a dark summer night, and we were lying on the grass in Joe's backyard when the stars were amazingly bright. Joe knew all the names of the ancient constellations. To him, they were like old friends. He knew their locations by time of day and month of year. He would say:

> *Take a trip with me through the universe. The light we see from the stars is ancient light. You have to understand the speed of light to give the universe any meaningful perspective. The speed of light is 186,000 miles per second, so it takes but one and one half seconds for light from the moon to reach Earth; two minutes from Venus to Earth, four*

minutes from Mars, Jupiter thirty minutes and Saturn one hour. Neptune is four hours away. The Oort cloud with a trillion comets is one light year away or about 5.9 trillion miles, while our sun is just eight minutes away.

Our nearest neighbor star is Alpha Centauri—you see it there on the southern horizon; it's just four light years distant. Man will go there some day. The Pleiades, the ancient Greeks' Seven Sisters, is 375 light years away. Remember, you're traveling at 186,000 miles per second. The Andromeda galaxy is two million light years distant. Get it? You're traveling at 186,000 miles per second for two million years to get to Andromeda. The light we see from it tonight left there when man first started to walk upright. Further out, light coming from the Hercules cluster of galaxies 500 million light years away left millions of years before dinosaurs walked the Earth. The end of the known universe is out there some ten billion light years plus. The light that left there with the Big Bang is over five billion years older than our solar system.

With trillions of stars in the universe, how many planets are there and how many of those planets have life? It would be the height of conceit to believe there's only one here on Earth. And what universes might lie beyond? Could we even calculate or fathom their distance with the speed of light as our crude and puny yardstick? Our Earth is in an outer spiral arm of our galaxy, the Milky Way, which has as many as a billion stars in it. Our known universe probably has as many as a billion galaxies. And remember, our galaxy, the Milky Way, is 100,000 light years across.

> *Astronomers believe that at the center of each galaxy is a black hole created by the death of a giant star. The black hole feeds and grows by consuming all that falls within its sphere of influence, its gravitational field. It will be our ultimate end, our oblivion, to fall prey to our own black hole, some billions of man-years hence. We, all of this, everything you see, will be drawn irretrievably closer and closer to the black hole in our galaxy. That is our destiny. At the point we pass the event horizon—the moment the gravitational pull of our black hole takes over, the point of no return—at that instant, you and I, and all we know, all of this around us, will be swallowed by the black hole. Within seconds, we will arrive at oblivion, the Great Singularity. Nothing passes the Great Singularity except pieces of atoms and fragments of light. It's all gone, everything! There is no way out.*

What Joe didn't know back then was that our universe is close to 13.7 billion years old and that half the universe is made of dark matter, invisible to the human eye. Joe would say, "The time will come when, discovery after discovery, science will reveal the secrets of the universe and man's place in it."

Was the black hole at the center of our galaxy a metaphor for life as Joe had come to know it? If we are the totality of our genetic blueprint and our life experiences, then the essence of Joe is the spirit that drives us on to wonder at it all. We owe much to our uncle Joe, as many of his genes predispose our curiosity, skepticism, sense of adventure, humanity, and mostly, our wonder of it all. We'll meet you at the Great Singularity, Uncle Joe.

XIV

Joe's Story in Pictures

Haan kids on burro, 1921

Joe is pictured here at age three in 1921, sitting at the front of a burro by the Haan home at 554 Rice Street in St. Paul. Bub, age five, and Kenny, age ten, sit behind Joe, while their mother and Sis, age eight, look on from the porch above.

Joe, on goat wagon, 1923

Joe is pictured here at the age of five in a wagon pulled by a goat near the Haan home at 582 Gautier Street in St. Paul. Joe's beloved mother would die unexpectedly two years later, leading to Joe's anguished poem, The Vagabond Road, "small frail hands on a coffin, gray."

Joe's mother

Joe's mother

Joe's mother, Marie Mamie Hlavac Haan, is pictured here about 1900

Danny Haan, age fifteen

Private Danny Haan, 1931, age twenty

Danny was sixteen when his mother died. He avoided the orphanage when his maternal uncle and aunt took him into their home until he was old enough to join the Army.

Aunt Sadie and husband Carl Kjeldsen

Aunt Sadie, devoted aunt who cared for the Haan children throughout her long life, is pictured here with her husband Carl (Charles) who died in 1915 at the age of thirty-two.

Kenny Haan, 1927, at the Hadley farm, age sixteen

Danny's machine gun unit, 1931

Danny liked the Army and served in the Pacific during World War II and later in Korea during the Korean War. He retired from the Army in 1960 as a Chief Warrant Officer (W-4).

Danny's camp, Fort Lewis, Washington, 1932 (Mount Rainier in background)

Danny loved the Pacific Northwest and eventually settled in Vancouver, Washington, after retiring from the Army.

Minnesota State Public School for Dependent and Neglected Children

540 West Hills Circle, Owatonna, MN 55060 | phone: 1-800-423-6466 | e-mail: museum@ci.owatonna.mn.us

Minnesota State School for Dependent & Neglected Children: The Owatonna Orphanage

Joe's "Cottage" State School Orphanage, Owatonna, Minnesota

Courtesy of Harvey Ronglien, State School Orphanage Museum—"Miss Morgan was the Cottage 11 Matron since it opened in 1923. She remained in that capacity until 1945 . . . Miss Morgan could be hard and cruel. Only rarely could she be kind and compassionate."

Joe Haan with baseball bat, 1927

Posed photo, Joe with bat at the Owatonna Orphanage.

Cottage Basement at State School Orphanage

Basement of "Cottage" C-11 at the Owatonna Orphanage. Courtesy of Harvey Ronglien, Owatonna Orphanage Museum—"We practically lived in the basement—each child had his own assigned chair for order and accountability."

Courtesy of State School Orphanage Museum

Picking apples

Courtesy of State School Orphanage Museum

Cecilia ("Bub") at St. Joseph's Academy in St. Paul, 1932

St. Joseph's Academy, St. Paul, Minnesota

Bub was fortunate in that she was indentured to a St. Paul family and enrolled in St. Joseph's Academy where she completed high school.

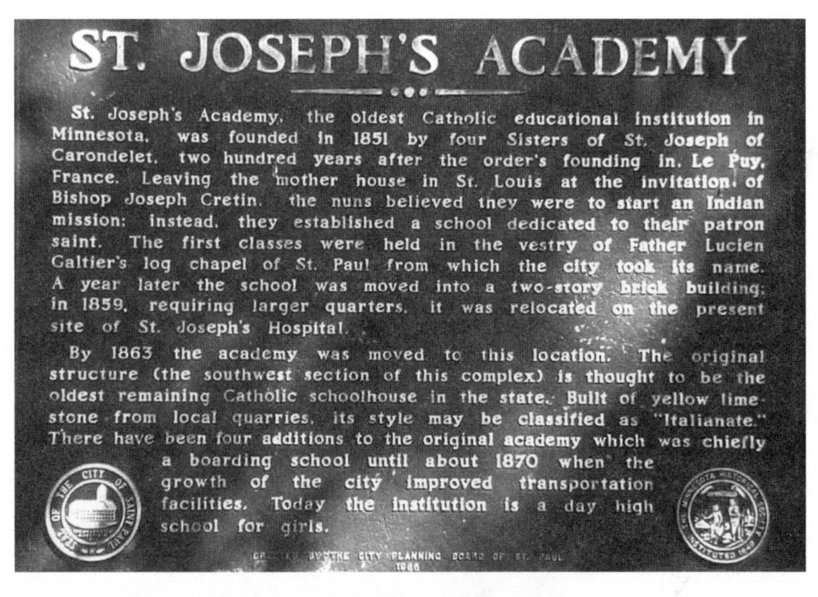

St. Joseph's Academy (plaque)

St. Joseph's was founded in 1851 and is the oldest Catholic educational institution in Minnesota.

The Farmhouse

Joe's windowless room was in the unfinished upstairs attic in the back of the house.

The Woodshed

Starting on his first day at the farm, Joe was beaten nearly every day in the woodshed by the sadistic farmer to whom he was indentured.

The Barn

Joe often slept outdoors and in the barn because it was more comfortable than his attic room, especially in the heat of summer. On his last day at the hated farm, Joe was repairing the barn when he hit the German farmer on the head with a two-by-four after a scuffle and ran to the nearest train junction a few miles away.

Cobb Creek

Cobb Creek was Joe's hunting and fishing refuge where he learned about wildlife and taught himself to become self-sufficient.

July 4, 1934, on the German farm

From left to right: Sis, Joe, Bub, and Kenny at the German farm on the fourth of July 1934. Joe's indentured master, a sadistic German farmer, is bending over in the background next to his wife.

Joe holding young pig, July 4, 1934, on the German farm
Joe is pictured holding a young pig with his sister Bub, who drove down to the German farm from St. Paul with Kenny and some of his friends. They picked up Sis in Faribault on the way to see Joe on the farm.

Joe's Bird Drawings

Joe loved to draw birds and other wildlife. He used the books Sis gave him to study mating calls and identify the sounds and colors of the various species of birds and animals.

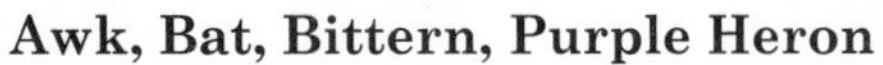

Awk, Bat, Bittern, Purple Heron

Blue Bird, Bob-O-Link, Brant, Bunting

Buzzard and Cockatoo

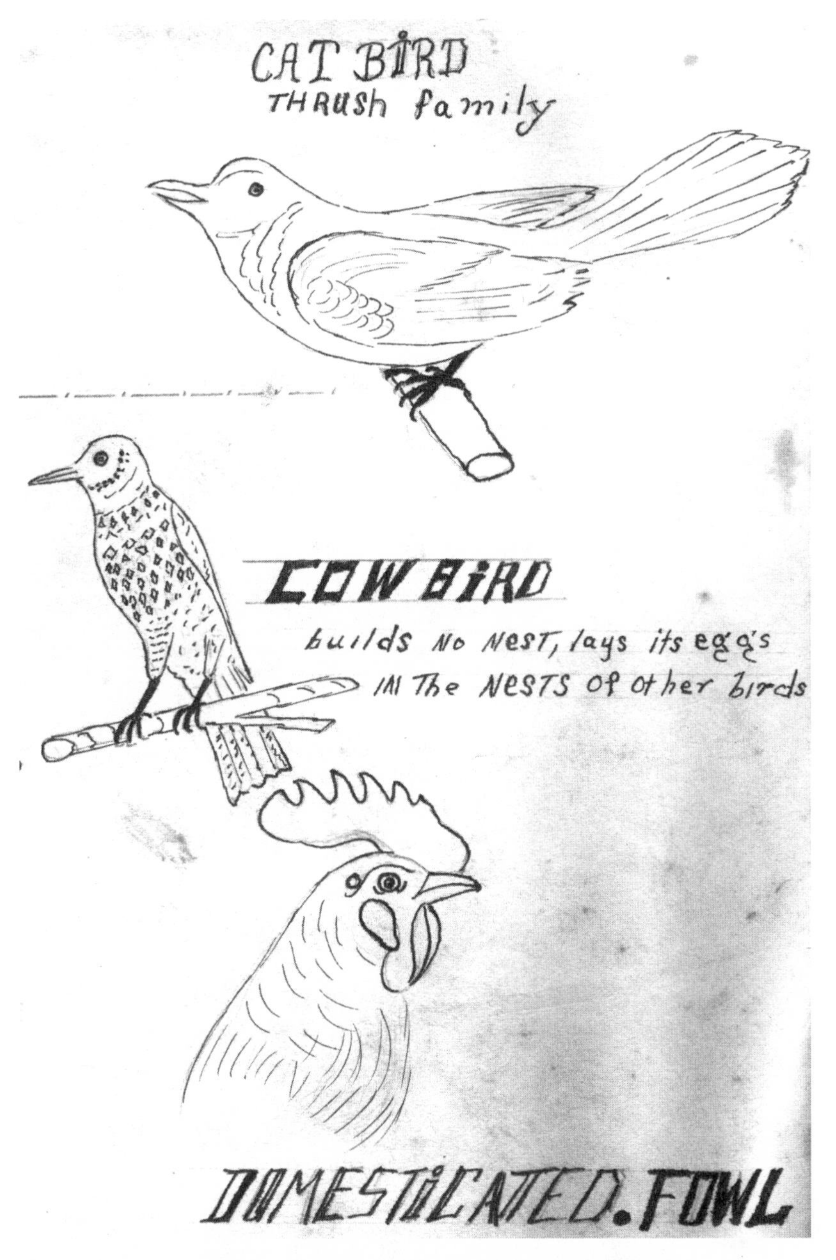

Catbird, Cowbird, Domesticated Fowl

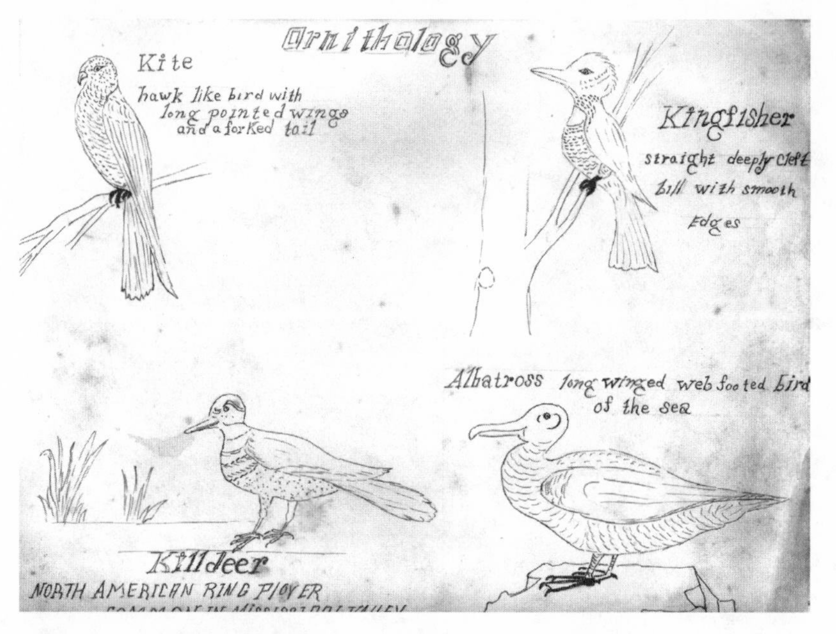

Kite, Kingfisher, Killdeer, Albatross

Dove, Eider Duck, White Egret, Falcon

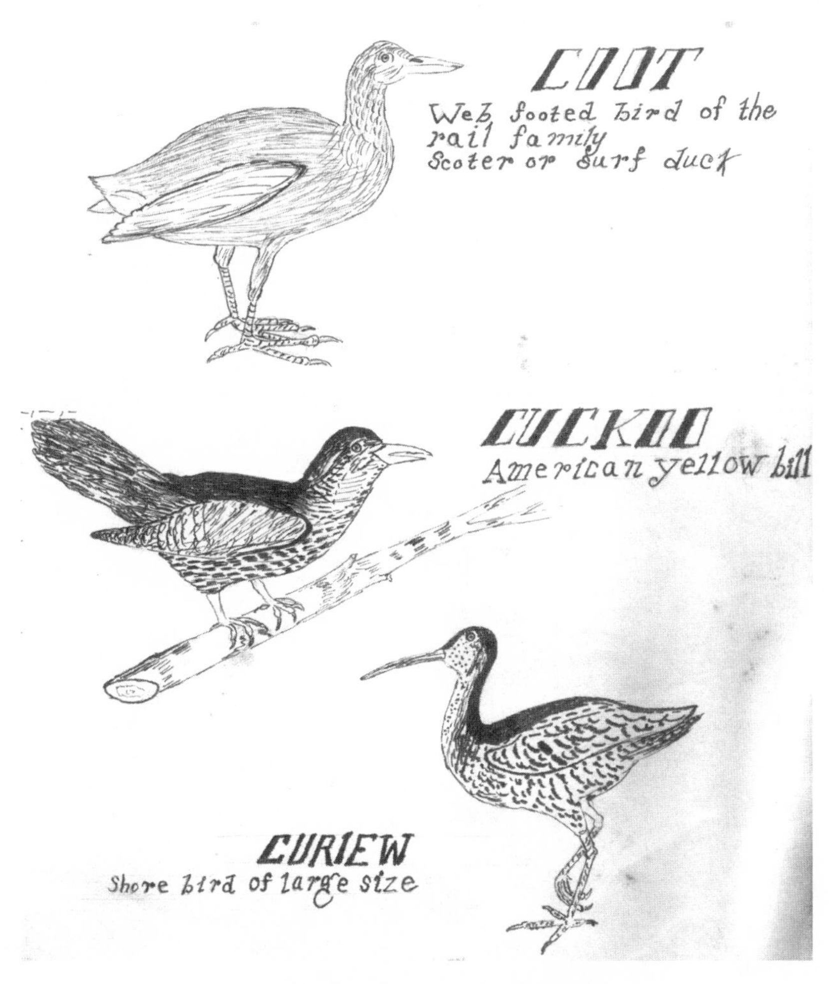

Coot, Cukoo, and Curlew

CONDOR
VUITURE OF THE HiGH ANDES
VUITURE OF CAliFORNIA SiMilAR

Condor

Finch, Flicker, Gannet, Goldfinch

Goshawk, Crested Grebe, Purple Grackle, Humming Bird, Grosbeak

Joe's Little Blue Books—Grammar

Pictured here are some of Joe's "Little Blue Books" that had their heyday in the 1920s and 1930s and sold for a nickel. The Little Blue Books were a series of small, staple-bound books that reprinted virtually all of the classics as well as general knowledge in a variety of subjects. They were designed to "bring education to the masses" and "strike a blow" for the freedom of the human mind. That philosophy appealed to Joe, and the books were cheap and could easily fit into your back pocket (three and a half inches by five inches)

Joe's Little Blue Books—Spelling

Joe's collection of Little Blue Books shows a great desire to learn about the English language and overcome his lack of education.

Riding the Rails

Joe at left, posing on a boxcar. The 1930s were hard times for all Americans, but for thousands of American teenagers, times were really tough "on the bum"—walking, hitch-hiking, hopping freight trains—"riding the rails" on the Milwaukee Road, Great Northern, Santa Fe, or Southern. Joe's hobo years riding the rails were frightening and often painful. Infamous railroad detectives were armed with guns and clubs and they used them frequently. Joe was hit more than once by the yard bulls and he recalled jumping into a boxcar one day as a bullet hit the wall just a foot from his head.

Joe, 1939

"... people are forever changed by the traumas of their youth ..."—Sigmund Freud

CCC Camp, Isabella, Minnesota, 1940

CCC Camp, 1940

Joe enlisted in the Civilian Conservation Corps on January 10, 1940 for the first of three six-month terms and was assigned to Isabella, Minnesota, located within the Superior National Forest in the remote Boundary Waters Area in Lake County. It was called the "Superior Roadless Area" at the time, and in 1940 Isabella was about as remote and isolated as you could get in the Upper Midwest.

Baptism Camp, Company 3703, F-54, Isabella, Minnesota

Joe was assigned to Company 3703, F-54. His serial number was CC7-272557, and his discharge paper dated June 25, 1941, listed him with "blue eyes, brown hair, medium complexion, five-feet six-inches tall, 120 pounds."

Joe and Buddies at CCC Camp

Joe is on the left. Minnesota had 148 CCC camps with 77,000 enrollees during the life of the program from 1933 to 1942. The Chippewa National Forest had twenty-three camps, and the Superior National Forest had thirty.

Isabella CCC Camp

Joe's pictures from Isabella show Army-style wooden barracks with a couple dozen men assigned to double-decked wooden bunks along each side of the one-story barracks.

Retreat, CCC Camp, 1940

Following reveille at 6:00 a.m., the troops would fall out at 6:30 in front of the flagpole and stand at attention while the flag was raised. At 7:00 they would march in step to the mess hall for breakfast and then back to the barracks for 7:45 inspection, followed by work duty in the wilderness from 8:00 to 5:00 and retreat in the evening before supper.

Guitar players, Isabella CCC Camp, 1940

Joe learned to play the guitar while riding the rails around the country from 1936 to 1940. At night Joe played his guitar and harmonica, listened to stories from his buddies and told his own, composed poems and sad love songs for everyone's amusement, and read a variety of books and magazines.

Work detail, Isabella CCC Camp, 1940

Work detail, Joe is pictured at left, with the axe. Joe's eighteen months in CCC camp were the happiest of his life up to that time, and he was putting money in the bank each month.

Remote forest camp, 1940

Joe genuinely liked the wilderness of the CCC program and its military camaraderie, even though strict military discipline threatened KP or even "dishonorable discharge," and Joe often pushed the limit when a "leader" tried to "lord himself" over Joe or one of his buddies.

Joe's buddies, CCC Camp, 1940

Very few of the men in Joe's company had even a year of high school and fewer still had any work experience beyond odd jobs, so Joe fit right in, even with his lack of formal education which he made up with his esoteric library studies on the road. And with eight years of hard independent farm work behind him as experience, plus what he had learned traveling around the country, Joe soon found that small as he was—five feet six and 120 pounds—he could wield an axe or saw better than most of his CCC camp buddies.

Joe Haan, 1940, CCC Camp 3703, Isabella, Minnesota

Sis, 1930, Faribault High School

Sis was very fortunate in being selected to live with Reverend Pinkham and his family at the St. James School for Boys in Faribault. The Pinkhams instilled a love of history in Sis and insisted that she complete high school and teacher's college.

Kenny and Sis, Minneapolis, 1934

Kenny proved to be a stalwart older brother who provided moral and financial support to the younger Haan children.

Sis and future husband Leonard Quist, 1934

Here Sis is pictured near Loring Park in Minneapolis with her future husband, Leonard Quist, who worked as a surveyor for the state highway department.

Rose Marie Haan ("Sis") Millersburg, 1934

Sis in Millersburg, 1934

Here Sis is pictured in Millersburg near her school in 1934

Millersburg Schoolhouse, 1935

Millersburg Schoolhouse, 1935. Sis and her class are pictured here at the end of the 1935 school year

"Sis" & husband Leonard 1935

Joe on bicycle in St. Paul, 1937

Joe would return to St. Paul as he crisscrossed the country riding the rails in the late 1930s.

Kenny, Ferris, Sis, Bub, and Joe in St. Paul, 1937

Here Joe is pictured with his sisters when he breezed through St. Paul in 1937.

Joe, Bub, and Ferris, 1937

Joe is pictured with Bub and Ferris in St. Paul in 1937.

Joe in St. Paul in 1939 just before going into CCC camp.

Joe and his nephew David Mahmood, 1941

Joe received his Honorable Discharge from the CCC program on June 25, 1941, and returned to St. Paul to see Bub, Sis, and Kenny. By this time, Bub and Sis were married and had started their families.

Joe 1942, Camp Chaffee, Arkansas

Joe enlisted in the Army shortly after Pearl Harbor and was transferred to Camp Chaffee, Arkansas, after basic training at Fort Snelling. Joe loved Arkansas and had his first chance to explore Indian artifacts with Native American Indians he met near the Army Post.

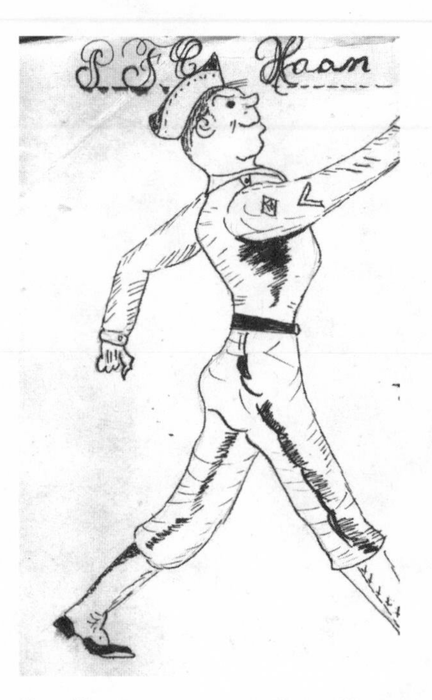

Pfc Joe Haan, cartoon drawing, 1942

Joe loved to draw and created this cartoon of a proud, stepping-out soldier named Pfc Haan.

Joe (on left) 1942, Fort Sill, Oklahoma

Joe was assigned to the 18th Field Artillery School at Fort Sill where he trained on the 105 mm howitzer that replaced old World War I French "75s."

Joe (in center) 1942, Oklahoma

Joe said he always liked Oklahoma because the people were so friendly and down-to-earth.

Joe (on left) 1942, Camp Hood, near Killeen, Texas

In August 1942, Joe was assigned to Company "A," 706th Tank Destroyer Battalion at Camp Hood, near Killeen, Texas.

Joe with machine gun, 1942

Here Joe poses with a machine gun while assigned to Company "A," 706th Tank Destroyer Battalion at Camp Hood, Texas.

Joe 1942 anti-tank unit

Joe (on left) with three of his buddies from Company "A," 706th Tank Destroyer Battalion at Camp Hood, Texas.

Joe's father, Dan McCann, 1942

One of the few surviving photos of Joe's father, Daniel F. Haan, taken in Northfield at Sis' home when Joe and Danny were home on furlough in 1942.

Sis, Joe, Danny, and Dan McCann, in Northfield 1942

In 1942, Kenny was stationed in Iceland and this reunion was the last time the family would be together with their father before his death the following year.

Joe, Bub, Dan McCann, Sis, and Danny—Northfield 1942

Joe was a buck private with no stripes on his sleeve, and Danny was a two-stripe corporal.

First Lieutenant Kenny Haan, 0-1799635

Captain Kenny Haan, 1950, Korean War

Kenny worked his way through high school and Macalester College and attended Harvard University after the war. He served in counterintelligence in Iceland during World War II and was recalled to active duty as a captain during the Korean War. Kenny retired from the Army Reserve as a lieutenant colonel.

Joe's WW II Army insignias

Pictured here are Joe's insignias from the Yankee Division and Company "A," 706th Tank Destroyer Battalion. Joe remained with the Yankee Division when he was transferred to the 101st Infantry Regiment in December 1944, just before the Battle of the Bulge.

Corporal Friedrich Hofmann (on left) and comrades

"Here I was thousands of miles from home on foreign soil, sharing this hole with a dead man, this creature I had been indoctrinated to hate. Somehow, I had never quite pictured the enemy as totally human. Gradually it became clear to me that here was a victim of circumstance like myself."—Private Joe Haan, Alsace-Lorraine, France, October 1944—thoughts while sharing a foxhole with the corpse of Friedrich Hofmann for three days while dug in at the front lines, unable to move in any direction.

Battle-weary Yankee Division Soldiers

Battle of the Bulge, December 1944 (Reprinted by permission, Yankee Division Veteran's Association, "The History of the Yankee Division" http://www.ydva.org/)

Friedrich Hofmann's identity papers

Friedrich Hofmann's papers indicate he was recently reassigned to the Western front in Alsace-Lorraine, France, to face Patton's advancing army.

Photo of young girl in Friedrich Hofmann's wallet

Picture of a young girl, most likely Friedrich Hofmann's sister or girlfriend.

Photo of young soldier in Friedrich Hofmann's wallet

Picture of an unknown youthful German soldier, found with Friedrich Hofmann's identity papers.

Photo of German officers in Friedrich Hofmann's wallet

Picture of unidentified German officers, found with Friedrich Hofmann's identity papers.

URLAUBER 50g R BROT | URLAUBER 50g R BROT | URLAUBER 50g R BROT | URLAUBER 50g R BROT | URLAUBER T 25g Nährmittel

URLAUBER 10g BROT (×5)

1 Tag

Reichskarte für Urlauber

Gültig im deutschen Reichsgebiet

Diese Karte enthält Einzelabschnitte über insgesamt:
350 g Brot, davon
200 g R-Brot
50 g Fleisch
30 g Butter
25 g Nährmittel

Ausgabestelle EA:

Name: ....

Wohnort: ....

Straße: ....

Abtrennen der Einzelabschnitte nur durch Kleinverteiler, Gaststätten usw.

Ohne Namenseintragung ungültig!
Nicht übertragbar!
Sorgfältig aufbewahren!

URLAUBER 50g BROT | URLAUBER 50g BROT | URLAUBER 10g Butter | URLAUBER 10g Butter | URLAUBER 5g Butter | URLAUBER 5g Butter

Ration card in Friedrich Hofmann's wallet

Gusen Concentration Camp, Austria, May 1945

Pictured here is a burial detail at the Gusen Concentration Camp in Austria shortly before its liberation by Joe's unit in May 1945.

Gusen Concentration Camp, Austria

Truckload of emaciated bodies at Gusen Concentration Camp, Austria, May 1945.

Joe and Helen, 1946

Joe and Helen, back in Minnesota, shortly after their marriage in early 1946.

Gulf of Mexico, 1949

During the summer of 1949, Sis and the Quist family drove from Minnesota to Houston, Texas, to see Joe, Helen, and the boys. Pictured here (L-R) are Wayne, Sis (holding James), Paul, Joe (with fishing rod), Jack, and Leonard.

Lunch on the Gulf of Mexico, 1949

Pictured left to right—Paul, Sis, Helen (holding James), Joe (with watermelon), Jack, and Wayne.

Joe, Goose Hunt, 1950

Joe was an avid hunter and took advantage of Houston's proximity to the central flyway for migrating North American waterfowl.

Joe Haan, 1950

Joe's taxidermy lab on Landor Lane in Houston.

James, Joe, and Jack, 1958
James and Jack are pictured with Joe and some of his Native American artifacts.

Joe with large black drum fish, 1959
Joe's motto was "I bring 'em back to life."

Joe's sons, Jack and James, 1959

Joe's stuffed bird collection, 1959

Antietam Battlefield, 1974

Wayne Quist, Joe, and Tim Carlson are pictured at Burnside's Bridge at the Antietam Battlefield in Maryland in 1974.

Joe at the Virginia battlefields, 1974. Fredericksburg and Spotsylvania National Military Park, Virginia

Joe Haan & Denny Carlson 1976

Joe with one of his many eccentric friends and ironworking buddies.

Joe, 1985

" . . . bring 'em back to life."

Joe, 1990

Pondering the future . . . "In the vastness of the sea of space, time is lost in an endless race."

Acknowledgments

This book was made possible through the many contributions of Joe's relatives and friends—James Haan for preserving Joe's poetry, artwork, war materials, pictures, and many mementos; Peter and Wendy Haan for collecting Kenny's letters and pictures; Paul Quist and David Mahmood for their support and vivid memories; Tim Carlson for his reminiscences, commentary, and devoted efforts throughout the summer and fall of 2009; Rose Reiter for laboriously translating the diary of Gerrit Niehaus, a German soldier Joe encountered in France during the late fall of 1944—a special thanks to all of you, for without each of your efforts and contributions, this book would not have been possible.

We also wish to acknowledge and thank many other people and organizations for their support and permission to quote from published materials—Harvey and Maxine Ronglien for permission to quote from *A Boy from C-11: Case #9164,* to print photos from the State School Orphanage Museum in Owatonna, Minnesota, and for their friendly and informative advice; Minnesota Historical Society for permission to quote from Michael Sanchelli's reminiscences of CCC camp in the "Greatest Generation CCC Camp 1940–41;" Margaret Haapoja and *Forest Magazine* for permission to quote information on life in CCC camp (August 2009); Al Kussmaul for permission to quote from *Life on the Bum in the 1930s;* Telegraph Media Group for permission to quote "Cavemen May Have Used Language," 20 October 2007; brave and daring ironworkers of Houston Local 84, *Ironworker* magazine, and Tom Dilberger for information on Joe's union membership and the ironworking trade; a special thanks to all veterans of World War II and to the veterans of Battery A, 952nd Field Artillery Battalion, the 26th Infantry Division (Yankee Division) Veteran's Association, and the veterans of the 101st Infantry Regiment; and to the essayists and authors of the wonderful old essays and poems, now in the public domain, that meant so much to Joe and that he so often recited—Rupert Brooke, Grant Allen, Langdon Smith, Edwin Arlington Robinson, Clarence Darrow, Theodore O'Hara, Titus Lucretius Carus—Joe would be overjoyed to know their words still resound with meaning.

Appendix

1. Haan Family Genealogy

Children of Daniel Frederick Haan and Marie Mamie Hlavac

HAROLD CARMODY
born December 20, 1908
date of death unknown
(father Edward W. Carmody)

DANIEL A. HAAN
born September 6, 1909
died July 24, 1969, in Vancouver, Washington

KENNETH W. HAAN
born June 3, 1911
died May 23, 1992, in St. Paul, Minnesota

ROSE MARIE HAAN ("SIS")
born April 8, 1913
died April 9, 1959, in Dundas, Minnesota

CECILIA FRANCES HAAN ("BUB")
born June 3, 1915
died 1985 in Seattle, Washington

JOSEPH BERNARD HAAN
born February 26, 1918
died January 7, 1992, in Houston

Addresses of Haan Children (1913–1930)

544 Rice St., St. Paul	1918–1923
Gaultier near Edmund	1923–1925
2013 Hudson Road	Summer 1925
1786 E. Minnehaha, St. Paul	September 1925
71 Edmund, St. Paul	October 1925–1926
345 Brimhall Avenue, St. Paul	1926
(Henry J. Borchers—Rose Marie's temporary home)	
670 Marshall Avenue, St. Paul	1926–1927
(Protestant Orphan Asylum)	
Owatonna, Minnesota	1927–1930
(Owatonna State School Orphanage)	

Joe's Father—Daniel Frederick Haan

Born Groningen, Midwolda Province, Nieuwolda,
The Netherlands, September 2, 1877
Died St. Paul, September 1943
Buried Oak Hill Cemetery, 243 16th Ave N., South St Paul,
MN 55075 (651-451-6161)

Joe's Mother—Marie Mamie Hlavac (Hadley) Carmody Haan

Marie Mamie Hlavac (Hadley) Haan (first husband was Edward W. Carmody)
Born in Iowa 1880, died St. Paul, MN, September 22, 1925, (three sisters, two brothers)
Residence at time of death: 1786 E. Minnehaha, St.Paul, MN
Funeral services held at St. Stanislaus Church, Kessler & McGuire Funeral Chapel, 733 West 7th Street, St. Paul, MN
Buried in Calvary Cemetery (651-488-8866), 763 Front St., St. Paul, MN (no marker)

Joe's Maternal Relatives

Aunt Sadie, Aunt Rose, Aunt Florence (Anna Walters), Aunt Maude (Hadley), Uncle Joe, Uncle Charlie

Joe Hadley (Maude), maternal uncle, 363 Harrison, South St. Paul, MN

Albert Hadley (Anna), maternal uncle, 646 Pleasant Avenue, St. Paul, MN

Mrs. Frances Sadie Kjeldsen (Charles) maternal aunt (sweet and kind "Aunt Sadie") 656 Pleasant Avenue, St. Paul, MN

Mrs. Arthur G. Walters (Anna Florence), maternal aunt (died March 3, 1939) 3918 Grand Avenue, Minneapolis, MN
Owned two four-family apartments, raised Harold Carmody, Joe's half-brother

Lawrence & Dorothy Poszal (maternal aunt) Mrs. C. R. Pozel (Rose) 1587 Brooklin Avenue, St. Paul, MN

HLAVAC* Monument (Calvary Cemetery, St. Paul, MN, Section 38, Block 28, Lot 2):

Rose Hlavac (Joe's grandmother)
b. 1852 d. June 15, 1900

Joseph Hlavac (Joe's grandfather)
b. 1846 d. April 26, 1916

Michael (Mathias) Hlavac (Marie's brother)
b. 1875 d. 1896

Anna Florence Walters (Marie's sister, no marker)
d. 1939

Charles Kjeldsen (Aunt Sadie's husband)
b. 1883 d. 1915

Marie Mamie Hlavac Haan (Joe's mother)
b. 1880 d. September 22, 1925 (on right of Charles, no marker)
**Albert and Joseph Hlavac, Marie Hlavac's brothers, changed their last name to Hadley during World War I. "Hlavac" comes from the Czech word for "head" (hlava), which is often a nickname for an important person or someone with a large head.*

HADLEY Monument (Calvary Cemetery, St. Paul, MN, Section 72, Block 26, Lot 15):

Albert Hadley (Marie's brother) lot owner
b. 1881 d. 1957

Anna Hadley (Wife of Albert)
b. 1884 d. 1960

Joseph A. Hadley (Marie's brother) wife Maude
(Sgt Co. C, 2nd Field Signal Btn, WW I)
b. 1889 d. 1954

Frances S. Kjeldsen (Aunt Sadie, Marie's sister)
b. 1886 d. 1969

Charles Kjeldsen (Aunt Sadie's son)
b. 1912 d. 1994

Marie M. Kjeldsen (Charles' wife)
b. 1910 d.?

Harold Carmody (Joe's half-brother)
buried in Calvary Cemetery, St. Paul, MN, Section 49, Block13, Lot 2).

Family of Daniel Frederick Haan in Holland

Father Derek Haan, lived in Eveneens in northern Netherlands

Rose Anna Haan (mother of Daniel F. Haan)

Brothers & Sisters of Daniel F. Haan

Geziena Haan

Alida Bertha Haan Doewes
Born 1870—Midwolda, Scheemda, Groningen, Netherlands
Died 12 February 1934 (Age 64)—Scheemda, Groningen, Netherlands
Married Albert Doewes, born 1872 in Duurkenakker, Muntendam, Groningen, Netherlands, and died September 6, 1928, (Age 56) in Groningen, Netherlands

Bertha Haan Drevel

Frederick Haan, moved to USA (6042 Dorchester Ave, Chicago, never married)

Bouko (Bouka) Haan (married Klasiena Rentema) died in Rendema

Henderikus (died as a child), Eveneems and Waarmede

Rienko Haan (married Efrietje Hamster)—oldest brother, died March 17, 1919, age 57
Wife Efrietje Hamster, died September 28, 1928
Daughter died January 7, 1917
Son, Fritz Haan, born November 5, 1897, lived on farm in Nieuwolda:

> Fritz married Effie Dallinga on June 15, 1921, (Effie's father was Simon Dirks); Fritz & Effie had three children:
>
> > Son, Rienko Haan, born 1923; Son, Dr. Peter Haan, doctor, born 1926; Son, Simon Dirks, born 1936, address in 1947 for Fritz Haan was Nieuwolda B-6, the Netherlands

Fritz Leep was a cousin of Daniel Frederick Haan; moved to Chicago in 1940, not heard from.

2. Joe's Little Blue Books

Spelling and grammar:

Spelling Self Taught by Lloyd E. Smith. Little Blue Books No. 681 Edited by E. Haldeman-Julius.

Grammar Self Taught by Lloyd E. Smith. Little Blue Books No. 682 Edited by E. Haldeman-Julius.

Punctuation Self Taught by Lloyd E. Smith. Little Blue Books No. 683 Edited by E. Haldeman-Julius.

A Book of Useful Phrases, selected and arranged by Lloyd E. Smith. Little Blue Books No. 734 Edited by E. Haldeman-Julius.

How to Improve Your Vocabulary by Lloyd E. Smith. Little Blue Books No. 821 Edited by E. Haldeman-Julius. (very used, taped, worn, Joe's notes).

Curiosities of the English Language by Lloyd E. Smith. Little Blue Books No. 1350 Edited by E. Haldeman-Julius.

Book of Striking Similes, selected and arranged after a new and practical system, by Heinz Norden. Little Blue Books No. 1354 Edited by E. Haldeman-Julius.

Prepositions and How to Use Them by Lloyd E. Smith. Little Blue Books No. 1367 Edited by E. Haldeman-Julius.

Clarence Darrow's debates and essays:

Are We Machines: Is Life Mechanical or Is It Something Else? A Debate between Clarence Darrow and Will Durant. Little Blue Books No. 509 Edited by E. Haldeman-Julius.

Can the Individual Control His Conduct? Is Man a 'Free Agent' or Is He the Slave of His Biological Equipment? A Debate between Clarence Darrow and Dr. Thomas V. Smith. Little Blue Books No. 843 Edited by E. Haldeman-Julius.

Is the Human Race Getting Anywhere? A Debate between Frederick Starr and Clarence Darrow. Little Blue Books No. 911 Edited by E. Haldeman-Julius.

The Skeleton in the Closet by Clarence Darrow. Little Blue Books No. 933 Edited by E. Haldeman-Julius.

The Ordeal of Prohibition by Clarence Darrow. Little Blue Books No. 974 Edited by E. Haldeman-Julius.

Facing Life Fearlessly: The Pessimistic versus the Optimistic View of Life by Clarence Darrow. Little Blue Books No. 1329 Edited by E. Haldeman-Julius.

Is the U.S. Immigration Law Beneficial? A Debate between Clarence Darrow vs. Lothrop Stoddard. Little Blue Books No. 1423 Edited by E. Haldeman-Julius.

Environment vs. Heredity. A Debate between Clarence Darrow and Albert Edward Wiggam (reported by George G. Whitehead). Little Blue Books No. 1581 Edited by E. Haldeman-Julius.

Other:

The Structure of the Earth by Carroll Lane Fenton. Little Blue Books No. 555 Edited by E. Haldeman-Julius.

Man's Debt to the Sun by Maynard Shipley. Little Blue Books No. 808 Edited by E. Haldeman-Julius.

Sayings of a Sourdough by William Sulzer. Little Blue Books No. 1757 Edited by E. Haldeman-Julius.

Historic Crimes and Criminals by Charles J. Finger. Little Blue Books No. 149 Edited by E. Haldeman-Julius.

Great Pirates by Charles J. Finger. Little Blue Books No. 558 Edited by E. Haldeman-Julius.

In one of his notebooks, Joe made the following notes and listed six books that were important to his self-education:

1. *The Outline of History* by HG Wells has enlightened me.
2. *The Story of Mankind* by Hendrik Willem Van Loon has added fuel to the fire.
3. *The Age of Reason* by Thomas Paine contributed much to my way of thinking.
4. *Civilization Past & Present* by Wallbank & Taylor has given me a panoramic view of man's known past.
5. *Infidels and Heretics: an Agnostic's Anthology* by Clarence Darrow provided sound reasoning and good humor.
6. *The Ruins and the Law of Nature* by CF Volney, published in England, is a wonderful publication that should be more widely circulated and made required reading for all seminary students.

3. XOTÄNEF Caveman Language

By Zulor X. Zep, alias Joe Haan

In an effort to determine how Neanderthal cavemen might have communicated tens of thousands of years ago, I composed a language called XOTÄNEF. It attempted to transcribe the sounds of cavemen, as I imagined them, into the Roman alphabet. I developed the language over a period of several years. It consists of a thirty-two-letter alphabet and working vocabulary, along with a two-part description of the grammar, twenty-five-page pronunciation guide, and accentuation rules. It is clear that Neanderthal man had the ability to use sophisticated language to communicate. XOTÄNEF was my attempt to show how these early primitive people communicated with each other tens of thousands of years ago.

XOTÄNEF Alphabet

Letters		Names	Pronunciation
1.	Ä	ÄTÄ	Ä ′ TÄ
2.	B	BËTÄ	BĀ ′ TÄ
3.	C	CÓTÄ	KŌ ′ TÄ
4.	CH	CHÏTÄ	CHĒ ′ TÄ
5.	D	DÜTÄ	DŌŌ ′ TÄ
6.	Ë	ËTÄ	Ā ′ TÄ
7.	F	FÄTÄ	FÄ ′ TÄ
8.	G	GÓTÄ	GŌ ′ TÄ
9.	H	HÜTÄ	HŌŌ ′ TÄ
10.	Ï	ÏÜTÄ	Ē ′ TÄ
11.	J	JËTÄ	JĀ ′ TÄ
12.	K	KÄTÄ	KÄ ′ TÄ
13.	KH	KHÓTÄ	KHO ′ TÄ
14.	L	LÜTÄ	LŌŌ ′ TÄ
15.	M	MÏTÄ	MĒ ′ TÄ

16.	N	NËTÄ	NĀ ' TÄ
17.	O	ÓTÄ	Ō ' TÄ
18.	P	PÄTÄ	PÄ ' TÄ
19.	Q	QÜTÄ	KWŌŌ ' TÄ
20.	R	RÏTÄ	RĒ ' TÄ
21.	S	SËTÄ	SĀ ' TÄ
22.	SH	SHÓTÄ	SHO ' TÄ
23.	T	TÄTÄ	TÄ ' TÄ
24.	TH	THÜTÄ	THŌŌ ' TÄ
25.	ȚH	ȚHÏTÄ	ȚHĒ ' TÄ
26.	Ü	ÜTA	ŌŌ ' TÄ
27.	V	VËTÄ	VĀ ' TÄ
28.	W	WÓTÄ	WŌ ' TÄ
29.	X	XÄTÄ	ZHÄ ' TÄ
30.	X	XÏTÄ	KSĒ ' TÄ
31.	Y	YÜTÄ	YŌŌ ' TÄ
32.	Z	ZËTÄ	Z Ä ' TÄ

The Rules of XOTÄNEF Grammar—Summary

Part I:
The Forming of the Plural to XOTÄNEF Nouns (three pages).

In the XOTÄNEF language, the plural of nouns is formed by one of three methods, all of which are similar. The three methods are accomplished by adding either the letters "N," "EN," or "TEN." When a noun in XOTÄNEF ends in the letter "N," an extra letter is typically added, which is the letter "T," in order to form the plural. The letters "EN" are added in most cases at the end of the word to make it plural. The "EN" method of plural formation is done when the noun ends in every consonant of the alphabet except the letter "N." The third type of plural in XOTÄNEF is the kind in which the singular noun ends in a vowel, and simply adds the letter "N" to form the plural. It should be noted that words ending in the letter "M" are not affected by the "TEN" rule, and receive their plural simply by adding the letters "EN" to the end of the word.

Part II: The Definite and Indefinite Articles, "KÄ" (the) and "O" (a or an) (three pages).

The word for the definite article "the" in XOTÄNEF is "KÄ." However, there is a slight change when "KÄ" comes before a word beginning with the letter "A," in which case the word "KÄ" adds the letter "T" and becomes "KÄT." There is one more rule concerning "KÄ," and that is in the formation of plural nouns. The word "KÄ" adds the letter "N" before all plural nouns to become the word "KÄN." The word "O" means "a" or "an" in XOTÄNEF and adds the letter "T" as does "KÄ," when it precedes a word beginning with the letter "O."

Pronunciation of the XOTÄNEF Alphabet (25 pages)—Summary.

This section summarizes the pronunciation of each of the thirty-two letters in the XOTÄNEF alphabet.

Rules of Accentuation of the XOTÄNEF Language (seven pages).

XOTÄNEF uses accent marks over the syllables of its words to indicate where the stress is to be placed on the word. However, accent marks are not used on all words, and not even on most words. Accent marks are predominantly used on words of three or more syllables, and on words of two syllables that are to be stressed upon the last syllable. Accent marks are not only placed over the syllable to be stressed, but also over the letter itself that should be stressed. There are no accent marks placed on words of one syllable.

On words of two syllables the only times there are accent marks on a word is when the word is accentuated on the last syllable. Some three-syllable words carry accent marks over the stressed syllable and some do not. In rare cases, some words may contain two accent marks in the word, but the syllable to be stressed the most is always the one with the double accent mark. The only word in XOTÄNEF like this is "KÄÄDÄKRÊNŚHÏN."

Bibliography

752nd Field Artillery Battalion. History, Verdun, France, 15 August 1945. Unpublished unit history included with Joe Haan's poems and notebooks in author's collection at Millersburg Schoolhouse Museum, Millersburg, Minnesota.

Clement, Priscilla Ferguson. "With Wise and Benevolent Purpose: Poor Children and the State Public School at Owatonna, 1885—1915." Minnesota History (Spring 1984). http://collections.mnhs.org/MNHistoryMagazine/articles/49/v49i01p002-013.pdf (accessed August 2010).

Dilberger, J. Thomas. Book # 873894, Local 361 (Retiree). "Blacks and High Steel: What affirmative action did to the trade." *The Ironworker,* June 2006.

Haan Family Records. Files #7993, #7994, #7995. Minnesota History Center. Minnesota State Historical Society Archives. Owatonna State School Records. St. Paul, Minnesota.

Haan, Joe. Unpublished Army records, poems, and notebooks in author's collection.

Haapoja, Margaret A. "Back to Work." Forest Magazine, Summer 2009. http://www.fseee.org/forestmag/1103haap.shtml (accessed August 2010).

Haahr, James C., *The Command is Forward: The 101st Infantry in Lorraine,* Xlibris, 2003.

Holmes, Lee. "Lucretius—On the Nature of Things." Atheist Foundation of Australia, Inc. http://www.atheistfoundation.org.au/lucretius.htm (accessed August 2010).

Holt, Dean. *American Military Cemeteries: A Comprehensive Illustrated Guide to the Hallowed Grounds of the United States, Including Cemeteries Overseas.* Jefferson, NC: McFarland & Co., 1992.

Ingersoll, Robert Green. *Great Speeches of Col. R. G. Ingersoll.* Chicago: Rhodes & McClure, 1895.

Johnson, Rossiter. "Martial Epitaphs." *The Century,* a Popular Quarterly Vol. 40, No.1 (May 1890): 156–57.

Kussmaul, Allen. *Life on the Bum in the Early 1930s.* AuthorHouse, 2009.

Linder, Douglas. "Clarence Seward Darrow, 1857–1938." University of Missouri-Kansas City (UMKC) School of Law. http://www.law.umkc.edu/faculty/projects/ftrials/Darrow.htm (accessed August 2010).

Lounsbury, Thomas R., ed. *Yale Book of American Verse.* 1912. http://bartleby.com/102/147.html (accessed August 2010).

O'Hara, Theodore. "Bivouac of the Dead." United States Government, Department of Veteran Affairs (March 2009). http://www.cem.va.gov/hist/BODpoem.asp (accessed August 2010).

Office of the Quartermaster General. Annual Reports of the War Department, 1822–1907. National Archives and Records Administration. RG 92, Microfilm (M997).

Office of the Quartermaster General. Roll of Honor. 25 vols. Washington, DC: Government Printing Office, 1868–71. Baltimore: Genealogical Publishing Co., 1994.

Rasenberger, Jim. *High Steel: The Daring Men Who Built the World's Greatest Skyline.* New York, NY: HarperCollins Publishers, Inc., 2004.

Rittenhouse, Jessie B., ed. *Little Book of American Poets: 1787–1900.* Cambridge: Riverside Press, 1915.

Ronglien, Harvey. *A Boy from C-11: Case #9164.* Minnesota: Graham Megyeri Books, 2006.

Ronglien, Harvey. Interviews with the author, May, October, 2009.

Sanchelli, Michael T. *The Greatest Generation.* Minnesota Historical Society, St. Paul, Minnesota (October 2006). http://people.mnhs.org/mgg/story.cfm?storyid=378&bhcp=1 (accessed August 2010).

Wilson, Robert Burns. "Theodore O'Hara." *The Century,* a Popular Quarterly, Vol. 40, No.1 (May 1890): 106–10.

Yankee Division. "26th Infantry Division —World War II." http://yd-info.net/page2/index.html#Bulge (accessed August 2010).

Index

JBH refers to Joe Haan. His poems are collected under "Haan, Joe, poems." Unattributed poems elsewhere are by Joe Haan. Photographs have page numbers in *italics.*

A

Abraham, 300
Adventure stories/reminiscences, 218–21
Alaska, 203, 215, 303, 312
Allah, 278
Allen, Grant, 14–15
Allosaurus, 283
Alsace-Lorraine, France, 151, 154, 161, *358–59*
Apostate, 300
Ardennes Forest, Luxembourg, 172–73, 175–77
Ardennes Offensive, 171–72, 175–76
Army General Classification Test (AGCT), 136n
Army service
  advancing through France, 152–57
  arrival in England, 146–49
  arrival in France, 149–52
  basic training, stateside assignments, 134–45
  Battle of the Bulge, 5, 129–30, 169–71, 173–78
  at Bey-sur-Seille, France, 159–61
  Bronze Star Medal for Valor, 23, 130–31, 133, 173–74, 178–81, 184, 196
  Camp Chaffee, Arkansas, *352*
  Camp Hood, Texas, *354–55*
  Christmas night patrol, 173–74, 179–81
  discharge records, 130–31
  Drive to the Rhine, 182–83
Army service *(continued)*
  enemies *seen* as human, 166–67
  equipment, supplies carried, 149
  Fort Sill, Oklahoma, *353*
  in foxhole with dead German, 23, 133, 162, 164–68, 195, *358*
  gasoline supplies, lack of, 152–53
  German surrender, World War II, 185
  at Gramercy, France, 157–60
  at Gusen Concentration Camp, 185
  Honorable Discharge, 189, 201
  insignias, *358*
  insubordination, fighting problems, 131–32, 136, 171, 196
  in 101st Infantry, 5, 130, 168–70, 173–85, 196–97, *358*
  on outpost guard duty, 156–60
  in Patton's Third Army, 23, 129–32, 148, 150–51, 169–70, 193
  questioning god, 161
  summary, letter to Kenny, 186–89
  survivor guilt, 222 wages, 134
Arsdorf, Luxembourg, 169, 173, 176, 179, 196
Artifact collections, 11–12, 186, 204, *366*
Artillery. *See* 752nd Field Artillery Battalion
Astralagus (Milk-Vetch), 71
Astronomy, star navigation
  Alpha Centauri, 310
  Andromeda, 310
  books from Rose, 82
  Jupiter, 310
  lunar calendar creation, 69
  Mars, 310
  Milky Way, 310–11

Astronomy, star navigation *(continued)*
"On the Nature of Things" (Lucretius), 122
nova, xii, 248, 253
Pleiades, 310
"Salute to the Stars," 243
sleep under stars, 64
spiral nebula, 255
star knowledge and navigation, 206
trip through the Universe with Paul Quist, 309–12
Venus, 310
Auruch bull, 17
Austria, 177, 184–85, 189, 198–99, *362*
Axis Sally, 146

B

Barr, Joe, 221
Bastogne, Belgium, 172, 175, 178–79, 181, 196
Battle of the Bulge, 5, 129–30, 169–71, 173–78
Bayonets, 102, 149, 189, 204, 305
Beer, homemade German, 62, 85
Belgium. *See* Bastogne, Belgium; Battle of the Bulge
Bible study, 57–58
Bird drawings, 329–35
"The Bivouac of the Dead" (O'Hara), 103–7
Black neighborhood, Houston house in, 306–8
"Blasphemy" (Quist), 300
Blattaria (cockroaches), 241, 282
Blitzkrieg tactics, 193
Blitzkrieg tactics, use of, 150–51
Boar, European wild, 172–73
Bolshevik Revolution, 98–99 A
Boy from C-11 (Ronglien), 53, 83–84
Brahmin, 278–79
Brokaw, Tom, 299
Bronze Star Medal for Valor, 23, 130–31, 133, 173–74, 178–81, 184, 196
Brooke, Rupert, 11–13
Bruno, Giordano, 271
Buddha, 278–79
Buffalo Bayou, 219–20
Burgess, Thornton W., 64

C

Calvary Cemetery, 37, 375–77
Camp Bowie, Texas, 137, 144–45
Camp Chaffee, Arkansas, 134
Camp Hood, Texas, 135–36
Camp Maxey, Texas, 138, 140–41
Camp McCoy, Wisconsin, 130, 189, 201
Camp Miles Standish, Massachusetts, 145
Cannons, 135, 159, 166, 192, 286
Caradoc drift, 16
Carduus marianus (milk thistle), 70–72
Carleton College, 56
Carlson, Denny, *369*
Carlson, Tim, 4, 96–97, 218–21, 225, 303–4, *368*
Carmody, Harold (half-brother), 32, 41, 50, 373
Carmody, Marie Mamie Hlavac. *See* Haan, Marie Mamie Hlavac (Hadley) Carmody
CCC (Civilian Conservation Corps)
camp, Isabella, MN, *339–43*
camp life description, 116–18, 120
enlistment in, 1940, 12, 113
and forest fires, 117
and *Forest Magazine,* 115–17
history and purpose, 114–15
JBH joined, 121
JBH's aptness for, 114, 118–19
and JBH's pneumonia, 117
Laager, Lowell, 116–17
Marshall, George C., 115
military-style discipline, 118, 120
shift of purpose toward defense, 123
survival of the fittest, 121
Chimpanzee-orangutan, 273
Chimpanzee-orangutans, 9
Choctaw Indians, 2, 135, 202–3
Chimpanzee-orangutan *(continued)*
Christ, Jesus, 7, 278–79, 300
Christian Communion, 9–10, 57–58
Christmas donations to homeless, Houston, 207, 294
Civil War area explorations, studies, 8, 57, 101–7, 221–22, 225–29, 294–95, *368*

Civilian Conservation Corps (CCC). *See* CCC
Cobb Creek, 65–66, 69, 85, 294, *327*
Cockroaches (*blattaria*), 241, 282
Collections / artifacts, 11–12, 186, 204, 216–17, 305, *365–67*
Combat casualties, 150, 161–62, 176, 187
Common-law marriage of parents, 35–36, 37, 42
Communion, 9–10, 57–58
Communist Party, 99
Compulsory military service, 127–28
Concentration Camps, 185, 199, *362*
Copernicus, 277
Coralline crags, 19 Court-y-Gellon, South Wales, 146
Cow-killing in Germany, 63
Cunningham, William, 47, 222–25
Curare dart, 262
Czechoslovakia, 37, 175–77, 184–86, 189, 193, 199

D

Darrow, Clarence, 100–101, 108
Darwin, Charles, 2, 24
David and Goliath, 65
Deafness. *See* Hearing problems
Democracy, 24, 99
Depression, Great, 36, 86–87
Dilberger, Tom, 208, 211–12
Dinosaurs, xiii, xvi, 216, 241–42, 258, 276, 283, 305, 310
DNA and language development, 229–31
Dodecahedron, 254
Dog attack and killing, 218–19
Dog Man, 220–21
Dominican Republic, 209, 232–35
Dos Passos, John, 99–100
Draft program (Army service), 127–28
Drawings and notes, 64–68, 329–35
Drive to the Rhine, 182–83
Drug dealers in Houston neighborhood, 306–7
Dumbo (elephant), 96–97
Dust Bowl rural migrations, 87–88

E

Earth as planet, xi, 5, 12, 122, 241–42, 261, 309–11
Eban Flood characters, 293–94
Eisenhower, Dwight D., 153, 174–75, 181, 185, 189
"Elegy Written in a Country Churchyard" (Gray), 31
Emotional scars from experiences, 3, 23, 25, 53, 86, 205
England, 129, 141, 146–48, 155, 186, 194
Europe. *See regions; specific cities*
"Evolution" (Smith), 14, 16–19, 108

F

Facing the Chair (Dos Passos), 99–100
Faribault, Minnesota, 54–57, 75–76, 82, 86, 328, 344
Farm indentureship
  alcohol, first experiences with, 84–85
  barn, *326*
  beatings and cruel treatment, 59–61, 85–86, 90
  butter story, 85–86
  farmhouse, *325*
  final day at farm, 90
  forfeiture of money, clothes due, 94
  game hunting, trapping, 65, 69
  German farmer, cruelty of, 59–63, 71, 83–86, 90
  German Orphan's Prayer, 60
  hatred for farmer, 61, 63, 74, 127
  Indian burial site excavation, 69
  isolation from State care, family, 73–77
  Joe holding pig, *328*
  laborious jobs, 61–62, 66
  living conditions, 61, 64
  schooling, lack of, 22, 61, 73, 78–79
  woodshed, *326*
Fer-de-lance, 262
"The First Idealist" (Allen), 14–15
Flood, Eben (fictional), 293–97
Forest Magazine, 115–17
Fort Sill, Oklahoma, 134
Fort Snelling, Minnesota, 130, 134

FOXP2 (language gene), 229–31
France, cities with Army presence, World War II
Bey-sur-Seille, 159–60
Brethany, 154
Chauffour, 152
Colombey, 156
Courbesseaux, 157
Courtenay, 151
Dembasle, 156
Dieuze, 169, 171
Epagne, 152
Germiny, 156
Guindercourt-aux-Ormes, 155
Haracourt, 156
Landivy, 151
Laneuville-devant-Bayon, 156
Lorey, 156
Montrevil-sur-Barse, 152
Nancy, 195
Ormes, 151
Sarreguemines, 171
St. Mere Eglise, 149
Ville-sur-Madon, 156
Frau, wife of German farmer, 60, 69, 74, 85–86
Freud, Sigmund, 24–25
Ft. Lewis, Washington, *319*
Ft. Snelling, Minnesota, 130, 134
Fubar (acronym), 226
Fulda, Germany, 184, 198

G

Galaxies, 2, 122, 163, 241–44, 247–48, 255, 310–11. *See also* Astronomy, star navigation
Galileo, 277
Game hunting, trapping, 65, 69
Gene for language, 229–31
Geology, 21, 82, 208, 241
German farmer, cruelty of, 59–63, 71, 83–86, 90. *See also* Farm indentureship
German Orphan's Prayer, 60
German surrender, World War II, 185
Germany
anti-German propaganda, 133
Ardennes Offensive, Battle of the Bulge, 170–80, 187
Germany *(continued)*
Army service (in JBH life overview), 23
cow-killing, 63
JBH wounded, 130
maps, 193, 197–99
memorabilia from, 189, 204–5
and memories of farm indentureship, 91
and Patton's Third Army, 150
rifle practice, 220
and survivor guilt, 222
U.S. declares war on, 123–24
Gettysburg, Pennsylvania, 8, 101–3, 222–24, 228
God
"Conflict of the Gods," 279
"Death of the Gods," 278
god compared to atom, 46
"In God We Trust," "Gott Mit Uns", 8–9, 87, 110, 161–62, 195
Greek gods, 24
JBH as "god's angry man," "last iconoclast," 10, 299
JBH's anger at, 57, 61, 74
JBH's questioning, xiii–xiv, 57–58, 63, 74, 78
perceived cruelty of, 57, 61
God's perceived cruelty, 57, 61
Goose hunt, *364*
Gorillas, 9, 273
"Gott Mit Uns," 87
Gott Mit Uns (German phrase), 8–9, 161–62, 195
Gramercy, France, 157–60
Gray, Thomas, 31
Great Depression, 36, 86–87
The Greatest Generation (Brokaw), 299
Great Singularity, 311–12
Greek gods, 24
Groningen, Holland, 36, 374, 377
Gunder, Iowa, 226
Gusen Concentration Camp, 185, 199, *362*
Guthrie, Woody, comparison to, 24, 304

H

Haan, Cecilia Frances "Bub" (sister)
cared for by Rose, 41
with family in Northfield, MN, *356*
4th of July visit with JBH at farm, 73, *327*
Haan children on burro, *313*
Haan family genealogy, 374
indentured from orphanage, 55
with JBH, St. Paul visit, *350*
with JBH holding pig, *328*
placed in orphanage after mother's death, 31–33, 50
at St. Joseph's Academy, *323*
Haan, Daniel A. (Danny) (brother)
at ages fifteen and twenty, *316*
Army enlistment at eighteen, 50
with family in Northfield, MN, *356*
Haan family genealogy, 373
military career, 127–29, 187
in Texas and at father's funeral, 140
with uncle after mother's death, 32–33, 41
Haan, Daniel Frederick (father) "Dan McCann"
alcoholism of, 32, 35–36, 39, 41–43
birth, 36, 374
common-law marriage to Marie, 37
death, 36, 139, 374
family visit, Northfield, MN, *355–56*
Haan family genealogy, 373
parents, siblings, 377–78
personality, salesmanship skills, 37–38
roast sold for liquor, 43, 50
visit, Rose and Cecilia, 55
Haan, Helen (Jessie) (wife)
acceptance of Joe's character, personality, 202
after Joe's death, 293
as Choctaw Indian, 2, 134–35, 202–3
pictured with Joe, *363*
visit, Julia and Paul Quist, 216
wedding, 203
Haan, Jack (son), 4, 203, 221, 293, *367*
Haan, James (son), 4, 203, 221, 293, *367*
Haan, Joe, Army service, overview, 129–33
Haan, Joe (Joseph Bernard Haan)
affinity for Indian spirituality, life-style, 83, 202
agility, 208, 210–11, 225
as agnostic / athiest, 207–8 *See also* Iconoclastic beliefs
alcohol issues, 84–85, 132, 196, 203, 205
anger at god, 57, 61, 74
anger at life issues, 5–6, 73, 78–79, 84, 205
aptness for CCC life, 118–19, 121. *See also* CCC
aversion to butter, 85–86
bird drawings, 329–35
birth, 1918, 31
circus, carnival jobs, 96–97
deafness. *See* Hearing problems
death, 293
defender of human rights, 213
drawings, *329–35*
early life in St. Paul, 31, 34–35
education, formal, 21–22
emotional scars from experiences, 3, 23, 25, 53, 86, 205
evenings with, typical, 303–5
and father's alcoholism, 31
funerals, distaste for, 36–37
hearing problems, 83, 130–31, 135, 204, 293, 304
iconoclastic beliefs, 3, 8–10, 21, 23–24, 121, 299
indentured to German farmer, 53. *See also* Farm indentureship
intuition, gift of, 225–26
joined CCC, 90–91. *See also* CCC
joined U.S. Army, 91. *See also* Army service
as last iconoclast. *See* Iconoclastic beliefs
lawsuit against farmer, State of Minnesota, 203
lecture prelude, 242
left ear, damage to, 57, 60
life-molding experiences summarized, 23
literature read while riding the rails, 107, 110

Haan, Joe (Joseph Bernard Haan) *(continued)*
living with Cecilia after marriage, 203–6
marksmanship / hunting skills, 219–20
memorabilia, World War II, 305
memorization skills, 81, 103, 120–21
met Helen Jessie, 134
mother's death, 41–42
move to Houston, 203
nature collections, drawings, notes, 64–68, *329,* 352
nicknames, 32, 204
"Notes on the Farm," 64–68
observational skills, 66–69
orphanage life. *See* Orphanage life
physical appearance, demeanor, 22
pneumonia at CCC Camp, 117
poverty, sensitivity to, 232, 306–7
Purple Heart, Military Order of, 23, 130–31, 182–84
questioning god, xiii–xiv, 57–58, 63, 74, 78, 161–62
return to St. Paul with Helen, 203
self-education, 1–2, 21–22, 66–68, 82–83
spirituality in nature, 70
as survivalist, 11–12
teaching aids from Rose, 64, 82
themes of poetry, 241
trip to Mexico, 141–43
wedding, 203
Haan, Joe, as ironworker
in Dominican Republic, 232–39
Ironworker's Local 84 member, 208
ironworking skills, 210–11
job descriptions, 212–13
pride in Houston development, 210–11
promotion reluctance, 213
El Tigre Chiquito, 4, 25, 209, 211
work habits as ironworker, 208–9
Haan, Joe, photographs
1939 photograph, *338*
at Antietam Battlefield, *368*
on bicycle, St. Paul, MN, *349*
CCC (Civilian Conservation Corps), *351*
at CCC Camp, *339–43, 340, 342, 344*
Haan, Joe, photographs *(continued)*
with Cecilia and Ferris Mahmood, *350*
with child, 1990, *370*
with David Mahmood, *351*
with deer head, *369*
with Denny Carlson, *369*
and drum fish, *366*
with family, *356*
on goat wagon, age five, *314*
Haan children on burro, *313*
at orphanage, *321*
riding the rails, *338*
with Rose, *345*
with sons and Native American artifacts, *366*
and stuffed bird collection, *367*
Haan, Joe, poems
"Allosaurus," 283
"The Axis Tilts," 281
"Birth of a Sun," 255
"The Carnivore," 260
"The Coconut Cartel," 284
"Cockroach: Blattaria Suprimus," 282
"Conflict of the Gods," 279
"Death of a Galaxy," 248
"Death of the Gods," 278
"Deception," 262
"Dinosaur Feast," 258
"Equality Dead," 58, 259
"Escape Smilodon," 272
"Evolution, or Geological Time," 275–76
"Fido's Fate," 111, 247
"The 4th Dimension," 254
"Free Thought," 251
"Futility I," 250
"Futility II," 252
"Gott Mit Uns," 9, 161–62
"Heresy's Crime," 277
"High Steel," 214–15
"Leopard's Feast," 269
"Memories of Death," 163–64
"The Mermaid," 40, 274
"The Nucleus," 261
"Oblivion," 33–34, 245
"Ode to Corporal William Cunningham," 223–25

Haan, Joe, poems *(continued)*
"The Open Mouth of Hell," 191–92
"Over Population," 263–64
"The Particle," 249
"Paradise Disorganized," 91–92, 270
"Pestilence," 257
"Pickett's Charge—July 3, 1863," 102
"Prejudice," 271 "
Quantum Jump to Within," 265
"The Question," 244
"The Round Game," 285
"Salute to the Stars," 243
"San Pedro, Dominican Republic," 236–39
"Shadow of the Past—the Ghost," 1–2, 25–30
"The Slaves," 268
"Soldier's Lament," 190–91
"The Spoiler Man," 266–67
"Stars' Atomic Divinity," 280
"A Star's Terminus," 253
"Survival Lesson," xi
"Thinker," 246
"Those That I Fight," 191
"The Vagabond Road," 31, 43–47
"Volcano," 256
"War," 125
Haan, Joe, songs by
"The Latin Lament," 289
"Infidelity," 288
"Love Lost," 287
"Suzanna," 290–91
"Why Soldier Why," 286
Haan, Kenneth W. (Kenny) (brother
age sixteen at Hadley farm, *318*
Bronze Star Medal awarded, 196
family visit, St. Paul, MN, *350*
4th of July visit with JBH at farm, 73, *327*
Haan children on burro, *313*
Haan family genealogy, 373
with Hadleys, 41, 50
Harvard University, 129, 202, *357*
in Iceland, 129, 139–41, 143–44, 146, 155, 182, 186, *357*
Macalester College, 127, 129, *357*
marriage, family, 129
military service, 127, 129
with uncle after mother's death, 32–33
Haan, Marie Mamie Hlavac (Hadley) Carmody (mother)
birth, background, 37
birth, death statistics, 375
death of, 32, 37, 41
genealogy record, 373
photographs, *314–15*
Haan, Nave (granddaughter), 293
Haan, Rose Marie "Sis" (sister)
caretaker for JBH and Cecilia, 41
death from ovarian cancer, 43
family visit, Northfield, MN, *356*
family visit, St. Paul, MN, *350*
at Faribault High School, *344*
4th of July visit with JBH at farm, 73, *327*
Haan children on burro, *313*
Haan family genealogy, 373
indentured to Pinkham family, 54–56
with Leonard Quist, *346, 348*
married Leonard Quist, 57
in Millersburg, MN, *347–48*
placed in orphanage after mother's death, 31–33
in Protestant Orphan Asylum and Owatonna Orphanages, 32, 50
Rose and Kenny, *345*
and self-teaching aids for Joe, 64, 82
as teacher, 57
Haan, Wendy, 8
Haan children addresses 1913-1930, 374
Haan family genealogy, 373–78
Haapoja, Margaret A., *Forest Magazine,* 115–16
Hadley (Hlavac), Albert (uncle), 37
Hadley (Hlavac), Joe (uncle), 33
Hadley, Marie Mamie. *See* Haan, Marie Mamie Hlavac (Hadley Carmody
Hadley, Maude (aunt), 33
Hadley monument, Calvary Cemetery, St. Paul, MN, 376
Haldeman-Julius, Emmanuel, 107
Hanau, Germany, 177, 197
Harmonica, self-taught, 83
Hearing problems
damage from artillery, 135, 304
near total deafness at death, 293

Hearing problems *(continued)*
partial deafness after Army service, 204
tinnitus in left ear, 83
VA total disability for, 130
"Heaven" (Brooke), 13–14, 107
Hector the Great (dog), 221
High Steel ironworking, 8, 210, 212–15
Hitler, Adolf, death of, 184
Hlavac, Marie Mamie. *See* Haan, Marie Mamie Hlavac (Hadley) Carmody
Hlavac anglicized to Hadley, 37
Hlavac monument, Calvary Cemetery, St. Paul, MN, 376
Hobo Cabbage recipe, 97
Hofman, Friedrich, 133, 162–68, 195, 304, *358–61*
Holy Communion, 9–10, 57–58
Hominid, 272
Homo sapiens, xi, 242
Houston, Texas, 207–9, 218–19, 306–9. *See also* Landor Lane house, Houston
Houston Astrodome construction, 217–18
Hunting and trapping, 81–82

I

Iconoclastic beliefs
atheists in Portland, Oregon, 99
Clarence Darrow on atheism, 101
criticism of organized religion, 3
description of to Wendy Haan, 8–10
god compared to atom, 46
Greek myth on democracy, 23–24
JBH as "god's angry man," "last iconclast," xiii–xiv, 10, 21, 299
poetry, songs about, 121
Robert Ingersoll lectures, 108–10
"In God We Trust," 87, 110
Indenture Contract, Minnesota, 51–53, 59, 73–74, 77, 83, 88–90
Indentured children, commonality of cruel treatment, 52–53, 83–84
Indian burial site excavation, 69
Indians as iron workers, 208
Ingersoll, Robert G., 108–10
Inquisition, xiii, 271
"Introducing Joe Haan" (Quist), xii–xiv
IQ test, 136 Iron Brigade, 222–24
"The Iron Man," 294
The Ironworker magazine, 208
"High Steel" poem, 213–15
job descriptions, 211–12
Ironworkers
in Dominican Republic, 222–39
High Steel ironworking, 8, 210, 212–15
Indians and, 208 job descriptions, 211–12
traits required, 208
See also Haan, Joe, as ironworker
Ironworker's Local 84, Houston, Texas, 208–10
Isabella, Minnesota, 113–14. *See* also CCC

J

Jalapeno peppers, 215–16
Jefferson, Thomas, 21
Jessie, Helen. *See* Haan, Helen (Jessie)
Jesus Christ, 7, 278–79, 300
Jurassic Period, 283
Juvenile Court, St. Paul, MN, 31–33, 35, 43, 49–50

K

Kimmeridge clay, 19
Kjeldtsen, Carl (uncle), *317*
Kjeldtsen, Sadie (aunt), 32, 49, *317*
Knife, sharpest in the world, 308–9
Korean Deathlock, 219, 305
Kussmaul, Al, 95

L

Laager, Lowell, 116–17
Laccolith, 256
Lafayette Escadrille, 5
Landor Lane house, Houston
drug dealers in neighborhood, 218–19, 306–7

Landor Lane house, Houston
(continued)
interior, 305–6
tiger next door, 219
tropical botanical garden, 215
Language development in Neanderthals, 229–31
LaRue, Lanny, 219
Lawsuit against farmer, State of Minnesota, 90, 203
Lazarus, 6–7
The Lectures of Colonel Robert G. Ingersoll (Ingersoll), 108–10
Lemurs, 276
Lentz, John M., 156–57
Leopold-Loeb case, 100
Letters
Cecilia to Kenny, 55, 129, 138
Daniel Haan to Cecilia, 38–39
German couple to Owatonna Orphanage, 88–90
Joe to Cecilia, 135–36
Joe to Helen, 232–35
Joe to Kenny, 80–82, 136–37, 140–45, 147, 154–55, 182–83, 186–89, 202–3
Joe to Tim Carlson, 6–7
Joe to Wendy Haan, 8–10
Joe's teacher to German couple, 78–79
Rose to Joe, 75–76
Rose to Kenny, 76–77, 79–80, 139
Life on the Bum in the Early 1930s (Kussmaul), 95–96
Linz, Austria, 177, 185, 199
Little Blue Books (Haldeman-Julius), 12–13, 107, *336–37,* 379–81
Liverpool, England, 146, 186
Louisiana, 141, 143
Lucretius Carus, Titus, 121–23
Luxembourg, 169–80, 187, 196, 201, 222

M

Machine gun unit, Danny Haan and, *319*
Maginot Line, 171
Mahmood, David (nephew), 203–7, *351*
Mahmood, Ferris, 205, *350*
Maps
Joe's trek across Europe, 193
(1) Utah Beach to Troyes, 194
(2) Nancy to Sarre-Union, 195
(3) Metz to Bastogne, 196
(4) Mertzig to Hanau, 197
(5) Fulda to Meiningen, 198
(6) Austria, Czechoslovakia, 199
Marshall, George C., 115, 128
Maternal relatives, 375
Maugham, Somerset, 309
McCann, Dan, 37, 39. *See also* Haan, Daniel Frederick (father) "Dan McCann"
McPherson's Woods, 223
Meiningen, Germany, 177, 184, 198
Memorabilia, World War II, 189, 204
Merzig, Germany, 197
Meson, 265
"Mess Song" (Lafayette Escadrille), 5
Methuselah, 7
Metz, France, 5, 153, 169, 196
Meuse River, 170, 174
Mexico, 141–43, 209, 289
Middle East, 24, 131
Milk -Weed (*selinum palustre*), 71
Milk-Thistle (*carduus marianus*), 70–72
Milk-Vetch (*astragalus*), 71–72
Milk-Wort (*polygala vulgaris*), 72
Millersburg School, Rose's class, 57, *346–48*
Milwaukee Road, 94
Minnesota. *See specific cities*
Minnesota Historical Society, 119
Mohammed, 279, 300
Monterrey, Mexico, 141–42
Moselle River, 153, 156, 160, 170, 173, 186, 195
Moses, 300
Mother Nature, 279
"Mr. Flood's Party" (Robinson), 293–97
Muir, John, 70

N

Native American artifacts, 11–12, 134, *366*
Native American skills, 83
Nature collections, drawings, notes, 64–68
Neanderthal man, 186, 229–31
Needles, California, 137, 140
New Deal, 114
Nightmares after Army discharge, 201, 205
Nomadic travels. *See* Riding the rails
Normandy invasion, 147–48
Northfield, Minnesota, 56
Northwoods CCC Camp. *See* CCC
Notes and drawings, 64–68, 329–35
Nucleus, 261

O

Oak Hill Cemetery, 36, 139, 374
Oblivion
  children's cemetery at orphanage, 52
  finality of death, 87
  in foxhole with dead German soldier, 167
  Great Singularity, 311–12
  poem about mother's death, 44
  poem on Civil War soldier, 224
  respite from thoughts of, 70
  return to ashes after death, 36–37
Oblivion, JBH's belief in, poem about, 33–34
Observations, nature studies, 64–68, 329–35
O'Hara, Theodore, 103–7
Oklahoma, 2, 87–88, 134–35, 202–4, 293, *352–53*
The Old Farmer's Almanac, 1891, 68, 70–72
Old Mother West Wind series (Burgess), 64
"On the Nature of Things" (Lucretius), 121–23
101st Infantry, 130, 170, 173–85, 196–97, *358*
Operation Market Garden, 153, 156
Oppenheim, Germany, 197
Ornithopoda, 283
Orphanage. *See* Owatonna (MN) Orphanage
Orphanage life, 22, 31–32, 51–52, 54. *See also* Owatonna (MN) Orphanage
Orphans, indentured, 52–53, 83–84
Oryx, 269
Ovarian cancer and Haan family, 33
Owatonna (MN) Orphanage
  apple picking, *322*
  censorship, withholding of orphans' mail, 55, 76–77
  cottage basement, *321*
  Haan children assigned to by Court Order, 32–33, 41–43, 50
  history, buildings, grounds, 52
  JBH's cottage dormitory, *320*
  Museum veterans' memorial, 54
  orphans photograph, *322*

P

Paabo, Svante, 230–31
Paris, France, 187–88
Parrish, Mary, 222
Passau, Germany, 189, 199
Paternal relatives, 377–78
Patton, George S., 150–57, 174–76, 178, 183
Patton's Third Army
  Alsace-Lorraine battle casualties, 161
  Ardennes Offensive, 171–72, 175–76
  Battle of the Bulge, 129–30, 169–71, 173–78
  blitzkrieg tactics, use of, 150–51
  JBH as private in, discharge record, 129–32
  JBH's battalion assigned to, 23, 148. *See also* Army service
  map, Third Army route in Europe, 193
  progress stopped by lack of fuel, 153
Paul, Willard S., 169, 178–79, 181
Pearl Harbor attack, 123–24
Pentagon, 254
Philosophy struggles, 294

Physiological resemblance, apes and man, 9
Pig roast for soldiers, 172–73
Pinkham, Victor E., 55–56
Plato, 254
Polygala vulgaris (milk wort), 72
Portland, Oregon, and radical ideas, 99
Praying under duress ("in foxholes"), 49, 125, 166, 207
Preface to poems, 2–3
Prehistoric animals
  brachiopod, 275
  Eohippus, 276
  Smilodon, 275
  trilobite, 275
  See also Dinosaurs
Prehistoric Periods, Eras, Ages
  Cambrian, 16, 275
  Carboniferous, 275
  Cenozoic, 276
  Cretaceous, 276
  Devonian, 275
  Eocene, 276
  Eolithic, 27
  Mesolithic, 28
  Neocomian 17, 195
  Ordovician, 275
  Paleocene, 276
  Paleozoic, 16, 275
  Permian Period, 281
  Proterozoic, 275
  Silurian, 275
  Triassic, 276
Prohibition, 34, 84–85
Protagoras, 24, 310
Protestant Orphan Asylum, 32, 50
Public libraries, use of, 107–10
Purbeck flags, 19
Purple Heart, Military Order of, 23, 130–31, 182–84

Q

Quark, 265
Quist, B. Wayne (nephew), 226–29, 300–303, *368*
Quist, Julia, 215–18
Quist, Leonard, 37, 57, *346, 348*
Quist, Paul (nephew), 215–18, 303–12
Quist and Haan families, *363–64*

R

Racism, 233
Ramsey County Juvenile Court, 31–33, 35, 43, 49–50
Rawhide, Arizona, 226
The Razor's Edge (Maugham), 309
Redball Express trucks, 156, 158
Reed, Jack, 98–99
Religion vs. spirituality, 2
"Remembering Joe at Vicksburg" (Quist), 226–29
"Requirements for Iron Workers" (*Ironworkers Local 84*), 209
Residences, Haan family, St. Paul, 35, 41
Rhine River, 182–83
Riding the rails, 90, 93–95, 97, 101, 107, *338*
Rifles, 11, 80–82, 130, 149, 189, 219–20
Roaring Twenties, 34
Robinson, Edwin Arlington, 293–97
Ronglien, Harvey, 53–54, 83–84
Roosevelt, Franklin, 123–24, 184
Runstedt, Gerd von, 172, 174, 196
Rush, Benjamin, 21

S

Sacco-Vanzetti case, 99–100
Sachem, 9–10, 246, 271
San Francisco, California, and radical ideas, 98
San Pedro, Dominican Republic, 232–39
Sanchelli, Michael T., 119–20
Sarre-Union, France, 169, 171, 195
Scopes trial, 100–101
Seabury Divinity School, 56, 75
Self-education, 1–2, 21–22, 66–68, 82–83
Selinum palustre (milk-weed), 71
Service, Robert, 110, 304
706th Tank Destroyer Battalion, 130, 135–38

752nd Field Artillery Battalion, 130, 143, 145–46, 151–54, 156, 169–70
"Sharing a Foxhole with Friedrich Hofman" (memoir), 163–68
Shinto, 278–79
Shiva, 278
Siegfried Line, 148, 151, 176, 181, 183, 197
Skid row, Houston, 207, 293–94
Slaves, indentured orphans compared to, 52–53, 83–84
Slingshot hunting, 65
Smilodon, 272
Smith, Langdon, 14, 16–19
Smoked meats and hides, 66, 69
Social services involvement, Haan children, 32–33, 35–36, 41–42
Socrates, 24
Southampton, England, 148–49
Spiral nebula, 255
Spirituality in nature, 2, 69–70
St. James School for Boys, 55–56, *344*
St. Joseph's Academy, St. Paul, MN, 55, *323–25*
St. Paul, Minnesota
  Haan residences, 35, 41
  JBH's birthplace, 31
  return after Army service, 203
St. Paul (MN) Protestant Orphan Asylum, 32, 50
State Agents, Minnesota, 73, 77, 84
State Public School for Dependent and Neglected Children. *See* Owatonna (MN) Orphanage
Steelworkers. *See* Ironworkers
Stockbridge, England, 148
Stuben, Czechoslovakia, 184–86, 199
Sûre River, 173, 176, 179–80
Survival
  in the Army, 127, 137, 149, 176, 189
  at CCC Camp, 121
  of earth, universe, 241–42
  lectures on methods of, 304
  vs. scope, depth of human heart, 294
  by self-education, life experience, 1–2, 11, 22–25, 205
  "Survival Lesson," xi
  while riding the rails, 97–99

T

Tank Destroyer, 129–30, 135, 137–38, 145, 187, *354–55, 358*
Taxidermy, hide tanning
  hide tanning on farm, 66, 69
  Houston house, stuffed animals, 216–17, 305
  leather breeches, shirt, 83
  as mostly self-taught, 21–22
  skunk hides, 205–7
  as source of venison, 4
  stuffed bird, animal collections, *366–67*
  taxidermy lab, Houston house, *365*
The Ten Days that Shook the World (Reed), 98–99
Texas
  Army training camps, 135–44, *354–55*
  See also Houston, Texas; Landor Lane house, Houston
Third Army. *See* Patton's Third Army
El Tigre Chiquito, 4, 25, 209, 211
Train, Spencer, 222 Train hopping. *See* Riding the rails
Trapping and skinning, 11–12, 63, 69, 82, 119, 205–6
Tremadoc beds, 19
Trench foot, 160–61
Tropical botanical garden, Houston, 215–17
Trot lines (fishing), 206
Troyes, France, 152, 186, 194
26th Infantry Division. *See* Yankee Division
26th Infantry Division records of events (1944-45), 168–69, 174–75, 176–78
Tyrannosaurus Rex in living room, 216, 305

U

Underdown, Simon, 231
Underwear, aversion to wearing, 22
Universe, relationship to Earth, 309–11
U.S. Third Army. *See* Patton's Third Army

USS Wakefield, 145–46
Utah Beach, Normandy, 149, 186

V

Vancouver Barracks, Washington, 128
Verdun, France, 161–62
Veterans Adminstration (VA), 131
Vicksburg, Mississippi River trip, 226–29
Virgin Mary, 234–35
Vishnu, 278–79
Vonnegut, Kurt, 6–7

W

Wales, 146, 186
Walters, Mrs. Arthur G. (aunt), 50
War. *See* Army service; Patton's Third Army
Wehrmacht, 162, 164–65
Wells, Minnesota railroad junction, 94
Whitman, Walt, xii
Wisconsin, 95, 130, 189, 201, 222–24
World War II
  declared, 123–24
  ended, 189
  See also Army service; Patton's Third Army

X

XOTÄNEF (created Neanderthal language), 83, 229–31, 382–85

Y

Yankee Division (26th Infantry Division), 181–85, 189, *358, 359*
  assigned to Patton, 168
  and Battle of the Bulge, Ardennes Offensive, 169–79
  capture of Fulda and Meiningen, 184
  capture of Stuben, Czechoslovakia, 185
  commanded by Major General Willard S. Paul, 169
Yankee Division (26th Infantry Division) *(continued)*
  eastern advance and Drive to the Rhine, 181–83
  Gusen Concentration Camp, 185
  insignias, *358*
  JBH served in, 130–31
  JBH's summary of service in, 187–89
  101st Infantry Regiment as part of, 170–71
  soldiers, Battle of the Bulge, *359*
  Vic-sur-Seille, Marimot, Dieuze, Sarre-union seized, late 1944, 169
Yuma, Arizona, 138, 140

Z

Zeus, 24, 279, 300

About the Author

B. Wayne Quist has recently coauthored two books on radical, militant Islamism and the ideology of al Qaeda—*Winning the War on Terror* and *The Triumph of Democracy Over Militant Islamism*—and has plans for a third book in the series, *A New Approach to the Greater Middle East.* He is a popular speaker on the subject of militant Islamism and lectured at the 2004 Nobel Peace Prize Forum.

He retired from the Air Force in the rank of full colonel and has written many publications in the fields of national security, political science, and American history. He is currently a partner with Northstar Industries, Inc. in Wayzata, Minnesota, where he specializes in the sale and recapitalization of privately held companies. He also serves on the boards of non-profit organizations in Minnesota and Washington, DC. Wayne graduated from St. Olaf College in Northfield, Minnesota and has advanced degrees from the University of Southern California and National War College, specializing in the Middle East.

Wayne is Joe's nephew. His mother was "Sis."